Recommended

COUNTRY INNS

The Midwest

"Puhala has captured the essence of these inns: welcoming and warm as a fire's glow."
—Rick Sylvain, travel editor, *Detroit Free Press*

"With an eye for detail and a talent for description, Bob Puhala has searched out and chosen some of the best in the Midwest. . . . A reference you will want to add to your travel library."
—Norman Strasma, *Inn Review*

"Reading Bob Puhala's *Recommended Country Inns: The Midwest* is like asking a good friend for vacation advice. He gets right to the heart of the matter and tells you exactly what you want to know. The book is comprehensive, well researched, and written in a warm, chatty, and highly readable style."
—M. Eileen Brown, travel editor, *The Daily Herald*, Arlington Heights, Illinois

"This unique, detailed guide will attract an audience seeking something different."
—The Midwest Book Review, WYOU–TV, Oregon, WI

"Puhala has opened a door to a Midwestern treasure house of travel gems—a spectrum of places not to be missed. One can almost smell the morning muffins and feel the sunshine."
—Gary Knowles, director, Bureau of Communication, Wisconsin Division of Tourism

''Recommended Country Inns'' Series

"The guidebooks in this new series of recommended country inns are sure winners. Personal visits have ensured accurate and scene-setting descriptions. These beckon the discriminating traveler to a variety of interesting lodgings."
—Norman Strasma, publisher of *Inn Review* newsletter

The "Recommended Country Inns" series is designed for the discriminating traveler who seeks the best in unique accommodations away from home.

From hundreds of inns personally visited and evaluated by the author, only the finest are described here. The inclusion of an inn is purely a personal decision on the part of the author; no one can pay or be paid to be in a Globe Pequot inn guide.

Organized for easy reference, these guides point you to just the kind of accommodations you are looking for: Comprehensive indexes by category provide listings of inns for romantic getaways, inns for the sports-minded, inns that serve gourmet meals . . . and more. State maps help you pinpoint the location of each inn, and detailed driving directions tell you how to get there.

Use these guidebooks with confidence. Allow each author to share his or her selections with you and then discover for yourself the country inn experience.

Editions available:
Recommended Country Inns
New England   •   Mid-Atlantic and Chesapeake Region
The South   •   The Midwest   •   West Coast
Rocky Mountain Region   •   The Southwest

Recommended
COUNTRY INNS™
The Midwest

Illinois • Indiana • Iowa
Michigan • Minnesota
Missouri • Ohio • Wisconsin

Third Edition

by **Bob Puhala**
illustrated by Bill Taylor, Jr.

A Voyager Book

The Globe Pequot Press

Chester, Connecticut

For Kate and Dayne, the joys of my life. Also special thanks to my wife, Debbie, whose tireless assistance and on-the-road companionship made it all easier; to Pa, who traveled thousands of Midwest miles with me on long research trips; to Ma, a source of endless encouragement and baby-sitter supreme; and to brother Mark, master kiddie entertainer and adventure-trip partner.

Is there anything better in life than a loving family?

Text copyright © 1987, 1989, 1991 by Bob Puhala
Illustrations copyright © 1987, 1989, 1991 by The Globe Pequot Press

Library of Congress Cataloging-in-Publication Data

Puhala, Bob.
    Recommended country inns. The Midwest / by Bob Puhala :
illustrated by Bill Taylor, Jr.—3rd ed.
      p. cm.—("Recommended country inns" series)
    "A Voyager book."
    Includes indexes.
    Contents: Illinois—Indiana—Iowa—Michigan—Minnesota—
Missouri—Ohio—Wisconsin.
    ISBN 0-87106-311-5
    1. Hotels, taverns etc.—Middle West—Guide-books. 2. Bed and
breakfast accommodations—Middle West—Guide-books. 3. Middle
West—
  —Description and travel—Guide-books. I. Title. II. Series.
TX907.3.M55P84 1991
647.947701—dc20   90-22313
                                                 CIP

Manufactured in the United States of America
Third Edition/First Printing

Contents

Indexes

About This Inn Guide

Country inns, historic hotels, and outstanding B&Bs are listed state by state and alphabetically by city, town, and village within each state. You'll find them in the following order: Illinois, Indiana, Iowa, Michigan, Minnesota, Missouri, Ohio, and Wisconsin. Preceding each state grouping is a map guide and handy index. There's also a complete alphabetical index at the end of the book.

Helpful guidebook features are the special inn indexes. These list particularly noteworthy inn activities, amenities, and features. They will help you select the inn that's right for you.

When you see a "B" (it stands for Bob) at the end of an inn selection, it means that I felt compelled to add one last personal comment before moving on.

There is no charge of any kind for an inn to be included in this guide book. I have chosen inns based on my professional experience and personal standards. I offer readers a choice among the finest, most interesting, and historic accommodations available in the Midwest. I thank those of you who have written me in the past, and I continue to welcome comments, questions, and information about your favorite inn—whether or not it's included in my selections—or newly opened and soon-to-be-opened inns. Please address all correspondence to Bob Puhala, *Recommended Country Inns: The Midwest*, The Globe Pequot Press, 138 West Main Street, Chester, Connecticut 06412.

Rates: Inns often change their rates without notice. The high/low prices I have quoted are meant to be used only as guidelines. They'll give you a reasonable idea of what a room might cost. I haven't included tax rates or service charges, which add to your bill; neither have I described tipping suggestions. Inquire upon making reservations.

Menu Abbreviations: The following abbreviations are used:

EP: European Plan—room without meals.

EPB: European Plan—room with full breakfast.

AP: American Plan—room with all meals.

MAP: Modified American Plan—room with breakfast and dinner.

BYOB: Bring Your Own Bottle.

Note that meal plans change often. An inn offering one of the quoted specialties may change chefs and, thus, their entire entree list. Other inns constantly adjust breakfast policies, some offering full breakfasts one season, then continental or buffet-style breakfasts the next. There are several inns offering lunch and dinner specials by reservation or request; this is noted under "Facilities and activities" preceding each inn description. Remember that it is always best to call ahead so that you know what to expect.

Innkeepers: Some inns remain in the same family for decades. Others change ownership more frequently. This might result in wholesale revisions of previous inn policies. Or inns might completely close their doors to the public as they convert to private residences. Be sure to call ahead to ensure that the inn of your choice still welcomes travelers.

Reservations and Deposits: Many inns maintain such a sterling reputation of excellence and service that they require reservations made months in advance. Even on average, it's advisable to call at least one month in advance, especially if you're planning to visit during the high-volume travel season (usually summer). Smaller establishments may require even more advance notice. And if you wish to stay at inns during annual town festivals, call *right now*.

On the other hand, it's always possible to make spur-of-the-moment reservations—possible, but not very likely.

As for deposits, this is such a common requirement that I do not mention specific inn policies. With few exceptions, you'll be required to pay a deposit to reserve a room, using a personal check or a credit card. Be sure to inquire about refund policies.

Credit Cards: Visa and MasterCard are accepted unless otherwise stated. Many inns accept additional credit cards, too. Others accept only cash or personal checks. Call ahead to be sure.

Children: Inns that offer special rates for children are duly noted. Several inns do not publicly advertise kid discounts, so ask about them. Also note that some inns specialize in quiet getaway weekends for couples; others are antique-filled treasures. I still cringe when my children get close to my baseball trophies; imagine how innkeepers might feel if your little ones are steamrolling toward a precious Ming vase. My wife and I are used to all types of kid-related noises (at all hours of the night), but some people are not. I guess what I'm trying to say is—please use your discretion when choosing an inn. Make sure it's one that the kids will enjoy. (See the "Inns Especially Good for Kids" index for some help.) As we and thousands of other parents have discovered, traveling with children is often a joy, but it's also tough work.

Pets: Spot usually won't be allowed inside. The rule: No pets unless otherwise stated. (See the "Pets Welcome" index.)

Minimum Stay: Two-night minimums on weekends and even three nights during holidays are requirements at several inns, as noted. This is a frequently changing policy.

Bed Size: Inns may use three-quarter beds, twins, doubles, queens, or kings. While a few historic selections may offer antique rope beds or other fanciful contraptions, exotica is usually not a worry. If you have a preference, make it known in advance.

Television, Telephones, and Air Conditioning: Are you the type of person who loves to travel deep into the heart of the wilderness but still must get a nightly fix of David Letterman? Were you born to live in air-conditioned rooms? I've noted which inns offer the above amenities in guest rooms. (Other inns offer these amenities in common rooms only.)

Food for Thought: A number of B&Bs are included in my selections. Oftentimes, innkeepers will have area restaurant dinner menus for guests to look over. At the least, the innkeeper should inquire about your food preferences and suggest an appropriate local restaurant. Most of the time, choices range from casual to fine dining. If you have any special dietary requirements, you should realize that such requests often are considered by inn restaurants. As for vegetarians, you'll usually find seafood and fowl entree selections. Therefore, if I do not mention restaurants as part of my inn descriptions, be assured that your hosts can advise you.

Wheelchair Access: Inns that have wheelchair access are noted in each "Rooms" listing; there is also a special "Inns with Wheelchair Access" index at the back of the book. Wheelchair access to restaurants and dining rooms only is listed under "Facilities and activities."

Bad Habits: More inns than ever prohibit smoking in guest rooms or common areas. You will find a special "No smoking Inns" index at the back of the book.

A Few Words About
Visiting Midwest Inns

Can it already be our third time around?

This third edition of *Recommended Country Inns: The Midwest* is the result of more than a half-decade of travel through eight Midwestern states to discover the finest and most interesting country inns, historic hotels, and bed and breakfasts around.

I rambled along more than 34,000 miles of Midwest roads—crisscrossing interstate highways, searching country back roads, maneuvering down gravel lanes—and personally visited nearly 700 inns to offer you the very best of America's heartland. And of those 700 inns, only 180 made the final cut.

Why go to all that trouble? Because there's no other way to do it. Simple as that. I have to see inns with my own discerning eye, talk to innkeepers, probe guests for their insights and impressions, sample the food, sleep in the beds, walk the grounds, explore the towns. Only then do I feel confident to recommend an inn and include it in this book.

Of course, my rewards for such rigorous travel are the discoveries: river-town inns perched atop high bluffs that afford magnificent views of mighty Midwest rivers like the Mississippi, Missouri, and Ohio; elegant Victorian mansions that charmed me with their opulent atmosphere; turn-of-the-century summer homes that bathed me in a fiery glow of Great Lakes sunrises and sunsets; log-cabin lodges surrounded by awesome North Woods wilderness that nestle on rivers with world-class white-water rapids; Southern gentility exhibited in fine estates and manors tucked deep into the Ozark Mountain foothills.

Then there are the people. Innkeepers who have fled big-city corporate life-styles, ex-soldiers, homemakers, teachers, lawyers, engineers, farmers—who tackle the day-to-day task of running a historic hostelry mostly for the pleasure of making travelers feel as though there's a little bit of home waiting for them no matter where they go. They have to love their innkeeping role; the work's too hard for any other reason to make sense. After all, even Bob Newhart gave up innkeeping after six years in the television "hospitality business."

Fellow guests are part of the attraction, too. Inn-hoppers seem to be friendly, interesting, and involved with the world around them, possessing a special drive to experience new things, explore the past, or relive a little part of history.

The wildlife surprises also please this big-city boy. A black bear stood up in the middle of the road in a remote corner of northwest Wisconsin and looked me right in the eye before scurrying into the brush. I saw eagles soar off bluff tops, foxes slink through the woods, deer stand frozen on the sides of numerous roads; I saw hawks, coyotes. . . .

There are lots of laughs. Consider the Minnesota inn that rents pussycats to make guests feel more at home during their stay.

But some things bother me about this burgeoning business. The "country inn" concept has exploded throughout the Midwest marketplace, and many entrepreneurs have exploited its drawing potential by shamelessly using the "inn" tag in their advertising. Therefore, I discovered major motel chains, hotels, condominium complexes, tiny B&Bs, restaurants, roadside cafes, and the like, calling themselves "inns."

I also dislike "underground homestays," houses that ignore zoning regulations to transform guest bedrooms into guest quarters unregulated (and mostly undetected) by any state or local authority. This can lead to confusion and disappointment for potential inngoers.

That's why it is more important than ever to seek out an authoritative travel guidebook whose author has actually visited all the inns recommended to you.

Another part of the problem is that there's no easy way (at least aesthetically speaking) to define just what a country inn is. In the Midwest, your choices include everything from historic log cabins to re-created Victorian resort hotels—and you'll still have a great time.

Even as Midwest state legislators begin to refine legal distinctions among B&Bs, inns, and hotels, this legalese is pretty much lost on the average inngoer. A vacationer doesn't much care how local government defines a hostelry or what category it's placed in. He or she does care about quality, style, class, hospitality, friendliness, cleanliness, and all the other tangibles and intangibles that make country inns so special.

Therefore, a trusted guidebook with an excellent track record of directing people to those very kinds of establishments is one of your most important tools in planning a getaway.

So I'll ask you once again to come with me and discover inns that have served travelers since the days of the stagecoach and steamboat as well as those that have called the railroad their best friend.

Some inns were magnificent private homes for local notables that might otherwise have been forgotten if not for the loving restoration of innkeepers; others were spacious summer retreats deep in the woods, used to flee big-city pressures, or fabulous "cottages" built to escape scorching Midwest sunshine by perching on lakes and coaxing cool breezes to the shore. Now they welcome guests to rediscover their charms. Still more were merchant buildings, grist mills, once-grand hotels, modest frontier homes. . . .

These are all country inns. They have something special and exciting to offer the traveler: atmosphere, charm, historical significance, architectural stylings, spectacular location, a certain feeling. Maybe even a little soul.

I've met several of you on the road as I traveled the country-inn circuit, and often you had my book in hand, telling me that you never knew about "this fabulous place" until you read about it in these pages. Thanks.

Many others have written and commended my choices; some have offered me inn-side information about places they've discovered and would like to see in the book. Thanks, again.

Eventually, we'll all bump into one another. Just look for the family with the beautiful wife, two fair-haired daughters—and a guy juggling enough suitcases to supply the entire 7th Cavalry. That guy will be me.

Maybe you can even give me a hand with the luggage!

Bob

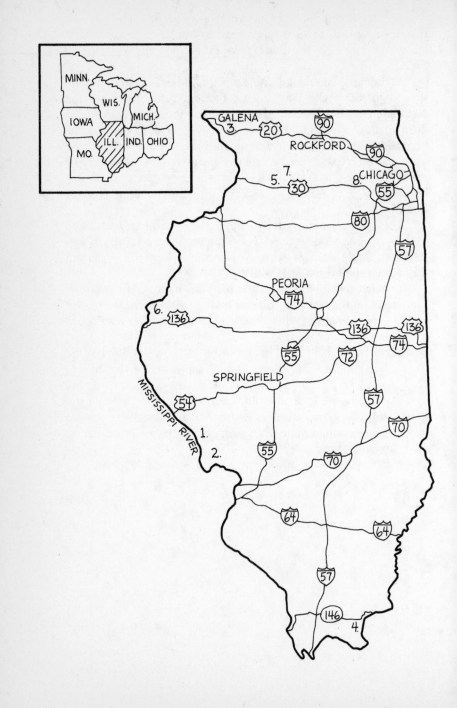

Illinois

Hobson's Bluffdale
Eldred, Illinois
62027

Innkeepers: Bill and Lindy Hobson
Address/Telephone: Hillview Road; (217) 983–2854
Rooms: 8, with 3 two-room suites; all with private bath and air conditioning.
Rates: $50 per person; $35 children ages 9–13, $30 kids 4–8, $23 under age 4; AP. $295 adults, sliding scale for children, for weekly farm vacations. Includes all activities and recreation. Three-night minimum Memorial Day, July 4, and Labor Day. Two-night minimum on all other weekends, June through September.
Open: All year for B&B; farm vacations, March through November.
Facilities and activities: Horseback riding and trail rides, cart rides, swimming in heated pool, hot tub, canoe day trips, hiking through private wooded bluffs, arrowhead hunting, wild blackberry picking, fishing in private pond or Illinois River, hayrides, square dancing, ice cream socials, bonfire roasts, workshops in forestry, archeology, pottery, ceramics, wildlife, and more.

"I'm a city girl," Lindy said. "Never set foot on a farm until I met Bill when we were both students at the University of Illinois." Bill steps right in with a zinger. "That's right. She saw giraffes and zebras at the city zoo long before she ever saw any of my farm animals."

Bluffdale is a 320-acre farm (soybeans, corn, wheat, and a few pigs) run by the Hobsons; it's been in Bill's family since 1828. It was named by his great-great-grandfather for bluffs that run through the property.

Lindy took me into the original stone farmhouse that still stands. It's cooking headquarters and also contains some of Bill's priceless family heirlooms, including a four-volume family history written by his great-great-grandfather.

Bill added: "Charles Dickens was one of his friends, and visited here in the 1840s. They had to pick up Dickens at the train in a spring wagon and bring him to the farm."

Bluffdale is a spectacular getaway for anyone—but especially for city slickers and kids. Bill and Lindy encourage everyone to help with regular farm chores—feeding the chickens and pigs, gathering eggs, moving geese, bottle-feeding calves, picking fresh blackberries, harvesting vegetables from Bill's two-acre garden, and more.

Lindy is the cook who takes all this delicious farm-fresh food and whips up great feasts. Family-style meals include eggs, French toast or pancakes, fruits, and home-baked breads for breakfast; maybe a picnic lunch packed for a trek through the woods; and supper table specials like fried chicken, baked ham, pot roast, barbecued pork chops, topped off with oven-fresh sweets and homemade ice cream.

Overnight rooms are comfortable enough, done in bandana red and blues with brass lanterns and wide-plank floors. But you don't come to Bluffdale for room-side splendor; there's far too much to do. The flexible schedule includes: archeological digs (this is historic Indian country); Saturday-night square dances; Sunday ice-cream socials; Monday ball games; Friday-night bonfire sing-alongs; and Tuesday-afternoon cookout picnics at Greenfield Lake.

How to get there: From St. Louis, take Missouri 367 north to Alton, Illinois. Continue north on U.S. 67, then head north on Illinois 267. Turn west at Illinois 208 and continue to Eldred. At Eldred–Hillview Road (at the bottom of a hill, opposite the Standard gas station), turn north, and proceed just over 3½ miles to the farm.

Green Tree Inn
Elsah, Illinois
62028

Innkeepers: Michael and Mary Ann Pitchford, owners; Paul McClintock, manager
Address/Telephone: 15 Mill Street; (618) 374–2821
Rooms: 9, with 1 suite; all with private bath and air conditioning, phone on request.
Rates: $65 to $90, single or double, EPB.
Open: All year.
Facilities and activities: Dining room, gathering room, private balconies; nineteenth-century-style mercantile store featuring fine arts and crafts; paddle wheeler offering riverboat excursions. In the heart of historic Elsah. Short walk to Mississippi River. Jogging or biking on Great River Road. Nearby is 16-mile-long Vadalabene bike trail. About 40 antique shops within 15 minutes' drive. Bald eagles winter along the river in great numbers from December through March. About 40 minutes from St. Louis.

I found it hard to believe that this 1850s-style river-town building is only five years old. "We designed it to convey nineteenth-century charm," Mary Ann said. "And since the entire town is on the National Register of Historic Places, we had to be very exact in matching the spirit of this building with its authentic nineteenth-century surroundings."

Guests at the Green Tree Inn are greeted with a complimentary carafe of chilled Catawba. Then it's off to one of the inn's charming rooms, each individually decorated.

My favorite is the Federal Room, done in Federal blues, boasting a canopy bed that copies 1850s Mississippi styles. Bedposts are draped with linens made in Lao Ping province in China. "It's interesting that linens are handmade in China but are copies of American nineteenth-century lace," Mary Ann said. Austrian and Swedish lace also grace windows. The Federal theme is carried through with two wing chairs and handsome wall portraits.

In the Victorian Room, a brass bed and Austrian lace curtains create an absolutely charming atmosphere. A quaint Country Room is equally stylish in its casual and relaxed nature that seems to well reflect the nature of this historic nineteenth-century village.

Or sample the elegant Governor's Suite, named for John Sevier, Tennessee's first chief executive in 1897, and Mary's great-great-great-grandfather. It's done in family heirloom antiques (including a canopied poster bed) and has two private balconies.

Other rooms have second-floor porches furnished with settee, table, and chairs. There are even ceiling fans.

A charming gathering room in the building's basement is a picture of country quaint. Red-checked tablecloths cover tables and chairs specially made by local craftspeople for the inn. Mary Ann serves breakfast here—everything from tasty omelets and homemade strawberry-tinged French toast to pastries from the renowned local bakery.

The innkeeper also runs monthly workshops at the inn, featuring everything from planting nineteenth-century spring and woodland gardens to a Victorian tea luncheon that includes a workshop on day-lilies. Of course, white gloves are required for this one.

For dinner, I'd recommend either Elsah's Landing or Fin Inn, a unique seafood restaurant in nearby Grafton, where huge aquariums filled with Mississippi River marine life (mainly turtles, carp, catfish) front dinner booths. Besides the lively setting, the inn offers specialties like turtle soup, white perch and spoonbill fillets, a 16-ounce whole catfish, fried turtle, and desserts like chocolate meringue and Kentucky Derby pie.

How to get there: From St. Louis, take Missouri 367 north to U.S. 67 and continue into Illinois. At Illinois 3, turn west and proceed to Elsah. There are only two major streets in the town, Mill and LaSalle streets.

Maple Leaf Cottage Inn
Elsah, Illinois
62028

Innkeepers: Patty and Jerry Taetz
Address/Telephone: 12 Selma Street (mailing address: P.O. Box 156); (618)
    374–1684
Rooms: 4; all with private bath, air conditioning, and TV; 1 with
    wheelchair access. No smoking inn.
Rates: $65, single or double, EPB; $90, single or double, MAP.
Open: All year.
Facilities and activities: Restaurant, seven-course dinner. English country
    garden, herb garden. Located in heart of historic Elsah, nineteenth-
    century Mississippi river town. Near Grant River Road, jogging and
    biking along the 16-mile Vadalabene bike trail. Nearly 40 antiques
    shops within a 15-minute drive. Bald eagles winter along river from
    December through March. About 40 minutes from St. Louis. Limo
    service to and from St. Louis Regional and Lambert International
    airports; will arrange for special trolly tours to St. Louis arch, Union
    Station, etc.; will arrange daily river and walking tours.

    Imagine stepping back into the steamboat era of the nine-
teenth century in a little Illinois village that appears much as it did
in pre–Civil War days. It is a peaceful, easy feeling I get when
driving into Elsah, on my way to Patty and Jerry's historic inn.
    This cozy country inn occupies an entire village block, sur-

rounded by blazing colors of a handsome English garden and facing the spectacular limestone bluffs that run down to the Mississippi River.

The rooms can be overwhelming, fashioned with seemingly every country accent and craft imaginable and available. Yet I found them to be some of the most relaxed and enjoyable lodgings I've encountered since I began inn-hopping years ago.

The Wash House is a charming cottage (the first ever of the Maple Leaf Inn, which has been open to travelers for nearly four decades.) In 1891 it was the Maple's summer kitchen, but after a fire it became the family wash house. Patty has carried this theme through to perfection, with quaint country decor that showcases an 1888 wooden washing machine, old-fashioned scrub boards, and even a clothes line. A wonderful rail bed adds to country charm. There are historic photos of the original Maples hanging on the walls. (And a featherbed is offered in the fall and winter!)

The most eye-catching decor in another room called the Maples is artful white pickets, the only survivors from the original home, which front handsome silhouettes on the wall. The room also boasts white wicker furniture and colorful antique quilts.

Guests especially enjoy the wall silhouettes of Elsah's historic buildings, Patty said. "They give the feeling of looking out across the fence or down the road."

A handsome dining room features maple-leaf wall stencils, hand-traced and painted by Patty from maple trees on the inn grounds. Lace tablecloths add to country elegance.

Let's not forget Patty's incredible meals. Breakfasts might include a special recipe of heart-shaped French toast, tarragon eggs, fruit cups, hot muffins, gourmet coffee and teas, and more; for dinner, consider boneless breast of chicken baked in herbs and butter, flounder stuffed with crab, Elsah Hills gravy, river-bluff rice with pecans, country-green vegetables, and scrumptious garden-house cheesecake.

A cozy screened front porch, filled with wicker chairs and tables, is a great place to enjoy a peaceful evening in this town that time forgot.

How to get there: From St. Louis, take Missiouri 367 north to U.S. 67 and continue into Illinois. At Illinois 3, turn west and proceed to Elsah. There are only two major streets in Elsah, Mill and LaSalle; Selma intersects both.

Aldrich Guest House
Galena, Illinois
61036

Innkeeper: Judy Green
Address/Telephone: 900 Third Street; (815) 777–3323
Rooms: 5; 3 with private bath, all with air conditioning.
Rates: Weekdays, $54 to $74, single; $59 to $79, double, EPB. Weekends,
$64 to $84, single; $69 to $89, double; EPB. Seniors, subtract $5.
Open: All year.
Facilities and activities: Double parlor, screened porch, gardens. Walk or
drive to restaurants and historic attractions of the old lead-mining
town of Galena, including U. S. Grant home and scores of antiques,
specialty, art shops, museums, historic homes.

I never expected innkeeper Judy Green to greet me at the door
of the Aldrich Guest House and then come out to my car and help
me inside with my bags. But that's just the start of all the
pampering guests receive here.

The Aldrich Guest House, an elegant 1853 Greek Revival
mansion with Italianate touches, is part of the Galena legend of
hometown-boy-made-good U. S. Grant. Tales say that Grant
mustered his Civil War troopers on the "green" next to the home.
So I sat on the inn's screened porch, gazing at the expansive yard,
trying hard to imagine the stoical figure of the bearded general

drilling his ragtag army collection of Illinois farmboys, readying them for furious battle. Now you can also enjoy wonderful spring and summer blossoms, thanks to Judy's green thumb; get set for an explosion of tulips, lilies, and other perennials.

Judy uses Victorian hues—green, mauve, and white—to brighten her delightful guest house. I especially like the parlor's tall, wide windows that wash the room in sunny daylight. There's a baby grand piano in the corner; I tested it by playing a few chords.

A broad fluted oak banister heads the stairway leading to the second-floor guest rooms. Judy led me to mine, and I immediately felt like the proverbial bull in the china shop. It was quite beautiful—soft pastel colors offset by white wicker furniture and an antique lace quilt gracing my bed. Old-fashioned pull-chain commodes in some of the bathrooms add to the feeling of historic authenticity.

However, my favorite is the Cyrus Aldrich Room, the oldest part of the house. Judy said that it was the home's sleeping loft, now charmingly decorated but still with its original plank floor, slanting roof, and tiny sliding window intact.

Breakfast here is a treat. There was lots of chatter among couples from the Chicago area, Brooklynites, and a doctor and his family from Rhode Island, all gathered around a long dining-room table. Fresh flowers, balloon-style draperies, and fancy china place settings all harkened back to a more elegant era.

Then came the food: delicious quiche, hot homemade bread, fresh fruit, eggs, and sausage. And Judy's home-baked coffeecake makes you forget about your waistline. She also will recommend restaurants to suit your dinner tastes; I found the Kingston Inn to be just about everybody's Galena favorite. But other crowd pleasers are Silver Annie's, The Log Cabin, and the new Cafe Italia, one of my favorites.

How to get there: Take U.S. 20 (across the bridge toward U. S. Grant's house) to Third Street. Turn left and go to the end of the block to the inn.

✺

B: *After a night of fun conversation, I found that my bedcovers had been turned down and a chocolate mint placed on my pillow. Just some more pampering.*

9

Brierwreath Manor
Bed and Breakfast
Galena, Illinois
61036

Innkeepers: Mike and Lyn Cook
Address/Telephone: 216 North Bench Street; (815) 777–0608
Rooms: 3, including 2 suites; all with private bath and air conditioning.
Rates: $60, single; $70, double; EPB. Three-night minimum on weekends,
   holidays. Special packages, off-season rates available.
Open: All year.
Facilities and activities: Sitting room, upstairs breakfast buffet; wraparound
   porch. Nearby: historic sites, art galleries, antiques shops, restaurants.
   Short ride to Mississippi Palisades State Park; riverboat rides, river-
   boat museum, and other attractions in Dubuque, Iowa.

A homey atmosphere with soft sofas, comfy guest rooms and
a great wraparound porch perfect for people watching in this
historic lead-mining town—that's Brierwreath Manor. And it's
only a half-block from all the shops lining Galena's Main Street.
   "People love our porch," Lyn said. "They do some sightseeing, come back and relax on the swing to recharge batteries, then
go right back out again."
   The 1884 home belonged to a local butcher who fought in the

Civil War. "It's a simple, big house built to hold his wife, five kids, and mother-in-law," Lyn said. "He didn't include a lot of elaborate decorations. It's just a comfortable house."

Lyn and Mike, who are from the Chicago suburbs, fell in love with this home after working for a year at Lyn's sister's Galena guest house outside of town. They've furnished it with relaxation in mind—not many delicate antiques or Victorian finery to worry about—and I felt right at home.

The Mayor's Room (named for the previous owner, who happened to be Galena's top honcho) offers lace curtains, a queen-sized bed, and a shower big enough for two. An antique pedestal sink graces the Country Charms Suite. My favorite is the Heirloom Suite, boasting the inn's finest antiques, including an Eastlake dresser, armoire, and clawfoot bathtub. (Lyn supplies the bubble bath!)

A typical breakfast might include pecan French toast, ham, watermelon slices, and more. For early birds, an upstairs buffet features a variety of teas and coffees that should hold you until breakfast. And Galena is graced with several fine restaurants: the gourmet-styled Kingston Inn; super pork chops at Silver Annie's; and fine fettucine Alfredo at the new Cafe Italia.

How to get there: From Chicago, take the Northwest Tollway (I–90) north to U.S. 20; then go west to Galena. Turn north on Main Street, west on Franklin, and south on Bench Street to the inn.

B: *Ask Lyn about eating breakfast with Gen. U. S. Grant!*

Captain Gear Guest House
Galena, Illinois
61036

Innkeeper: Alyce Green
Address/Telephone: 1000 South Bench Street; (815) 777–0222
Rooms: 3; all with private bath and air conditioning.
Rates: $64 to $89, single or double, continental breakfast. Two-night
minimum on holiday weekends.
Open: All year.
Facilities and activities: Two sitting rooms, library. Patio, expansive grounds.
Nearby: Main Street shops, restaurants, antiques stores, art galleries.
Short drive to skiing, hiking, golfing, Dubuque's riverboat rides and
museums.

I'll bet many veteran Galena visitors have never seen this
handsome inn. That's probably because of its off-the-beaten-path
location (at the end of Bench Street). Yet it's less than a mile's
walk from this 1855 mansion to all the Main Street hubbub of the
historic town.

Alyce told me that a Galena captain in the Blackhawk
(Indian) War, Hezekiah Gear, built this Federal-style house, which
now rests on four secluded acres. "He carried his money under his

hat and would give it away to the needy," Alyce said. "Apparently he was kind of a character."

Gear, who also founded one of the area's largest lead mines, was a visionary. "When the railroads offered to link up with Galena and town officials turned them down in favor of riverboat traffic, it was Captain Gear who predicted, 'Grass will grow in your streets.' " By the 1890s, once-bustling Galena was virtually a ghost town, and Gear had been proven correct.

Alyce discovered the house on a spontaneous weekend trip from the Chicago suburbs to Galena. "On a fluke, I started looking at old homes," she said. "I walked in the front door, got to the sitting room, and thought the home had lots of potential."

All rooms are warm and inviting. A huge double parlor boasts 14-foot ceilings and is graced with Victorian-inspired furniture. Guests breakfast in a handsome dining room bathed in English-styled, paisley Waverly wallcoverings.

My favorite guest room is named Clarissa; it has a queen-sized bed with a 7-foot-tall walnut Victorian headboard, pine plank floors, French doors, and a double whirlpool bath. Hamilton's Room includes exposed brick walls and a window view of the patio. And there's a fireplace and twin beds in Mary's Room.

How to get there: From Dubuque, take U.S. 20 east to Bench Street, turn right, and proceed up the hill to the end of the long block.

The Comfort Guest House

Galena, Illinois
61036

Innkeepers: Tom and Connie Sola
Address/Telephone: 1000 Third Street; (815) 777–3062
Rooms: 3 share 2 baths; all with air-conditioning, TV and phone on
   request.
Rates: $60 to $65, single or double, continental breakfast.
Open: All year.
Facilities and activities: Drive or walk across bridge over Galena River to
   restaurants, historic sites, antiques and specialty shops, and art
   galleries in architecturally preserved Civil War–era town.

In the six years Tom and Connie have owned the 1856
Comfort Guest House, this inn near the Fever (Galena) River has
established itself as a comfortable place to stay while exploring
historic Galena.

The couple has named guest rooms for spirits—the alcoholic
kind, that is. "When we first moved in here, Connie constantly
would tell me to move cartons upstairs to the bedroom," Tom told
me. "I always said, 'Which one? We have three, you know.'
Finally, I just decided that they needed names. Saved me lots of
extra walking."

The Wine Room is Tom's favorite, decorated in deep burgundy colors and graced with antique furnishings, including a beautiful red-and-white striped hand-tied bed quilt. Connie is thoroughly knowledgeable about all the antique furnishings, and she told me that the quilt design became popular in England during the mid-1800s. She has personally designed and made by hand the attractive quilts that brighten each guest room.

The Champagne Room is done in soothing beiges and has an iron-rail bed, long blue drapes, and a tall bay window looking out onto the tree-lined street. I found it airy and inviting.

In the Ale Room, a huge brass bed seems to invite you to jump right on it. Lace curtains on two big windows, charming wall borders, and an unusual basket-weave quilt add to the lighthearted atmosphere. It also overlooks beautiful perennial gardens.

Hearty, healthful breakfasts of granola, seasonal fruit platters, muffins, breads, juices, and other beverages—served on antique dishes—are offered in the dining room, handsomely decorated with crown ceiling moldings, a brass chandelier, and a fireplace made of fine marble.

"That fireplace is another story," Tom said as he ran his hand along the marble mantel. "This home belonged to a local banker who insured riverboats that ran the Fever River and the Mississippi. The captains reciprocated by presenting him with marble carried as freight on their ships. And that's how our home got this marvelous hearth."

Tom and Connie, gourmets of note, will recommend the town's best restaurants for discriminating tastes. They both agree that the Kingston Inn offers Galena's finest dining experience. Specialties include *cioppino*, seafood served in a spicy tomato-based sauce; redfish and fettuccine; and French silk chocolate pie or homemade strawberry cheesecake for dessert. Another fine choice is Cafe Italia, with great Italian selections.

How to get there: From Chicago, take the Northwest Tollway (I–90) to U.S. 20 and continue west into Galena. Before you cross the bridge, turn left on Third Street. The inn is on the corner.

❋

B: *A new way to enjoy The Comfort Guest House—rent the entire house! It's a cozy way for families and friends to experience Galena hospitality.*

DeSoto House
Galena, Illinois
61036

Innkeeper: Daniel Kelly
Address/Telephone: 230 South Main Street; (815) 777–0090
Rooms: 55, with 2 suites; all with private bath, air conditioning, TV, and
    phone. Wheelchair access.
Rates: $69 to $99, rooms; $99 to $109, suites weekdays; $109 to $119,
    suites weekends; EP. Special weekend packages.
Open: All year.
Facilities and activities: Three full-service restaurants, tavern, indoor court-
    yard, courtyard specialty shops. On Main Street in historic Galena.
    Nearby: tour home of U. S. Grant; see preserved Civil War architec-
    ture; visit specialty shops and museums.

General U. S. Grant stood in front of the grand DeSoto House.
He was unmistakable in his heavy navy-blue Union Army great-
coat, wide-brimmed hat, full beard, and ever-present cigar.

I walked up to him, aimed my camera, said, "Smile," and
clicked the shutter. The General wasn't even startled. In fact, he
said, "You need another shot? I'll strike my presidential pose for
ya." Now I was the one who was quite surprised.

I didn't expect to find Grant at the DeSoto House, even
though he made it headquarters for his 1868 presidential bid. But
Galena is full of surprises.

Of course, "Grant" turned out to be local actor, Paul LeGreco, who portrays the General at special functions including breakfast, dinner, and meetings at the hotel. The likeness is striking. And it's a stroke of advertising genius for the hotel.

Not that the massive 1855 structure—opened during the period when unprecedented lead-mining profits transformed Galena into a trade and commerce center rivaling Chicago—needs any gimmicks. More than eight million dollars was poured into the restoration project. That kind of money is reflected in the elegance evident throughout the building, which was once billed as "the largest hotel in the West."

On my way to the guest rooms, I passed through an enclosed courtyard with high skylight windows that sent a rush of sun toward diners enjoying an elegant al fresco buffet in its open space. The guest rooms are decorated in various shades of soothing blues and beiges. Some of the furnishings include high-back chairs, dressers, and writing desks. Even the inside rooms have views, with windows overlooking the Grand Court.

The hotel offers breakfast and lunch in its indoor courtyard; or try a down-home country meal at the Steakburger Inn, a local breakfast favorite.

For elegant formal dining, head for the hotel's General Dining Room, located on the lower level; it's a romantic showplace with exposed brick walls and original ceiling beams. Menu choices include the finest steaks and seafood.

Or sample the French, Spanish, and Mediterranean delicacies at the Kingston Inn. Others choose Cafe Italia for wonderful pasta.

And how can you pass up a chance to relax in the Einsweiler Library with a cognac nightcap in front of a roaring fireplace—an elegant way to end a day.

How to get there: Take U.S. 20 to Galena. Turn north on South Main Street. The DeSoto House is halfway up the block, at the corner of Main and Grand.

෯෧

B: *Nine presidents have stayed at the DeSoto House, as well as the likes of Mark Twain, Ralph Waldo Emerson, Susan B. Anthony, and Horace Greeley.*

DeZoya House
Bed and Breakfast
Galena, Illinois
61036

Innkeepers: Bill and Carol Preston
Address/Telephone: 1203 Third Street; (815) 777–1203
Rooms: 4; all with private bath and air conditioning.
Rates: $60 to $65, single; $70 to $75, double; EPB. Two-night minimum on weekends.
Open: All year.
Facilities and activities: Sitting room, library, screened porch, lawn activities, garden. Short walk to Main Street shops and restaurants. Nearby: skiing, golfing, fishing, riverboat rides, historical attractions, state park.

If you want to stay overnight in one of Galena's more historic settings, try the DeZoya House. Built before 1830 by a local financier, the 4,000-square-foot structure is "the largest stone residence in Jo Daviess County," Bill said.

"It's significant because it remains the only Virginia-style Federal home in Galena," he added. "And unlike most homes around here, it was built wholly at one time. There are no later additions."

Bill and Carol know what they're talking about. They worked at historic preservation of homes in Chicago before moving to Galena. What's amazing is that their superb collection of Federal antiques (1780–1820) perfectly matches the character and period of this handsome house.

I noted some items in their collection: Guests breakfast on a Chippendale dining-room set dating from 1800; inn walls are graced with antique prints, including original Audubons; and other Federal-style furnishings carry visitors back to the fine household stylings of Colonial New England.

Two guest rooms on the second floor feature unusual cypress floors (probably brought up the Mississippi River from New Orleans by riverboat, Bill said) in addition to hand-carved four-poster beds. Two third-floor rooms, both with original plank floors, boast a sleigh bed (my favorite) and a pine cannonball bed.

The home rests on two acres, with Muddy Hollow Creek gurgling somewhere down the bluff. A screened porch is the center of conversation and games during summer months; guests also enjoy a small balcony that overlooks the property.

Carol is from southern Louisiana and makes sure nobody goes away hungry. Breakfasts might include ham, eggs, and grits (of course); homemade fruit breads and muffins; even eggs Benedict.

How to get there: From Dubuque, take U.S. 20 east to Third Street, turn right, and continue all the way down the block to the inn.

Farmers' Home Hotel
Galena, Illinois
61036

Innkeeper: Tom Ogie-Kristianson
Address/Telephone: 334 Spring Street; (815) 777–3456, (800) 373–3456; FAX, (815) 777–3470
Rooms: 9, with 2 suites; all with private bath and air conditioning, phone and TV on request.
Rates: May 15 through October 31, $65 to $115, single or double; November 1 through May 15, $50 to $105; EPB, plus drink at bar. Children $10 extra per night. Midweek and weekend packages, also business traveler rates Sunday through Thursday, include full breakfast, complimentary drink, Chicago paper, fax and copier service, coffee to go.
Open: All year.
Facilities and activities: Lunch, dinner, tavern, room service, concierge, hot tub, special arrangements for in-room flowers, champagne, balloons, or "whatever." Nearby: walk or drive to historic Main Street architecture, shops, boutiques, art galleries, museums, summer theater; short drive to skiing, hiking, riverboat rides, and museum. Near all the historic attractions of Galena, a mid-1800s lead-mining boom town and home of U. S. Grant.

The first thing I noticed about the Farmers' Home Hotel was the "frontier" atmosphere established by the high ceilings and long corridors. That's easy to understand, because this long brick building was built in the fall of 1867, housing a bakery and a boarding house for area farmers bringing their produce to the town market.

Tom has restored the Farmers' Home Hotel while retaining its nineteenth-century charm. He proudly pointed out the original pine plank floors—a throwback to the hotel's old commercial days. I could even see the original hand-painted numbers faintly visible on the doors of the guest rooms.

Period antique furnishings add to the charm of the guest rooms. I saw high walnut, iron-rail, and four-poster beds adorned with handmade quilts, rich armoires, dressing tables, and period-print wallpaper and hand-stenciling. Original window glass was retained when window frames were restored; I could see the wavy lines in the old lead glass.

Spicy hobo hash, steak and eggs, down-home biscuits and gravy, and even eggs Benedict will get you started in the morning. All food is homemade, prepared from scratch; and the hotel's breakfast meats are from Tom's own naturally raised hogs, so absolute freshness is assured. The inn restaurant offers breakfast and lunch to both overnight guests and the public.

A nice way to unwind from a day of exploring historic Galena is by enjoying a cocktail at the hotel's Spring Street Tavern. It offers ten varieties of beer on tap, a large selection of champagnes, and the area's largest selection of single-malt scotches and cognacs.

Finally, notice the extremely tall front door of the hotel. Its panels are carved to resemble a cross with an open Bible at the foot. Tom told me that this represents an old German folk custom used to bless a house.

How to get there: Drive into Galena heading east on U.S. 20 west and follow the road as it turns into Spring Street, the hotel is located 1½ blocks west of the bridge in Galena.

Hellman Guest House
Galena, Illinois
61036

Innkeepers: Merilyn Tommaro; Rachel Stilson, manager
Address/Telephone: 318 Hill Street; (815) 777–3638
Rooms: 4; all with private bath and air conditioning.
Rates: $64 to $84, single; $69 to $89, double; continental breakfast.
   Two-night minimum weekends and holidays. Special discounts
   November through March.
Open: All year.
Facilities and activities: Parlor, library. Porch, patio, and gardens. Nearby:
   Main Street shops, antiques, restaurants, historic attractions. Short
   drive to Dubuque's riverboat rides, museums, Mississippi River.

Some of the best views of Galena can be enjoyed from the
Hellman Guest House, built into the hillside of Horseshoe Mound
and overlooking church steeples, gingerbread turrets, turn-of-the-
century merchant buildings, and surrounding bluffs. Just one
glance of the spectacular views convinced me that the entire town
had actually been suspended in time.

   Merilyn fell in love with the house as soon as she laid eyes on
it in 1986. The sun-filled attic, with its turret room, inspired the
painter in her; soon she'll be converting it into her private art
studio.

The 1895 home, built by a wealthy local merchant, boasts a magnificent interior. I can't remember being more impressed by what appears from the outside to be a modest home but inside offers cherry and oak woodwork, stained and lead glass, and an incredibly opulent foyer—complete with its own fireplace.

A huge window in the formal parlor reveals spectacular views of Galena. For a closer peek, I fixed my eye to the brass telescope, a 1942 U.S. military surveyor's tool that brought the town within arm's reach.

Guest rooms are equally distinctive. The Hellman is the original master bedroom of the home. Besides Victorian antiques and a queen-sized brass bed, it boasts a tower alcove with more incredible views.

Other rooms are named for Hellman's daughters: Pauline offers a queen-sized iron-and-brass bed; Irene features a Victorian oak bed and sapphire-tinted accents; and Eleanor is a great afternoon sun room, with a Victorian bath that includes a claw-footed bathtub.

Yes, both Merilyn and Rachel allow guests to luxuriate in the spectacular view from the house's main tower. Get your cameras ready; you won't want to miss this shot.

How to get there: Although the house is located on Hill Street, guest parking is on High Street. From Dubuque, take U.S. 20 east into Galena and turn left on High Street (up the steep hill) to the inn's parking area (marked with a sign).

*

B: *A visual fantasyland inside and out.*

Log Cabin Guest House
Galena, Illinois
61036

Innkeepers: Linda and Scott Ettelman
Address/Telephone: 11661 West Chetlain Lane; (815) 777–2845
Rooms: 4 authentic 1800s log cabins; 2-room historic Servant's House; all with air conditioning and TV, 1 with wheelchair access.
Rates: Cabins $65 to $85, single or double; Servant's House $50, single or double; EP. Two-night minimum on weekends (Friday and Saturday).
Facilities and activities: Near old barn, fields, woods. Short drive to historic attractions, specialty shops, museums, and restaurants of Galena.

It's not often Midwesterners get to step inside an authentic log cabin. Most have been destroyed by man's "progress." The few that remain usually belong to local historical societies, and most of these can be viewed only from the outside. That's why these cabins are so special.

One was built in 1865 by a Civil War veteran who later came to the booming lead-mine frontier town of Galena to carve a fortune out of the ground. The other two cabins, dating from 1850–1860, were found by Linda and Scott north of Plattville, Wisconsin, dismantled there, and then reassembled and restored on their historic homestead.

I pulled open the old latch door to the soldier's cabin and found a room dominated by a huge stone hearth, with a massive stone floor covered by a braided rug. A large antique spinning wheel sat in one corner, and black kettles hanging from iron rails hovered over the remains of a toasty fire in the hearth.

The logs are whitewashed inside to give the quarters a bright, airy look, with cheery tieback curtains on the small windows. An antique spindle bed is tucked into the far corner of the room.

Upstairs is a sleeping loft, furnished with two three-quarter-sized rope beds—real pioneer spirit, here. I tried one out, and it actually felt quite comfortable. (Scott explained that it's all in how the ropes are strung.) A small corner crib adds more sleeping space for babies. Two other cabins are ideal romantic retreats that each accommodate one couple. Their stone fireplaces add to the coziness; so do the upstairs whirlpools.

And one cabin, which is just one story, is completely wheelchair-accessible.

The Servant's House was built on the property between 1832 and 1834 by the father of Civil War General Augustus Chetlain, one of nine Galena native sons who reached that rank in the Union Army's war against the South.

Inside the Servant's House a charming potbellied stove caught my fancy. I also liked the original plank floors, spindle beds adorned with quilts, lace curtains on the windows, and floral-print wallpaper. A kitchenette and indoor plumbing are the only bows to the twentieth century.

No breakfast or dinner is served here, but Scott recommends the Farmers' Home Hotel for hearty, reasonably priced morning meals and the Kingston Inn for evening feasts. Both are located downtown, a short drive away, and Scott will give you directions.

How to get there: Take U.S. 20 west through Galena to Chetlain Lane and turn left. Go ¼ mile and you'll find the farmstead on the left.

～

B: *I feel as though I'm in a private, history-laden village that's all my own.*

Park Avenue Guest House
Galena, Illinois
61036

Innkeepers: Sharon and John Fallbacher
Address/Telephone: 208 Park Avenue; (815) 777–1075
Rooms: 3, including 1 suite; all with private bath and air conditioning.
Rates: $65, single or double; $95, suite; continental breakfast. Two-night minimum on weekends. Midweek discounts available.
Open: All year.
Facilities and activities: Two parlors, screened porch, gazebo, and Victorian garden. Short walk to Galena historic attractions, shops, and restaurants. Short drive to Dubuque riverboat rides, bluff scenery, Mississippi River.

Besides the imposing architecture of this 1893 Queen Anne home, the first thing I noticed were the "porch people"—wrought-iron chairs fashioned into likenesses of an entire family.

"They're dressed for all the holidays," Sharon said. "Halloween costumes, Uncle Sams on the Fourth of July, you name it."

As you probably guessed, holidays play an important part at the Park Avenue. Especially Christmas, when each room boasts its own decorated tree, and the house is festooned with more than

200 feet of garlands, 1,400 holiday lights, and 27 window candles.

Guest rooms are charming. The Miriam Room, named for the original owner's daughter (who still lives in town at age ninety-six), offers Victorian furniture, including a gray iron-rail bed. The Lucille Room is bright and cheery, with a queen-sized iron-rail bed and an Eastlake dresser.

But sunlight lovers should choose the Anna Suite, boasting six huge windows, Victorian and Eastlake antiques, and an extra trundle bed.

Count on breakfast in the home's formal dining room or on the wraparound (and partially screened) porch. It might include fresh fruit, homemade breads and muffins, cereal, and more.

And ask the innkeepers to tell you about Admiral Bias Sampson, the home's first owner. He is believed to have been aboard the battleship USS *Maine* prior to the Spanish-American War.

How to get there: From Dubuque, take U.S. 20 east to Park Avenue, turn left, and continue to the inn.

Pine Hollow Inn
Galena, Illinois
61036

Innkeepers: Sally and Larry Priske
Address/Telephone: 3700 North Council Hill Road; (815) 777–1071
Rooms: 5; all with private bath and air conditioning. No smoking inn.
Rates: $85 to $90, single or double, continental breakfast. Two-night minimum on weekends.
Open: All year.
Facilities and activities: Picnic basket lunches available. Dining room, porches. Hiking, birding, wildlife watching. Nearby: Galena Main Street shops, restaurants, historic attractions. Drive to Dubuque for riverboat rides on Mississippi, fishing, museums.

This newly built inn might be one of the best-kept secrets of northwestern Illinois. Located on a 110-acre Christmas-tree farm in the heart of Galena's historic lead-mining district, it is a gold mine for travelers who want to enjoy the splendor of country living while having Galena's treats only a three-minute-drive away down Main Street.

My pa and I turned up Pine Hollow's long driveway, crossed Hughlett's Branch (creek), and stopped near a patch of black walnut trees that surround a picture-perfect country inn.

Andy and Molly, a pair of golden retrievers, greeted us with wagging tails.

"Samuel Hughlett owned this valley in Galena's lead-mining heyday," Sally explained, "and you can still find some 'sucker holes' in the ground." One old mining hole is now used as a den by coyotes.

Sally and Larry planted 9,000 evergreen trees that should be ready for the "U-chop" Christmas season in 1993. They planned to build a shed for tree sales, then changed that to a warming hut, and finally settled on a country inn.

"I still don't have that shed," Sally said.

This is a landscape and wildlife wonderland with wild turkeys galore, blue heron, deer, and howling coyotes. Hike the bluffs for panoramic views of the countryside. Or poke around the valley for mining artifacts; an archeological dig a few years ago turned up a few historic items.

I prefer a guided tour with Andy, who beckoned me to follow him up a hill. "Guests have told me he's such a good leader, we should hang up a sign reading GUIDE DOG TOURS EVERY HOUR," Sally said.

Most country-charming guest rooms are huge, with four-poster canopy beds and wood-burning fireplaces. I like Number 3, which also boasts two skylights. Number 5 offers a beamed ceiling and a clawfooted tub, while Number 2's allure is a large whirlpool.

Sally's hearty country breakfast might include blueberry pancakes and sausage, sticky buns, and more.

How to get there: From Dubuque, take U.S. 20 east to Main Street and proceed 1½ miles north (Main Street changes into Dewey) to reach Pine Hollow. Turn left at the sign and continue up the driveway to the inn.

❋

B: *This valley used to be called "Hughlett's Bottom," and Sally contemplated that as the name for the inn. "But I decided there'd be too much explaining to do," she said with a chuckle.*

Queen Anne Guest House

Galena, Illinois
61036

Innkeepers: Kathleen Martin and Cary Mandelka
Address/Telephone: 200 Park Avenue; (815) 777–3849
Rooms: 3; all with private bath and air conditioning. No smoking inn.
Rates: $45 to $50, single or double, continental breakfast. Special multi-
   night and midweek discounts.
Open: All year.
Facilities and activities: Double parlor, library, video, entertainment room.
   Short walk to Grant City Park, Main Street shops and restaurants.
   Nearby: hiking, biking, state park, riverboat rides, horseback riding,
   skiing, golfing.

Tucked away on a quiet corner in a residential neighborhood, this gingerbread-crazy showplace is impossible to ignore.

Its elaborate turrets, knobs, fretworks, and overhangs combine to create a graceful snapshot of past elegance. Built in 1891 by William Ridd, an Englishman who became a prominent Galena merchant selling window, sash, and door treatments, it "served as his showpiece," said Kathleen. "He put extras everywhere to impress his customers."

Now one hundred years later, Kathleen and Cary's "customers" are still impressed. Stained, lead, and beveled glass is everywhere, oak floors and woodwork lend more elegance, and the home has a very comfortable and relaxing atmosphere—thanks to these two friendly and gracious innkeepers.

Guest rooms, furnished with antiques and reproductions, are unnamed "because we have three rooms and four grandmothers," Kathleen joked. I especially liked Number One, with an antique crazy quilt on the bed and three windows that brighten up the room. Number Two claims the home's tower, while Number Three boasts a white, iron-rail bed and a private bath (down the hall) with clawfooted tub and pedestal sink.

A family-style continental breakfast is served in the dining room atop a long, antique, farmer's harvest table that was handmade in Dubuque, Cary said. The couple, however, is most proud of their 1920s Magic Chef stove, a white porcelain beauty that still cooks up goodies today. By the way, I think the inn's "continental breakfast" might be a modest misnomer, for it could include fresh fruit, eggs, homemade muffins, and maybe one of Kathleen's coffeecakes.

Galena nights mean fine dining. Newest is Cafe Italia, with great Chicago-style Italian specialties; The Log Cabin, a favorite of locals, serves great steaks; and the Kingston Inn, with its singing waiters, serves gourmet-style selections.

How to get there: From Chicago, take the Northwest Tollway (I–90) north to U.S. 20 and go west to Galena. Turn right on Park Avenue (the street before the bridge) and continue to the corner of Park and Adams to the inn.

๛

B: *Kathleen and Cary are two of the most outgoing innkeepers around.*

The Victorian Mansion
Galena, Illinois
61036

Innkeepers: Robert George McClellan, owner; Joan and Kurt Cable,
  managers
Address/Telephone: 301 High Street; (815) 777–0675
Rooms: 9; all with private bath.
Rates: $70, single or double, continental breakfast.
Open: All year.
Facilities and activities: Library, dining room, card room with TV. Nearby:
  historic attractions of Galena, U. S. Grant home, tours of historic
  houses; art, antiques, and specialty stores.

Robert led me into his twenty-three-room, 1861 Italianate
mansion, long a prestigious address for entertaining important
guests in this former boom town along the Fever (Galena) River.

We sat down in the library to chat about this incredible inn,
furnished and preserved with museum-quality antiques so authentically displayed that it's as if a photograph of the home in the
1860s had come to life.

I noticed soldiers' boots standing next to a tall coatrack and
Civil war–era Union Army greatcoats slung over the high backs of
elegant chairs in the dining room. That's not surprising because
General Grant was a confidant of the home's original owner,

wealthy smelter Augustus Estey; and a group of the General's cronies often gathered to discuss political issues of the day with the cigar-chomping soldier in the very library where Robert and I were sitting.

"See that black grate above you?" Robert asked, pointing to the ceiling. "Estey had that built into his library ceiling to suck cigar smoke out of the air."

The house is immaculate. Walking through the front door, I passed a beautiful 10-foot-high Victorian oil painting depicting the wife of the first mayor of Princeton, Illinois. What especially intrigued me was the hallway's unusual chandelier, which has four graceful swan figurines supporting a large glass shade. But even these wonderful items are overshadowed by the grand oval staircase that spirals all the way up to the third floor.

Second-floor guest rooms exhibit exquisite antique furnishings. My favorite is the Grant Room, with its invitingly huge walnut bedframe, marble-topped bureau, and deeply colored floral-print carpeting. Robert's collection of antique *Harper's Bazaar* political caricatures sniping at the General hang on the walls.

I found elegance everywhere in this magnificent showplace. Plank floors are covered by oriental-style carpets, some original to the home. Pocket doors (which slide unobtrusively into walls) separate many of the rooms. Historically correct wallpaper, four marble fireplaces, and opulent chandeliers are just some more of the extras.

The Kingston Inn is probably Galena's finest spot for dining. You'll enjoy everything from its special *cioppino*, seafood bathed in spicy tomato-based sauce, to redfish and fine steaks. The home-made cheesecake is a scrumptious dessert.

How to get there: Take U.S. 20 west to High Street and turn left. Go all the way to the top of a steep hill to the mansion, which stands on the left side of the street.

☀

B: *One of the most historically correct inns of the Midwest.*

The Mansion of Golconda

Golconda, Illinois
62938

Innkeepers: Don and Marilyn Kunz
Address/Telephone: Columbus Avenue (mailing address: P.O. Box 339); (618) 683–4400
Rooms: 3, plus fishermen's cottage; all with private bath, rooms with air conditioning.
Rates: $75 to $90, single or double, EPB.
Open: All year except Christmas Day.
Facilities and activities: Full-service dining room with wheelchair access. Lounge with TV, sitting room; patio, gardens. Short walk to Ohio River, levee. Short drive to Shawnee National Forest, park, fishing, marina, houseboat and pontoon boat rental. Horseback riding, hiking; cross-country skiing in area during winter.

I wandered down to southern Illinois' Ohio River country, some of the most beautiful scenery in the Midwest. This historic corner of the state is also rich in legend, from the trail-blazing George Rogers Clark expedition to the Ohio river pirates of the 1790s who preyed on flatboats from infamous Cave-In-Rock.

Right in the heart of a small river town is The Mansion of

Golconda. I was surprised to find that the innkeeper of this 1895 mansion was from my old neighborhood back in Chicago.

Don and Marilyn have established a tradition of fine dining and hospitality. The rose, gold, and blue dining rooms, furnished largely with period antiques, set the mood for what Marilyn proudly calls "The Mansion's dining experience." In fact, Illinois' Governor Jim Thompson has dined here several times. "I had a chance to do some show-off cooking," Marilyn said. And many others drive more than 100 miles just to eat here.

Dinner means candlelight and elaborate meals. Selections include sautéed chicken livers, honey-crisp chicken, steaks, and fresh seafood. I recommend catfish Camille, a spicy, grilled touch of heaven; or the orange roughy St. Germain graced with hollandaise sauce. Marilyn serves dinners on antique China platters, and loaves of steaming-hot bread on rough-hewn breadboards add to the home-style "flavor" of the meal.

But hold on! You can't walk away without trying one of The Mansion's homemade desserts, which are prepared daily. The favorite of the moment: Almond Glory Pie—all custard, milk chocolate, and almonds, of course.

Marilyn knows that sometimes travel-weary inn hoppers "want the breakfast to be good" at a country inn. So she caters to both light and hearty eaters. Juice, fruit, toast, and croissants satisfy some; eggs over easy, spicy southern Illinois pork sausage, and biscuits and gravy satiate hungrier guests.

Did I forget to mention lunch on the back porch? How about red snapper with cream sauce or chicken with tomato-wine sauce?

Original stained-glass windows, six fireplaces, fine wood-work, and pocket doors are all architectural features of the inn. The guest bedrooms on the second floor contain Victorian and other antiques dating from the 1880s to the 1920s.

The Camellia room boasts a 7-foot-high, hand-carved Victorian mahogany headboard draped in lace curtains. "It's our fantasy room," Marilyn said. Azalea has two canopied four-poster beds. Most popular is Begonia, with its 1892 iron stove warming a two-person whirlpool tub.

How to get there: From north, east, and west, follow Illinois 146 into Golconda and turn right after the courthouse.

Colonial Inn
Grand Detour, Illinois
61021

Innkeeper: James Pufall
Address/Telephone: 8230 South Green Street, Grand Detour (mailing
   address: c/o Dixon, Illinois 61021); (815) 652–4422
Rooms: 12; 4 with private bath.
Rates: $28 to $40, single or double, continental breakfast. No credit cards.
Open: All year.
Facilities and activities: Sitting rooms, expansive lawns. Walk in quaint
   New England–style village. John Deere historic site a short walk
   away down country village roads. Restaurants and 3 state parks
   within a short drive; hiking, boating, fishing, swimming, golfing,
   biking, cross-country skiing.

   Driving into this historic town is like wandering through New
England back roads. Quaint houses are strewn about tiny streets,
shaded by tall trees; a little stone church built in the 1840s stands
amid the homes, still welcoming visitors; friendly people tend to
their gardens; families prepare country barbecues in their back
yards.
   Then there's the charming Colonial Inn, an 1850 redbrick
Italianate house sitting on an expansive 2½-acre lawn with huge
shade trees, low hedges, colorful flowers, and chirping birds.

Owner James Pufall was waiting for his weekend guests when I arrived.

The guest rooms are on the second floor, reached via a labyrinth of angling corridors. "Just when you think they're going to end, they start all over again," he said with a chuckle. They have high ceilings and are furnished with many antiques from James's personal collection, along with an eclectic mix of other styles. You'll find quaint country-floral wallpapers, some Victorian headboards, iron-rail and brass beds, Empire dressers, oak crosscut 1920s furniture, and bright curtains on tall windows.

One of my favorite inn treasures is the solid brass chandelier hanging over the stairway in the second-floor hallway; it was handcrafted in England, James told me.

All that wonderful flooring is the original pine plank used in 1850. Most of the other wood in the home is walnut; even the beams that support the house are made of that valuable wood.

In the morning a seven-clock symphony greets breakfast guests on the hour; even reluctant risers manage grins as a French timepiece chimes "Frère Jacques," amid a cacophony of cuckoo chirps, deep bell tones, and rousing Victorian dingdongs. James serves a continental breakfast featuring homemade croissants, fruits, sweet rolls, English muffins, and beverages. For dinner, he can direct you to nearby small towns that have charming restaurants with quaint riverside settings.

How to get there: From Chicago, take the Eisenhower Expressway (I–90) west to I–88. Continue west to Illinois 26 at Dixon and head north. Pass under Dixon arch and immediately turn right onto Illinois #2; continue into Grand Detour, where Illinois #2 becomes River Street.

※

B: *I found a walk around the village very soul-satisfying.*

Hotel Nauvoo
Nauvoo, Illinois
62354

Innkeepers: The Kraus family
Address/Telephone: Route 96, P.O. Box 398; (217) 453–2211
Rooms: 8, with 2 suites; all with private bath, air conditioning, TV.
Rates: $45 to $65, single or double, EP.
Open: Mid-March to mid-November.
Facilities and activities: Wheelchair access to restaurant. Located in historic Mormon, French Icarian, and German town. Tours of historic homes and architectural attractions including site of old Mormon temple. Walk to glass works, bookstore, woodworking boutique, antiques shops, restaurants, historic buildings. Short drive to Mormon and Christian Visitor Centers, Icarian Museum, old temple, historic sites, vineyards. Great River Road scenic drive hugs the Mississippi River. Verity Riverboat Museum, Lock and Dam #19 in Keokuk, Iowa. About a 1½-hour drive to Mark Twain's hometown, Hannibal, Missouri.

The Kraus family bought this 1840 landmark example of early Mormon architecture in the mid-1940s and have been extending their family-style hospitality ever since.

But first some history: Nauvoo continues to be a family-conscious community, largely in keeping with its historical roots.

This town on the Mississippi River was the center of the family-oriented Mormon culture in the mid-1800s. Founder Joseph Smith had a general store not far from here. In fact, bricks from that historic structure are said to have been used in the construction of the Hotel Nauvoo.

The hotel itself was built by J. J. Brendt, a Mormon, and was completed by Adam Swartz, a German immigrant. Another link to the town's rich Mormon history: Fragments of a sun-and-moon stone from the old Mormon Temple are said to rest in the hotel's yard.

So the fact that the hotel, along with many other historic buildings, is still sturdy and strong is no surprise. Just what you'd expect from enterprising, industrious Mormon, German, and French Icarian pioneers.

Guest rooms are simple and functional, with original period decor sprinkled with near-antiques.

But the special treat is the Hotel Nauvoo Restaurant (with seven dining rooms!), where the Krauses serve up splendid buffet and menu orders. I devoured delicious blueberry muffins, among my favorite sweet treats. Then it was down to real business—dinner featuring choices like channel catfish (a local specialty) and home-baked turkey served with the inn's fabulous wild rice—and I shouldn't forget Nauvoo grape jelly served with home-baked cinnamon rolls and breads.

Later I toured some historic Mormon sites, including town orientations at the Nauvoo Restoration Visitor Center, Latter Day Saints Center, and chamber of commerce. I also drove to the old jail in Carthage (20 miles southeast), where Smith and his brother died at the hands of an angry mob before his followers abandoned Nauvoo and headed for Utah.

How to get there: From Chicago, take I–55 to Illinois 136. Go west to the Mississippi River; then north on Illinois 96 to Nauvoo. The inn is on this road, in the center of town.

B: For breakfast try the blueberry pancakes with homemade sausage at Kraus Restaurant across the street from the hotel.

Pinehill Bed & Breakfast Inn
Oregon, Illinois
61061

Innkeeper: Sharon Burdick

Address/Telephone: 400 Mix Street; (815) 732–2061

Rooms: 5; all with private full or half bath and air conditioning. No smoking inn.

Rates: $65 to $100, single; $75 to $110, double; EPB. $10 per child extra for more than two children aged 10 or older.

Open: All year.

Facilities and activities: Afternoon tea, Sunday ice-cream social; picnic basket lunches and dinners available. Sitting room, music room, screened and open porches. Croquet, bocce ball, badminton. Nearby: biking, cross-country skiing, golf, horseback riding, kids playground, Rock River water activities—fishing, boating, water skiing, water slide. Short drive to 3 state parks, John Deere Historic Site, Sinissippi Christmas Tree Farm.

My pa couldn't resist Sharon's banana nut muffins, whose scrumptious aroma filled this mansion atop Jackson Hill. He ate two, then walked off his bounty on the inn's handsome three acres of manicured lawns.

Later we explored the 1874 house, built by one of the first merchants in Oregon. I imagined how the home's tall tower once offered panoramic views of the lush Rock River Valley, a prime location for autumn colors.

Walking through the house's huge front doors is like traveling back into the nineteenth century. Floor-to-ceiling windows grace the sitting room; the music room boasts a grand piano engulfed by sheet music and fine-arts books covering ballet and modern dance; and a staircase leading to guest rooms is highlighted by ostentatious wheel windows boasting delicate blown glass.

"A way for the original owners to show off their money, I guess," Sharon said.

Guest rooms are delightful. The Somerset Maugham Room is named for that man of letters who often visitied Pinehill in the 1930s; he probably enjoyed the wood-burning marble fireplace on chilly nights, though I doubt that the whirlpool tub was around back then.

The Emma Lytle Room, named for a former owner, offers a marble fireplace, a Jenny Lind dressing table, and an unusual cannonball four-poster bed. A family favorite is the two-room Lincoln Suite; kids love to sink into its European double feather-bed.

But most popular is the Fischer Room, former servants' quarters now graced with an antique Victorian queen bed—and the best outside view of any room in the house.

Did I mention Sharon's delicious breakfasts that might feature freshly baked muffins and crumpets, eggs, breakfast meats, juice basket, fresh fruits, and two Pinehill specialties—granola pancakes and hazelnut creme coffee?

How to get there: From Chicago, take Illinois 64 west into Oregon; then turn right on Mix Street and go up the hill to the house.

❋

B: *A super inn for kids: Consider week-long Easter egg hunts, teddy bear teas, ice-cream socials, storytelling, and more.*

The Wheaton Inn
Wheaton, Illinois
60187

Innkeeper: Judy Shipanik
Address/Telephone: 301 West Roosevelt Road; (312) 690–2600
Rooms: 16; all with private bath and air conditioning. Wheelchair access.
Rates: $99 to $160, single or double, EPB. Weekend packages.
Open: All year.
Facilities and activities: Patio, lawn area with croquet course and gardens, sitting room, dining area. Near McCormick's Cantigny war museum, Prairie Path hike and biketrail; Herrick Lake paddle boating and fishing; Wheaton Water Park; Fox River and Geneva famous shopping districts; horseback riding; Morton Arboretum; Wheaton College's Billy Graham Center; golf courses; tennis courts; polo grounds. Also short drive to Drury Lane Theatres.

I enjoy The Wheaton Inn because it weaves so well today's sophistication with yesterday's elegance. The inn, completed in 1987, relies on opulence in the Colonial Williamsburg tradition for its distinctive flair.

Guest rooms are named after famous Wheaton citizens. Eleven have gas fireplaces, many boast Jacuzzi tubs, and each has an elegantly distinctive personality. All have European towel warmers in their bathrooms—another thoughtful touch, especially for travelers who venture out in Chicago winters.

Rooms boast oversized styles often found in European concierge hotels. The Woodward Room is one of my favorites, with its Jacuzzi situated in front of a large bay window that overlooks the inn's gardens. The fireplace marble came from the face of Marshall Field's department store in downtown Chicago. (By the way, the room's namesake, Judge Alfred Woodward, is the father of newspaperman Bob Woodward, who broke the Watergate scandal for the *Washington Post* along with Carl Bernstein.)

Vaulted ceilings in the third-floor McCormick Room, along with its huge four-poster bed and windows overlooking the garden, make this another guest favorite. In fact, the mayor of Nairobi, Kenya, chose to stay in this room on a visit to the Chicago area. Another charmer is the Morton Room, with its alcoved ceiling, cozy fireplace, and 4½-foot-deep Jacuzzi, perfect for guests who yearn for a relaxing soak.

Only the Ottoson Room, named after the inn architect, departs from the Williamsburg theme. A brass-topped black iron-rail bed is dwarfed by cathedral ceilings that harbor a skylight.

In a cheery, window-lit breakfast room, guests enjoy Judy's European-style buffet of imported coffee and teas, hot egg dishes, seasonal fruits, and delicious pastries and muffins. Personal service is a trademark here, so expect amenities like afternoon cheese and crackers, freshly baked cookies and milk, 24-hour coffee, and bedtime turn-down service with chocolate treats left on your pillow.

How to get there: From Chicago, take I–294 to Roosevelt Road, then go west to inn.

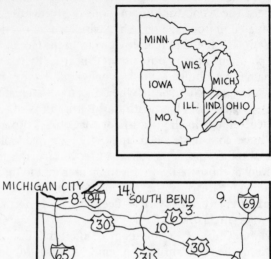

MICHIGAN CITY
8. 94 14. SOUTH BEND 9. 69
30 6 3. 69
10.
65 30
31
41
69
63 74
36 INDIANAPOLIS 5.
4. 70 70
37 74
COLUMBUS 7.
46 11. 1. 421
54 15. 65 50
231 6.
50
41
37
64
12. 13. 2.

Indiana

The Columbus Inn
Columbus, Indiana
47201

Innkeeper: Paul Staublin
Address/Telephone: 445 Fifth Street; (812) 378–4289
Rooms: 34, including 5 suites; all with private bath, air conditioning, TV and phone. Wheelchair access.
Rates: $79 to $175, single; $89 to $185, double; $225, Charles Sparrell Suite; EPB.
Open: All year.
Facilities and activities: Afternoon teas and sumptuous buffet breakfasts. Columbus is self-proclaimed "architectural showplace of America." Fifty significant contemporary works in one of the richest, most concentrated collections anywhere—a Who's Who of contemporary architects, designers, and sculptors. Horse-and-buggy tours of town stop at inn's front door. Historic-district tour map provided upon arrival. City's Visitor Center across the street. Walk or drive to restaurants.

Don't fight city hall. Just sleep in it.

This huge 1895 Romanesque-style brick building with its tall bell tower served as the city's seat of government for almost one hundred years. When it fell deserted, it seemed too august to simply demolish.

46

A Pittsburgh-based development company that specializes in historic preservation and restoration purchased the building in 1985—and the result is one of the most unique and elegant inns around.

Just stepping into the long entry hall is like entering an earlier era of elegance and gentility. Ornately engraved tin ceilings, handcarved oak woodwork, and original Victorian terra-cotta floors are graced with Victorian and Gothic-style love seats, huge brass chandeliers, and mahogany claw-footed banquet tables.

Guest rooms are magnificently furnished, with handsome teal or peach wall coverings and American Empire-style antique reproductions fashioned in France. I especially like the cherry-wood sleigh beds and second-floor rooms with floor-to-ceiling windows.

Most spectacular is the Charles Sparrell Suite (named for the architect of the old city hall), a stunning 1,200-square-foot chamber that is reached by ascending twenty-seven steps. It has 21-foot ceilings, 12-foot-tall windows, a sleeping loft (that's seventeen more steps), a second bedroom on the lower level hidden by mirrored French doors, and two and a half baths.

I forgot to mention the large Victorian parlor furnished in fine antiques.

Breakfast in the handsomely restored basement means a stylized buffet that might include fresh fruits and juices, homemade pumpkin bread, English muffins, apple and cherry strudel, and egg casseroles with meat and cheeses, fresh vegetables, and New Orleans–style bread pudding served piping hot.

If you still have an appetite for dinner, Paul or his staff will recommend several good restaurants.

How to get there: From Indianapolis, follow U.S. 31 south into Columbus and turn south on Washington Street. At Fourth Street, turn west, then go north on Franklin Street to the inn.

❋

B: *"A sense of quality has rubbed off all over Columbus."*—Time *magazine*

Kinter House Inn
Corydon, Indiana
47112

Innkeeper: Mary Jane Bridgewater
Address/Telephone: 201 South Capitol Avenue; (812) 738–2020
Rooms: 14, with 4 suites; all with private bath, air conditioning, and phone. No smoking inn.
Rates: $61 to $94, single or double, EPB.
Open: All year.
Facilities and activities: Parlor, sitting room, porch. Near Old Capitol building, Old Capitol Square antiques and crafts shops, art galleries, restaurants, Hayswood Theatre. Short drive to historic buildings, Battle of Corydon Civil War Site, historic Branham Tavern, Squire Boone Caverns and Village, Blue River canoeing, Marengo Cave Park, Wyandotte Caves, and Harrison-Crawford State Forest.

In 1837, Jacob Kinter opened the doors of the Kinter House as Corydon's finest hotel. Today it remains the historic village's best hostelry and one of the most handsome inns in the Midwest.

Old-fashioned hospitality is the hallmark of this carefully restored National Historic Landmark. From the rockers on the front porch to the fine period antiques gracing guest rooms named after historic Corydon figures, you're treated in first-class style.

Many guest-room antiques are museum quality. The Josiah

Lincoln Suite (named for Abe's uncle, who was a frequent guest here) boasts an 8-foot walnut headboard circa 1800 and a marble-topped walnut dresser hand-carved in an elaborate grape-vine design.

In the Governor's Room (named for Jonathan Jennings, the state's first chief executive, who toiled for an annual salary of $1,000), an 1850 four-poster walnut-and-mahogany bed with intricate leaf hand carvings is magnificent.

Yet my two favorites remain the huge Squire Boone Room (Squire Boone was an early Indian explorer and brother of Daniel), with its pencil-post cherry beds, plank floor, and exquisite inlaid star-pattern game table; and the President William Henry Harrison Room (Harrison, a one-time landowner here, was per-sonally known by every citizen of early Corydon), with its 1880 hand-carved mahogany grapevine dresser that looks as though it belongs in the Smithsonian. (The clawfooted mahogany shaving stand would also be mighty handy for trimming mustaches like mine.)

Third-floor guest rooms reflect a country theme, with plank floors, brass beds, and antique quilts.

The inn's homemade breakfast treats are legion. It might include goodies like ham-and-egg puffs, sausage cheese grits, cocoa banana bread, and sock-it-to-me cake (a house specialty).

How to get there: From Indianapolis, take I–65 south to I–64, go west to Indiana 135 (exit 105), then south to Indiana 62; turn east on Indiana 62, following that road to the inn at Capitol Avenue and Columbus Street.

⮎

B: *A special southern Indiana town, fitting for such a special inn.*

The Checkerberry Inn
Goshen, Indiana
46526

Innkeepers: John and Susan Graff, owners; Chris Graff, manager
Address/Telephone: 62644 County Road 37; (219) 642–4445
Rooms: 12, with 2 suites; all with private bath and air conditioning. Wheelchair access.
Rates: $85 to $165, single; $115 to $165, double; continental breakfast.
Open: All year except first three weeks in January.
Facilities and activities: Full-service dining room, swimming pool, arbor, croquet court, tennis court, hiking trails, cross-country ski area. In the midst of Amish farmlands; offers horse-drawn buggy tours of Amish surroundings, sleigh rides in winter. Near Shipshewana auctions, Middlebury festivals.

"We wanted to create a European feel to the inn," Susan said. "After all, being surrounded on all sides by Amish farmlands is more than enough country ambience."

The fine appointments of this northern Indiana inn do remind me of intimate, elegant European hotels I've stayed at. In fact, the handsome photographs adorning inn walls were taken by John during his travels in the French Bordeaux region.

Amish straw hats hang over beds, lending a nice regional touch to luxurious guest rooms that boast fine-arts prints, furniture with definite European flair, wide windows that allow views of the rolling countryside, and amenities like Swiss goat-milk soap in the baths. Rooms are named for flowers; my favorite is Foxglove, with its sitting-room fireplace, whirlpool bath, and six windows.

Queen Anne's Lace is another handsome room; its most interesting feature is a primitive secretary, made in the 1850s. "It consists of 1,200 individual pieces," Chris told me, pointing to the chest that had been delivered to the inn just that day. "And it took three years to complete." Its geometric designs put that craftsman far ahead of his time.

The inn's restaurant leans toward country-French cuisine. Four-course meals begin with a fresh garden salad, followed by a fresh fruit sorbet, entree, and dessert. An inn specialty is double duck breast sautéed and served over sweet onions, topped with an orange and Port wine sauce, accompanied by *Pommes* Anna and a bouquet of fresh vegetables. The vegetables, herbs, and spices are grown specially for the inn. Other favorites include chicken basil, veal medallions, and rack of lamb served off the bone with herb cream-and-garlic cheese.

The inn sits on one hundred acres, so there's plenty of quiet and relaxation. It's just a walk through French doors to the swimming pool, and the woods contain numerous hiking trails.

How to get there: From Chicago, take the Indiana Toll Road (I–80/90) to the Middlebury exit (#107). Go south on Indiana 13, turn west on Indiana 4, then go south on County Road 37 to the inn. It's 14 miles from the toll-road exit to the inn.

❧

B: *The inn boasts Indiana's only professional croquet course. So now is the time to perfect your game.*

Walden Inn
Greencastle, Indiana
46135

Innkeeper: Matthew O'Neil
Address/Telephone: 2 Seminary Square; (317) 653–2761
Rooms: 55, with 5 suites; all with private bath, air conditioning, phone and TV. Wheelchair access.
Rates: $60.50 to $71.50, single; $66 to $77, double; $118 to $125, suites; EP. Two-night minimum on DePauw University parents' weekend and graduation weekend.
Open: All year except Christmas Day.
Facilities and activities: Full-service restaurant, handsome sitting room and library, bar; short walk to DePauw University events, attractions.

"The inn doesn't have a lake, or pond, or anything like that," Matt said. "All we have is our integrity of service and cuisine." I can tell you both are excellent.

From Dublin, Ireland, Matt is a classically trained European chef who doubles as the innkeeper. The meals he now prepares have "roots in indigenous American regional cooking" but also reflect touches of his classical continental background.

He is especially proud of his Cape scallops, which he calls "absolutely the world's finest," served in cream-and-saffron sauce or sautéed with dill or raspberry butter. Another specialty is loin of lamb, wrapped in a puff pastry with duxelles of mushrooms and spinach. Then there's Chicken Pecan—a boneless chicken breast breaded with Dijon mustard, coated with chopped pecans, and sautéed—served with della Nonna sauce and a rainbow of vegetables.

Matt's appetizers are equally appealing. The game pâté is served with pistachios and truffles and wrapped in a puff pastry, and the puree-of-lobster-and-scallop soup features julienne of smoked salmon.

Dessert? Try the Fair Queen Chocolate Pie, with brandied raisins and orange zest, or the strawberries with caramel-and-bourbon sauce.

Is it any wonder people drive hours on end to dine at Matt's table?

Guest rooms are bright and comfortable, featuring furnishings with simple Queen Anne lines built by Amish craftsmen of northern Ohio. Bedspreads are handmade by Wisconsin craftswomen. There's also a flower box outside most every window. One of my favorite rooms is in the Cole Porter Suite, which has a sitting-room fireplace and canopy bed.

The inn library is another handsome attraction, with its salmon-colored tile fireplace that endlessly crackles with a fire during winter, large Palladian window, and Queen Anne antiques and reproductions. Or repair to the inn's bar, the Fluttering Duck, for a nightcap.

How to get there: From Indianapolis, take I–70 west to U.S. 231. Go north into Greencastle. At Seminary Street (a green sign signals directions to DePauw University), turn left and go 4 blocks to the inn.

The Teetor House
Hagerstown, Indiana
47346

Innkeepers: Marjorie Meyer, owner; Jack and Joanne Warmoth, managers.
Address/Telephone: 300 West Main Street; (317) 489–4422
Rooms: 4; all with private bath, air conditioning, and TV.
Rates: $65 to $70, single; $75 to $85, double; EPB.
Facilities and activities: Catered lunch and dinner. Sitting room, library, large screened porch, acres of lawn. Nearby: restaurants and specialty shops. Short drive to Centerville antiques mall, golfing, swimming, fitness center.

Locally, The Teetor House's staircase is legendary. I'll let Joanne tell the story.

"Ralph Teetor, the engineer and inventor who built this home, was accidentally blinded at age five," she said. "Later, when he visited New York City and stayed at the Waldorf-Astoria Hotel, he noticed how easy and comfortable it was to climb the hotel's staircase. It was the unusual rise of the steps that he liked. So he had an exact copy of that staircase built here."

Constructed in 1936, the handsome home is among the largest in Hagerstown, resting on ten acres. Teetor, who invented many ingenious devices including cruise control for automobiles, apparently spared no expense on his residence. Butternut and cherry paneling throughout lend a regal touch to this retreat.

(See if you can find the "secret" door in the cherry-paneled foyer that leads to the basement.)

The parlor's Steinway grand piano is a rare player, and the home has scores of music rolls to choose from. I picked the theme from *Cats* as my evening selection.

An expansive screened porch is another popular gathering place for guests.

Upstairs guest rooms are comfortable and cheery, with twin beds and airy spaces. A home-style breakfast might include omelets, waffles, or scrambled eggs and bacon.

How to get there: From Indianapolis, take I–70 east to Indiana 1 and continue north 5 miles until reaching Indiana 38; turn west and continue 1 mile; then turn in at the home's stone-pillared driveway.

Cliff House
Madison, Indiana
47259

Innkeeper: Lynda Jae Brierweister
Address/Telephone: 122 Fairmont Drive; (812) 265–5272
Rooms: 6; all with private bath and air conditioning.
Rates: $50, single; $75, double; continental breakfast.
Open: All year.
Facilities and activities: Sitting room, music room. Veranda. Short drive to
    historic downtown buildings; crafts, antiques, and specialty shops;
    restaurants; Lanier Mansion State Historic Site; tours of historic
    homes (September); Chautauqua; Ohio River scenic road.

I stood on the inn's second-story veranda overlooking the
great bend of the Ohio River and was swept away by thoughts of
pioneers in keelboats floating to frontier settlements. How exciting
(and dangerous) that must have been.

I also realized that the Cliff House might have the most
spectacular big-river vista of any Midwest inn.

Before discussing the inn, you must know a bit about the
town. Nestled in a valley surrounded by 500-foot-high, tree-
studded hills and limestone cliffs overlooking the Ohio River,
Madison is deeply rooted in its past. Perhaps the greatest legacy of
its 170-plus years is well-preserved architecture, with 133 city
blocks listed on the National Register of Historic Places.

Pick a street at random and you'll find stately turn-of-the-century buildings in a variety of styles ranging from Federal and Gothic to Greek Revival and Italianate.

You must tour the Lanier Mansion, a grand estate on the Ohio that emanates Southern gentility. It might boast the most spectacular location of any similar landmark building in the region.

Talking about location, from the Cliff House's perch on the ridge of the hill, you can see much of Madison and the Ohio. Built in 1885, this large antebellum home with tall white pillars facing the river resembles plantation houses of the South.

Guest rooms on the second and third floors include the Pink Room, with a four-poster full tester bed (complete with horsehair mattress) and a nice view of the river; the Yellow Room, with *all* windows facing the river; and my favorite, the Red Room, a romantic retreat with a queen-sized four-poster canopy bed and a panoramic view of the Ohio from bay windows.

Breakfast is served in the formal dining room on antique Haviland china and pearl-handled flatware. It might include homemade muffins, breads and morning cakes, croissants, juices, and coffee.

How to get there: From Indianapolis, take I–74 south to U.S. 421 and continue south into Madison. Turn right on Milton, and follow as it turns into Michigan Road. Watch for Fairmont, turn right up the hill, and follow the gravel pathway to the inn.

❋

B: *Maybe you can get Lynda to tell you about the love affair between the home's original owner and James Whitcomb Riley.*

Main Street B & B
Madison, Indiana
47250

Innkeepers: Sally and Ken McWilliams
Address/Telephone: 739 West Main Street; (812) 265–3539
Rooms: 3, with 1 suite; all with private bath and air conditioning.
Rates: $50, single; $72.50, double; continental breakfast.
Open: All year.
Facilities and activities: Sitting room, parlor, enclosed porch. Nearby: historic buildings, antiques and specialty shops, restaurants. Short drive to historic homes, riverboat rides, Ohio River scenic road.

The telephone kept ringing, and Sally kept jumping off her chair to answer it. "More reservations," she said on yet another return to the living room, eyeing me like some kind of life-sized good-luck charm. "Maybe you should come more often."

Sally told me that this Federal-style home, located in the heart of the Historic District, was built between 1843 and 1846 and has always been a private residence. Its size is deceiving—from the street, it doesn't look as though it would contain 5,000 square feet of space.

But all that room has been put to good use. In fact, the historic house, complete with "recent" ornamentations added in 1870, was featured in *Colonial Homes* magazine in October 1988.

The innkeepers were corporate gypsies, having lived on both coasts, Texas, and Washington, D.C., before settling in tranquil Madison. "My aunt had a houseboat on the Ohio, and every summer I'd come down here to visit her," Sally said. "It was always so peaceful. When we decided to slow down, the old memories of Madison just came back. We still liked the town, so. . . . "

Classical music wafted through the house as I sat in the living room, resplendent with its wood-plank floors, manteled fireplace, and comfortable sofas and chairs.

Guest rooms are upstairs, and one glance made it easy to understand why *Colonial Homes* so liked this inn. Four-poster beds, poplar plank floors, wing chairs, and handsome ceiling borders ensure that visitors enjoy classy and cozy confines.

Sally's homemade granola and coffeecakes, yogurt, muffins, fruits, currant jellies, and other fruit jellies, make up breakfast treats. A special bit of pampering: On request, Sally will bring a wake-up coffee tray to your room before the meal.

How to get there: From Indianapolis, take I–74 south to U.S. 421 and continue south to Madison. Proceed to Main Street and turn right, traveling through town to the inn.

The Thorp House
Metamora, Indiana
47030

Innkeepers: Mike and Jean Owens
Address/Telephone: Clayborne Street; (317) 647–5425 or (317) 932–2365
Rooms: 5; 3 with private bath.
Rates: $50, single or double, shared bath; $60, single or double, private
  bath; EPB.
Open: April through mid-December.
Facilities and activities: Full-service restaurant and 5 craft shops on first
  floor. Nearby: more than 100 fine arts, crafts, and specialty stores;
  historic houses; old grist mill; canal boat rides; excursions on the
  Whitewater Valley Railroad.

   This historic 1838 canal town looks much as it did more than
150 years ago, with clapboard-covered buildings, log cabins, and
general stores lining the narrow Whitewater Canal that originally
stretched 76 miles from Hagerstown through the village to Law-
renceburg.
   I couldn't resist a ride on the *Ben Franklin III*, the town's
newest horse-drawn canal boat that carried me over the only
operating aqueduct in the country to an authentic canal lock. I also
couldn't resist giving the horses, Tony and Rex, a pat on their
muzzles for a job well done.

Eventually I crossed the canal footbridge and came to The Thorp House, an original 1840 canal home transformed into a delightful inn by Mike and Jean.

"Though Thorp didn't build the house, he began living here in 1856 after bringing his family from Pennsylvania via the canal system," Jean said.

The innkeepers did most of the restoration work, uncovering fancy cast hinges on the front door and original pine and poplar plank floors. Five guest rooms (all named for the innkeepers' first paternal Indiana settler ancestors) are country-cozy—dotted with crafts, dried flower bouquets, and antiques.

My favorites: The William Rose Room, with stenciled walls, country quilt on the bed, and a window view of the canal; and Shedric Owens, boasting an antique pie-safe dresser.

Breakfast is an all-you-can-eat affair, with selections off the inn's regular menu. "We just fill up the plates, and if you want more, we'll fill 'em up again and again," Jean said. That's quite generous, considering that selections might include everything from homemade biscuits and sausage gravy, and egg and cheese casseroles to French toast, Belgian waffles, black raspberry pie and sourdough pecan rolls.

How to get there: From Indianapolis, take I–74 east to the Batesville exit; then proceed north on Indiana 229 to Metamora. Cross the canal footbridge to Clayborne and the inn.

∽

B: *A unique treat: Arrive in Metamora via the scenic route aboard the steam-powered Whitewater Valley Railroad, and the innkeepers will pick you up in a horse and buggy for a ride back to the inn.*

Creekwood Inn
Michigan City, Indiana
46360

Innkeeper: Mary Lou Linnen
Address/Telephone: Route 20–35 at Interstate 94; (219) 872–8357
Rooms: 12, plus 1 suite; all with private bath and air conditioning. Wheelchair access.
Rates: $85 to $100, single; $90 to $105, double; $140 to $150, suites; continental breakfast.
Open: All year except two weeks in mid-March and Christmas Day.
Facilities and activities: Dinner served in parlor on weekends to guests only. Short drive to restaurants, southeastern shore of Lake Michigan, Indiana Dunes State Park, Warren Dunes State Park in Michigan. Charter fishing, swimming, boating. Antiquing in nearby lakeside communities. Area winery tours. Old Lighthouse Museum. A short drive to heart of southwestern Michigan's "Fruit Belt" for U-pick fruit and vegetable farms.

The Creekwood Inn is nestled amid thirty-three acres of walnut, oak, and pine trees near a fork in tiny Walnut Creek. The winding wooded roadway leading to the inn is breathtaking, especially in the fall when nature paints the trees in rainbow colors.

Done in English Cottage design, the inn is warm, cozy, and

classically gracious. Massive hand-hewn wooden ceiling beams on the main floor were taken from an old area toll bridge by the original owner, who built the home in the 1930s. The parlor has a large fireplace, surrounded by comfortable sofas and chairs—a perfect setting for afternoon teas or intimate midnight conversation. Wood planking covers the floors. And you can gaze out a bay window that overlooks the estate's lovely grounds.

Mary Lou said she wanted to combine the ambience of a country inn with the modern amenities that people have come to expect. She has done better than that; she has established a first-class retreat. Twelve large guest rooms are tastefully decorated in a mixture of styles; some have fireplaces and terraces. All have huge beds, overstuffed chairs, and mini-refrigerators.

Last winter my wife and I stayed here during an especially snowy stretch. We simply walked out the front door, slipped on our touring skis, and beat a path to the inn's private cross-country trails that wind through deep woods and past Lake Spencer, the inn's private lake. Average skiers, we completed the loops in about twenty minutes, returning with a hearty breakfast appetite. Mary Lou serves a tasty continental breakfast of freshly baked breads, pastries, fruit, and coffee.

Late-afternoon tea in the parlor offers cookies and some delicious pastries. You may even have a cup of hot chocolate at bedtime on a blustery winter night, stretching before the fire and toasting your toes.

Mary Lou can arrange for special weekend dinners at the inn. She'll also recommend area dining spots. I suggest that you take a short drive along the lake to New Buffalo, where Miller's serves interesting *nouvelle cuisine*; the owner was a network foreign correspondent, and the restaurant draws a big-league Chicago media crowd.

How to get there: Heading northeast to Michigan City on I-94, take exit 40B. Then take an immediate left turn onto 600W, and turn into the first drive on the left. The inn is at Route 20-35, just off the interstate.

*

B: Mary Lou recently returned from Oxford, England, and was inspired to plant an English perennial garden on the east side of the inn. Things just keep getting better.

Essenhaus Country Inn
Middlebury, Indiana
46540

Innkeepers: Bob and Sue Miller, owners; Wilbur and Rosalie Bontrager, managers
Address/Telephone: 240 U.S. 20; (219) 825–9447
Rooms: 32, including 5 suites; all with private bath, air conditioning, phone and TV. Wheelchair access.
Rates: $55, single; $70, double; $80 to $110, suites; continental breakfast on Sunday only. Children under 13 free; cribs, cots available.
Open: All year.
Facilities and activities: Large enclosed porch, game room, kids' playground. Renowned restaurant, Das Dutchman Essenhaus, also owned by Millers, nearby. Villagelike setting, specialty and country stores a short walk away. Located in heart of Indiana Amish country. Amish quilt-and-crafts shops throughout Crystal Valley. Near Shipshewana, where numerous festivals are celebrated during year.

This handsome inn resembles a large Amish farmhouse—no coincidence since it's located in the heart of Indiana's Amish country. I saw black buggies pulled by horses clip-clopping down main highways, little girls with long black dresses and prayer bonnets, and boys wearing the familiar broad-brimmed hats.

Up and down side roads of the Crystal Valley you're likely to find Amish quilt shops, bakeries, and crafts stores. Best bet for sightseers: The inn offers a package deal that includes three-hour guided tours of Indiana's rich Amish heritage; you'll visit a cheese factory, buggy shop, Amish furniture factory, and hardware store, and learn about the new Menno Hof Center in Shipshewana.

So it's great to have the Essenhaus Country Inn as a base to explore Amish life. The inn has pure country styling, with handcrafted pine furniture specially made by craftsmen in nearby Nappanee, another heavily Amish settlement.

The main floor resembles a huge great room that's open to the rafters high above. It boasts all kinds of high-back sofas, rocking chairs, game tables, and sitting areas that truly have the feel of home. I also enjoy gazing about the fine country crafts and antiques that decorate the room.

I especially like the silver-plated potbelly stove, a decorative gadget my kids loved to snuggle next to.

The second floor resembles an open country meadow. A white picket fence corrals the second-floor balcony; and a white clapboard, one-room country schoolhouse, complete with desks and strewn with handsome country crafts, adds to the charm. It's a great spot for kids.

Guest rooms are elegantly country, with handcrafted pine furnishings. I'm always hooked by four-poster beds, as comfortable to lie in as to look at. Rosalie made all the attractive country drapes. Quilts and spreads were done by local artisans.

For a real treat, try the Heritage Country Suite, boasting cathedral ceilings, antique lamps, and a whirlpool tub.

As inn guests, you may make dinner reservations at Das Dutchman Essenhaus, the popular Amish-style restaurant that normally seats on a first-come, first-served basis. (A wait in line often stretches toward thirty minutes.) Count on delicious family-style fare, with heartland meats, potatoes, dressing, heaping bowls of vegetables, and steaming loaves of homemade bread. Dessert includes tasty old-fashioned apple dumplings, my favorite.

How to get there: From South Bend, take U.S. 20 east to the inn in Middlebury.

253 East Market Guest House
Nappanee, Indiana
46550

Innkeepers: Bernard Mishler and Jean Janc
Address/Telephone: 253 East Market; (219) 773–2261
Rooms: 6; 4 with private bath, air conditioning, and TV. No smoking inn.
Rates: $60, single; $65, double; continental breakfast. Off-season (November 1 to May 1) $40, single; $45, double; continental breakfast. Rates higher during Amish Acres arts festival in August.
Open: All year.
Facilities and activities: Short drive to Amish Acres' historic buildings, restaurant, and shops; downtown stores, Amish tours, and related attractions.

One of the inn's most appealing features is its rich stained-glass windows. "They are authentic, designed by George Lamb," Bernie said. "Experts have told me that they are rare and almost as valuable as Tiffany's."

Bernie and Jean have fashioned a comfortable English feel to their 1922 Georgian-style redbrick building. Bold rose print wallpapers, brass chandeliers, hardwood floors, and wedges of color thrown by stained glass make it a pleasant hideaway while you explore the Amish-influenced town.

Guests are served breakfast (juices, cold cereals, rolls, cherry and apple turnovers, or blueberry and cinnamon muffins) like royalty. That's because Bernie and Jean use original antique French china. Bernie showed me their service for forty. Get him to tell you the story of how he unearthed the treasure at a garage sale!

Rooms are named after candy, with a sampling of their namesakes available on each bedside table. Gumdrop features an iron-rail bed topped with brass; Lemon Drop is the brightest room, done in lemon yellow (of course), washed in light, and crowned with a stenciled headboard on the bed.

I like Melon Ball, with its 7-foot-tall Victorian walnut headboard and large walnut wardrobe. It is by far the home's most formal room.

Wintertime guests can curl up by the parlor fireplace to share some good conversation or just plain relax. Summer-season wayfarers should especially like the television room, entered from the parlor through French doors and loaded with wicker furniture, greenery, menus of area restaurants, and a VCR. The innkeepers keep a list of current videotapes available at the town library. All guests have to do is pick out their favorites, and Bernie and Jean will go get them for evening viewing.

How to get there: From Chicago, take the Indiana Toll Road (I–80/90) east to Indiana 15. Go south to U.S. 6; then go west to Nappanee. (U.S. 6 is Market Street in Nappanee.)

The Victorian Guest House
Nappanee, Indiana
46550

Innkeeper: Kris Leksich
Address/Telephone: 302 East Market Street; (219) 773–4383 or 773–7034
Rooms: 4; 2 with private bath, 1 with private half-bath.
Rates: $40 to $60, single or double; continental breakfast. $7 per child for
   rollaway cot.
Open: All year.
Facilities and activities: BYOB. In heart of Indiana Amish country. Nearby:
   restaurants, Amish Acres, Amish quilt shops, specialty stores, antiques, Borkholder Dutch Village. Near Shipshewana, famous for
   auctions of antiques and livestock and flea markets with more than
   900 vendors. Numerous festivals throughout year.

   Kris had enjoyed stays at inns on both coasts and throughout
England. Then the bug set in.

   "Four years ago on the Fourth of July, I was visiting relatives
not far from Nappanee," said Kris, "when the subject of owning a
B&B came up.

   "Soon I was ringing the bell of a Nappanee Victorian mansion,
asking the owner if she wanted to sell her home to me. Understand
there was *not* a FOR SALE sign out front."

It was only after discovering that Kris was planning to restore the handsome home and transform it into a gracious inn everyone could enjoy, that the owner agreed to sell. "The house meant too much to the town," Kris said.

Kris has done quite a job on the old Coppes House, completed in 1893 after taking five years to build. That patience is evident in the craftsmanship used to turn the home into Nappanee's showplace.

The front door, graced with lace curtains in the style of the period, opens to an etched-glass entryway. Original brass hardware shines everywhere, while rich panels of golden oak, cherry, and sycamore, found throughout the home, add to its luster.

"Lamb" stained glass, once made locally and said to rival Tiffany in its value, is found everywhere. I love the rose pattern set against a royal-blue background in the master bath of the Coppes Suite; more handsome stained-glass windows grace the front-hall stairway in a spectacular display of elegance.

The Coppes Suite is the guests' favorite, Kris said. Its most unusual attraction is a custom-made, freestanding bathtub, built for the 6'3''-tall original owner. "It looks like a huge trough, but it's beautiful," Kris said. So big that it holds fifty gallons of water; so big that Kris had to run a second set of pipes to fill it up in a reasonable amount of time.

The Wicker Room, with brass bed and lots of white lace, boasts its own balcony; while the Loft (old servant's quarters) features a tub that fills "from the bottom up," Kris said. "The water comes out from where you'd expect the drain to be. It fascinates all our guests."

An elegant continental breakfast is served in the imposing dining room (look for the servant call-button under the rug) or in bed. I suggest the Country Table, downtown, for good Amish-cooked dinners.

How to get there: From South Bend, take U.S. 31 south, then turn east on U.S. 6. Continue into Nappanee to the inn.

❋

B: *Get Kris to tell you about the secret staircase found during restoration and to share other house tales with you.*

The Allison House Inn
Nashville, Indiana
47448

Innkeepers: Bob and Tammy Galm
Address/Telephone: 90 South Jefferson Street; (mailing address: P.O. Box 546); (812) 988–0814
Rooms: 5; all with private bath. No smoking inn.
Rates: $85, single or double, continental breakfast. Two-night minimum year-round. No credit cards.
Open: All year.
Facilities and activities: Sitting room, porch. Walk to restaurants, specialty shops, craft stores, and boutiques. Summer theater. Brown County State Park a short drive away.

Tammy has added quaint touches to her country-charmed inn, nestled in the rolling hills of southern Indiana and just a stone's throw from Nashville's boutiques.

For example, her Victorian dollhouse near the sitting-room fireplace has decor that changes with the seasons. (Tammy pointed out that the miniature painting in one of the dollhouse's rooms is an original called *Bluebird in Sumac,* done by the same artist that executed the handsome paintings hanging in guest rooms.)

Then there's the folk-art rendering of the Allison House, done by a local artist, that depicts the entire Galm family—including Allison, the inn's dog.

I found the inn delightful. It was built in 1883, and the original owners had one of the first automobiles in Nashville. "Of course, no one in that family knew how to drive," Tammy said, "so they had to hire someone to tool them around town."

Guest rooms are named for the wildlife paintings that grace each of them. Some of my favorites: Eagle, with its iron-rail beds, quilt wall-hanging, and Brown County crafts; Bluebird in Dogwood, with its sandpiper ceiling-borders; Moor Hen, featuring an authentic, World War I military field desk; and Bluebird in Sumac, with a lovely, full-sized quilt wall-hanging fashioned by Bob's great-grandmother in the 1800s.

You can take breakfast in the dining room and share some of your town adventures with other guests; or you can sun on the large deck, where colorful flowers add to the country charm. Besides the usual fare, Tammy serves a caramel-nut roll that will make your mouth water. There are several restaurants that serve down-home family-style dinners; the innkeepers can recommend one that's right for you.

Be sure to explore Nashville, one of the Midwest's most famous folk-art-and-craft colonies. Scores of galleries and boutiques line downtown streets. Or obtain a map and take a driving tour of Brown County's many log homes, several dating from the 1880s.

And for some of the best rolling-hill panoramas in the region, visit nearby Brown County State Park. Its fall colors are spectacular.

How to get there: From Indianapolis, take I–65 south to Indiana 46. Go west to Nashville. Turn north at Indiana 135 and proceed to Franklin Street. Turn left, go to Jefferson Street, turn right to the inn.

The New Harmony Inn
New Harmony, Indiana
47631

Innkeeper: Nancy McIntire
Address/Telephone: North Street; (812) 682–4491
Rooms: 90; all with private bath and air conditioning. Wheelchair access.
Rates: $45 to $60, single or double, EP. Children under age 12, free; 12 and over, $10. Special winter packages.
Open: All year.
Facilities and activities: Entry House, indoor swimming pool. Located in historic town renowned for early nineteenth-century Utopian society community. Modernistic visitor center distributes information on historic buildings that dot settlement and conducts audio-visual presentations and walking tours. Nearby: specialty shops, fine restaurants.

As I drove across a bridge leading from southern Illinois into Indiana, a scripted sign arching high above the steel girders proclaimed *New Harmony, Ind.* Now I know why the town elders make that announcement. Driving into quiet New Harmony can lead to culture shock.

Amid the historic structures that are a reminder of a long-ago Utopian religious community stands The New Harmony Inn, blending harmoniously with its cultural surroundings. It's all dark brick, and its simple lines immediately call to mind Shaker stylings. Surrounded by tall trees, it looks unbelievably peaceful.

I talked with Nancy in her office across the street before I entered the inn. She said The New Harmony's goal is to provide "simple rest and relaxation" for its guests. That's exactly what I experienced.

Like all guests, I walked into the Entry House, a welcoming area that features a large open sitting area, high balcony, and a chapel intended for meditation. Rooms are located in buildings (referred to as "dormitories") across expansive lawns.

My favorites are rooms with wood-burning fireplace and a sleeping loft that's reached by a spiral staircase. Others have kitchenettes and exterior balconies overlooking the grounds.

The spartan furniture reflects the strong influence of Shaker design. Rocking chairs, simple oak tables, some sofa beds, and area rugs on hardwood floors complete the decor.

I immediately headed for the "greenhouse" swimming pool that's open all year. It's just a short walk from the rooms and a great way to relax after a long drive; there's also a newly completed health spa, with whirlpool, sauna, tennis courts, and Nautilus exercise equipment.

The inn's Bayou Grill serves breakfast in the coffee shop. Nancy recommends the nearby Red Geranium for wholesome dinner delicacies. You can choose from down-home dishes like baked chicken, grilled ham steak, and braised brisket of beef with vegetables.

How to get there: New Harmony is located at the point where Indiana 66 meets the Wabash River, 7 miles from I–64. In Indiana, take the Poseyville exit; in Illinois, take the Grayville exit.

TAYLOR

The Rockport Inn
Rockport, Indiana
47635

Innkeepers: Emil and Carolyn Ahnell
Address/Telephone: Third Street at Walnut; (812) 649–2664
Rooms: 6, all with private bath, air conditioning and TV.
Rates: $32 to $40, single; $36 to $46, double; continental breakfast. No credit cards.
Open: All year. Restaurant closed Monday and Tuesday.
Facilities and activities: Full-service restaurant with wheelchair access and cocktails available. Nearby: Ohio River bluff-filled landscape, Abe Lincoln Pioneer Village (mid-1800s homestead), Old Rockport Little Theater, fishing, boating, cross-country skiing.

When I arrived at the charming Rockport Inn, a wedding-shower party had just gathered in the lobby, waiting to be seated in a private dining room. The room vibrated with friendly chatter, which seemed to perfectly characterize the quaint small-town atmosphere that the inn calls to mind.

I met Emil back in the kitchen, where he was helping the cook ready luncheon plates and Mimosas for the shower. In between slapping tomatoes and lettuce on sandwiches, he told me that the 1855 inn is one of the oldest remaining buildings in this history-filled Ohio River town.

He excused himself and took a platter of sandwiches out to the dining room. When he returned, Emil told me that the building still rests on the original hand-hewn logs and beams used to build the house. I could see the old square-shaped iron nails that hold it together.

Later, as we walked up the stairs and down a long hallway to reach the guest rooms, we discovered that we're "Big Ten" brothers, both having completed studies at Northwestern University's graduate school. So we had lots of catching up to do before we proceeded any further.

Inside the rooms, I first noticed the original poplar hardwood floors that have survived all kinds of renovations. Emil and Carolyn have decorated with antique beds, oak dressers, sitting chairs, and oriental-style rugs. Even with the party going on downstairs and a dining room full of customers, it was quiet and peaceful here.

The inn prides itself on excellent food. Prime rib, tournedos, beef *bordelaise*, and stuffed pork chops are just some of the entrees offered here. A daily special is announced by waiters at the dining tables.

Homemade pies and cookies are another treat at the Rockport. A good way to work off dessert is to walk to the base of the 200-foot bluff at the end of Main Street. A historical marker notes that it was from here that young Abe Lincoln left on his famous flatboat trip to New Orleans.

How to get there: From Evansville, take Indiana 66 into Rockport; then turn right on Linda. At Main Street, turn left and continue to Third Street. Turn right to the inn.

*

B: *The Rockport Inn was one of the first area buildings to have glass windows. If you look closely, you'll see wavy lines in the old lead glass.*

Queen Anne Inn
South Bend, Indiana
46601

Innkeepers: Pauline and Bob Medhurst
Address/Telephone: 420 West Washington; (219) 234–5959
Rooms: 5, with 1 suite; all with private bath, air conditioning, and phone.
Rates: $60 to $80, single; $65 to $85 double; EPB. Two-night minimum
  on Notre Dame football and graduation weekends.
Open: All year.
Facilities and activities: Parlor, library, porch. Open House first Sunday in
  December. Located in West Washington Historic District. Nearby:
  Century Center, Tippecanoe Place, Covelski Stadium, Studebaker
  Auto Museum, Copshalom, Oliver House Museum. Short drive to
  restaurants and Notre Dame campus and its events and activities.

Bob is a former Marine Corps officer who now sports a
handlebar mustache; Pauline was a college professor of education.
Both delight in revealing the history of their wonderful inn.

The seventeen-room Queen Anne Victorian was built in 1893
by Sam Good, a South Bend contractor who became wealthy in
the California gold rush. Bob said Good was friends with famed
architect Frank Lloyd Wright who built the nearby Wright house.
(Well, of course!)

"A result of that friendship is this," Bob said, as he led me into the library, revealing an exquisite lead-glass bookcase designed by Wright.

There are other elegant touches here: Silk wallpapers, crystal chandeliers, lead glass, and a carved oak staircase imported from Italy with an ornate newel post all offer glimpses into the house's masterful craftsmanship.

Also surviving is a porte cochere, with handsome fluted columns, which was used for guests arriving in coach and buggy.

It's hard to believe that the house, at one time called the best example of Queen Anne neoclassical architecture within 100 miles, was once traded for a single Commodore computer! Get Bob to tell you *that* story.

Bob said there are ten kinds of oak used throughout the house, and the dining room is done in solid mahogany. The crystal chandelier in the music room is original to the home. "Didn't know what we had until I went up there to polish it," Bob said. "Turned out to be solid sterling silver."

Guest rooms, named for common birds of the area, are attractive and filled with period antiques and reproductions. A few favorites: Scarlet Tanager Room, with its twin sleigh beds and bed quilt made by Pauline; Cardinal Suite, with fireplace, cozy window seat, and queen-sized brass-and-pewter bed; and the Humming-bird Room, with its huge Jenny Lind bed donned with eyelet-lace covers.

Pauline is a great chef, and her baking fills the air with a scrumptious aroma. A full breakfast may include blueberry pancakes, Texas French toast, bran muffins, fruit, juice, beverages, coffeecake, and more.

The porch, with its comfy wicker furniture, is a nice place to relax after breakfast or sip iced tea or homemade lemonade on late afternoons.

How to get there: From Chicago, take I–94 east to U.S. 20, then continue east. At U.S. 31, exit north into South Bend. Go to Washington, turn left, and continue to the inn.

❀

B: *Bob can tell you how the house was moved 7 blocks to save it from the wrecker's ball; it is the largest and heaviest house (350 tons) ever to be moved in the county.*

Story Inn
Story, Indiana
47448

Innkeepers: Benjamin and Cyndi Schultz, owners; Susan Barrett, manager
Address/Telephone: State Road 135 South (mailing address: P.O. Box 64);
  (812) 988–2273
Rooms: 5, including 3 suites, plus 6 cottages; all with private bath and air
  conditioning, some with TV. No smoking inn.
Rates: $55 to $75, single; $65 to $85, double; EPB.
Open: All year.
Facilities and activities: Gourmet restaurant serves breakfast to public every
  day except Monday; dinner, Tuesday through Sunday. Tea time
  (including homemade desserts) 2:00–5:00 P.M. daily. Nearby: Edges
  Brown County State Park for hiking, biking, relaxing. Nashville, with
  scores of specialty stores, antiques shops, and art galleries, is 14 miles
  north.

"Now I'm gonna tell you the story about Story," said Susan,
a country girl with an Indiana twang whose sparkling eyes and
quick smile reminded me a lot of Dolly Parton.

She almost never had the chance. My wife and I had driven
from Nashville, down twisting backroads and through dense forest
in search of the Story Inn. We finally came to a "T" in the road,
and there was Story, Indiana—a tumbledown old mill, a few

cottages, and a dilapidated, tin-sided general store that looked like something straight out of the *Beverly Hillbillies*.

That general store was the Story Inn. It even had two old American Oil gas pumps on its front porch, their red-and-gold glass crowns lighted and shining, along with a collection of broken stoves and other geegaws.

We fought the urge to flee and walked inside. Fresh flowers graced tables in an expansive dining room whose ceilings, walls, and timbers are crammed with antiques, kerosene lamps, patent medicine bottles that promise cures for the grippe, and all kinds of gadgets. A big wood-burning stove sits in the center of the room. And the menu reads like a gourmet's wish list.

"There's been a general store here since the 1850s," Susan said, although this building went up in 1916. "During the 1920s, Studebaker chassis were assembled on the second floor." Upstairs she pointed to where workers used to slide them out from the loft to the ground below.

I'll let Susan tell the rest of the story when she sees you. Or maybe you'll talk with Cyndi, who also is the chef. She often chats with guests during dinner. So does Benjamin; he is known to sometimes speak animated French to bilingual visitors.

Food. That's the real story. Cyndi's gustatory delights change every Friday. Maybe you'd enjoy her steak *au poivre* (an 11-ounce rib eye marinated in wine, garlic, and pepper, and deglazed in brandy); *poulet printemps* (chicken breast breaded in pecan meal, sautéed and finished in rhubarb, rosé wine, and savory sauce); or medallions of baked pork stuffed with apricots, currants, pine nuts, herb bread crumbs, and marinated mustard seed, glazed with maple syrup and honey mustard, and topped with orange sauce.

Many vegetables and herbs come from Cyndi's garden. Benjamin's expertise in the kitchen has come from cooking stints in restaurants spanning the globe, including North Africa, Greece, and France.

The restaurant also offers a selection of California, French, and Australian wines. And the house dessert is Turtle Cheese Cake, tinged with coffee liqueur and topped with toffee, crushed pecans, and chocolate.

I don't think I ever want to leave here.

How to get there: From Nashville, take Indiana 46 east, then Indiana 135 south into Story. You can't miss the inn.

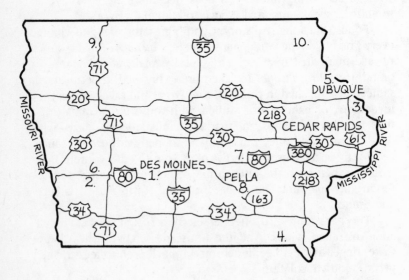

Iowa

Numbers on map refer to towns numbered below.

Walden Acres
Adel, Iowa
50003

Innkeepers: Phyllis and Dale Briley
Address/Telephone: R.R. 1, Box 30; (515) 987–1338 or 987–1567
Rooms: 2 share 1 bath; both with air conditioning.
Rates: $45, single; $55, double; EPB. $5 per child, $10 per teenager. Pets
    boarded, $7. No credit cards.
Open: All year.
Facilities and activities: Recreation room–solarium. Outdoor trampoline,
    badminton, volleyball. Forty acres of rolling hills with 6-acre horse-
    shaped lake for fishing. Four-room antiques shop. Stable for 18
    horses; kennel runs. Hawkeye Antique Acres and restaurants nearby.

Many people just might see an old barn standing on the
historic Bob Feller homestead. But I see history, because inside the
weathered structure, the Hall of Fame pitcher for the Cleveland
Indians threw that incredible fastball to his dad when he was just
an Iowa farmboy with a live arm.

The farmstead, with its English cottage and historic barn, is
home to Phyllis and her country-vet husband, Dale (who has a
small cottage clinic for his animals far away from the main house),
and to their guests who stay overnight at this idyllic 40-acre
spread.

On my visit, Dale was tending to his patients; an Irish setter was an especially happy fellow, licking his owner's face in thanks that she'd come to retrieve him. What with a kindly, soft-spoken country vet, horses in a corral behind the main house, and bales of hay strewn in the fields, I couldn't help but feel that I'd stepped into a scene right out of James Herriot's animal tales.

Phyllis showed me the charming guest rooms: One was soft and delicate, with oriental rugs, ceiling fans, a lacy bedspread and curtains, and a fireplace; another was more rough-hewn, laden with attractive antiques and folk art.

I was particularly taken with a large antique basket hanging on the wall. Phyllis told me that it had been used by field hands harvesting tobacco.

If you like farm breakfasts, you're in for a treat. Phyllis serves "stick to your ribs" Iowa breakfasts to guests in her English country kitchen. That means eggs, sausage, flapjacks, bread, rolls, and hot coffee. (It's just a short ride to Des Moines for "big-city" attractions; or stick around and enjoy excellent steaks at a popular roadhouse restaurant nearby.)

Of course, I toured the historic barn that is crucial to the Bob Feller legend. The one-hundred-year-old building also boards horses, as Walden Acres is a kind of long-term B&B for four-legged travelers, too! I especially liked watching the animals being turned out to pasture daily.

Phyllis said that people often stop along the road just to take a glimpse inside the Feller barn and soak up some baseball history.

Funny—that's exactly how I discovered Walden Acres.

How to get there: Take I–80 to the Waukee/Booneville exit (#117) and go south on Rural Route 22 for 1 mile. At the top of the hill, turn right down a gravel road and proceed for 1 mile until you come to the barn and home on the left side of the road.

∽

B: *Bob Feller sometimes stops by the home during summers to visit. Wouldn't it be great to run into a Hall-of-Famer on "Backroad, U.S.A." Or travel to his hometown of Van Meter, which is building a Bob Feller baseball museum with many of the ballplayer's awards and mementos on display.*

Victorian Bed and Breakfast Inn
Avoca, Iowa
51521

Innkeepers: Jan and Gene Kuehn
Address/Telephone: 425 Walnut Street; (712) 343–6336 or (800) 397–3914
Rooms: 4 share 2 baths.
Rates: $55, single or double, EPB.
Open: All year.
Facilities and activities: Lunch, dinner. Just east of Avoca is the "biggest little antiques center in southwest Iowa," with several shops. An hour's drive away is Carstens Memorial Farm, a 100-year-old farmstead; DeSoto National Wildlife Refuge; Elk Horn Danish Windmill; and Botna Bend Park.

I immediately liked this gracious turn-of-the-century Queen Anne Victorian. The magnificent Southern yellow pine woodwork and floors that literally sparkle are easily the most outstanding features of the home.

Finely carved pine columns in both the parlor and elegant dining room are highlighted by large windows that let the sunlight in, adding luster to the pine adornments. Beautiful flower arrangements brighten both rooms.

All the guest rooms have names of flowers, like Jasmine and Apple Blossom, and they're reached by climbing a hand-turned pine staircase. One room has fine antique walnut Eastlake treasures, while others boast brass beds, floral-print wallpapers, and other decorating goodies. They're happy and friendly spaces.

Jan pointed out the handmade quilts and handsome wallpapers to match those wonderful treasures. Many of the quilts are done by Mennonite neighbors.

My favorite is the Wild Rose Room, resplendent in pink pastels and washed in white furniture that includes an iron-rail bed; what makes it so is the little alcove with tall windows that look out onto the quiet street.

Jan and Gene are very proud innkeepers, excited about the prospect of owning a historic inn after operating motels in New Mexico and Wyoming. "I like doing beautiful table decorations that I specially change during the seasons," Jan said. "I also prepare gourmet meals and desserts." A typical dinner might feature medallions of beef in mushroom sauce, a dazzling cream-of-broccoli or chilled avocado soup, glazed carrots, rice pilaf, and scrumptious French dessert puffs topped with cream cheese, powdered sugar, and whipped cream. A current dessert favorite is the Orange Blossom Torte.

This feast is served on lovely Lenox china, with sterling silver flatware and beautiful table arrangements that have earned this inn quite a reputation.

Hearty breakfasts include eggs Benedict, quiches, fruit compotes, and beverages. There's simply no way you can go hungry here.

The best way to describe this inn's personality is "county comfortable." "I'll do what people want to make them feel very much at home," Jan noted.

How to get there: Take I–80 to U.S. 59. Go south to Avoca. U.S. 59 turns into Walnut Street in town. The inn is just past the downtown section, on the right side of the street.

✳

B: *Look for the Murphy-type bed hidden in an oak cabinet and the imposing Northwind walnut sideboard, both dating from the 1800s.*

Mont Rest Victorian House of Bellvue
Bellvue, Iowa
52031

Innkeepers: Christine and Robert Gelms, owners
Address/Telephone: 300 Spring Street; (319) 872–4220
Rooms: 5 share 2¾ baths; all with air conditioning. No smoking inn.
Rates: $50 to $90, single or double, EPB.
Open: All year except Christmas Eve and Day.
Facilities and activities: Sitting room with fireplace, gourmet meals, thera-
    peutic massage, panoramic views of Mississippi River due to inn's
    bluff-top location. Situated in one of the most picturesque river towns
    in Iowa. Nine parks nearby (several with great bluff-top river views),
    trout streams, 9-hole golf course, Young Museum, tours of Lock and
    Dam No. 12, butterfly garden, antiques shops, hiking, biking, Indian
    cave. Fests include Fourth of July Heritage Days and Tom Sawyer
    Days in August.

"This house was once lost in a poker game," Christine said.
    That was in 1896, just three years after Seth Baker built Mont
Rest, a nine-acre estate nestled halfway up a wooded bluff
affording one of Iowa's most panoramic views of the Mississippi
River.

Locals nicknamed the imposing white house, with its round, white tower protruding like a periscope from the home's belly, Baker's Castle—a moniker that has stuck into the 1990s.

I cannot overemphasize that the inn's vista of the Mississippi is truly breathtaking.

The Bellvue Room is the inn's largest sleeping quarters and has a great view of both the river and the quaint town. It has a 9-foot headboard on the bed and matching furniture with pink marble tops. The room's a favorite for honeymoon and anniversary couples.

A guest favorite is the Great River Room, all done in delicate blues with print ceiling borders, a pinwheel-style bed quilt, and marble-topped dresser; it's a terrific spot from which to gaze out endlessly over the mighty "Miss'sip."

Eagle's Nest, a charming room with hand-stenciled hardwood floors and an iron-rail bed, is another of my favorites. Sometimes you can see eagles making their nests in the trees.

The Baker Room, located in the building's tall tower, offers one of the Midwest's best river vistas, but, Christine said, "It's not for the faint of heart." Oak antiques, hooked rugs, and a roof garden are some additional perks.

A full country breakfast awaits overnight guests. Imagine country-style eggs with green peppers and cheese, smoked sausage, homemade banana-nut bread and coffeecakes, fresh fruit, orange juice, and beverages. Dine at Potter's Mill, built in 1843 on the edge of Big Mill Creek and now carefully restored and transformed into a unique restaurant; it serves some of the best prime rib and pork loin in these parts. Not to mention catfish and trout from local rivers and streams.

How to get there: From Dubuque, take U.S. 52 south into Bellvue. Turn right on Spring Street and continue to the inn.

❀

B: *Maybe you'd rather stay at the innkeeper's "new" 1800s boat house, across the road from the river?*

Mason House Inn
Bentonsport, Iowa
52565

Innkeeper: Dr. William and Sheral McDermet
Address/Telephone: Rural Route 2, Box 237, Bentonsport, Keosauqua,
  Iowa 52565; (319) 592–3133
Rooms: 10; 2 with private bath. No smoking inn.
Rates: $45 to $65, single or double, EPB. No credit cards.
Open: All year.
Facilities and activities: Located in village declared National Historic District
  in 1972. Walk to shops (open April through November, Sunday–
  Saturday) that include native crafts, antiques, blacksmith, weaver,
  and potter. Nearby: bike, hike, canoe on Des Moines River. Short
  drive to restaurants, Shimek State Forest, cross-country skiing.

If you look upstream from the 1882 bridge in this historic
river-front village, you'll see ripples on the water marking the site
of the old dam. It's a reminder of the days when the Des Moines
River teemed with riverboat traffic, mills lined the winding banks,
and nearly 1,500 people lived in the town. Today the year-round
population numbers 31.

The Mason House Inn was built in 1846 by Mormon craftsmen who stayed in Bentonsport for one year while making their
famous trek to Utah. It mainly served steamboat passengers
traveling from St. Louis to Des Moines.

No wonder the inn still stands sturdy, its cozy Georgian stylings providing a warm welcome for big-city visitors who want to experience a quiet and restful stay.

Many of the rooms appear as they did in their heyday, with several original furnishings. Especially interesting is a memorial-hair-wreath measuring 3 feet by 4 feet that hangs in the parlor. Here you can also pump and play tunes on an 1882 Estey organ.

William (a former pastor for the Christian Church) and Sheral (who boasts a degree in hotel and restaurant management) did extensive remodeling in 1990, connecting the inn with the old railroad station; now it boasts two extra rooms: the Wash House and Old Country Store, each with period furnishings.

Other guest quarters include the Lincoln Room, with its 9-foot-high walnut headboard, and the Mason Room, with matching bedroom set, 9-foot French mirror, fainting couch, and wood-burning stove—all original to the inn.

I especially like the Bonaparte Room with its burl walnut bedroom set and windows offering a good view of the river.

The innkeepers' breakfast, served in the Keeping Room next to the 1803 cook stove, is a special event. How does eggs and sausage, blueberry waffles, peach crisp, and Mason House sticky pecan rolls sound? Sheral serves dinner, including dishes like smoked brisket of beef, orange roughy filet, and roasted chicken breast, with advance reservations.

How to get there: Bentonsport is in the southeast corner of Iowa's Van Buren County between Keosauqua and Bonaparte on J40, a paved county road. Take Iowa 1 south through Keosauqua, cross the river, and go uphill to J40. Then go east to Bentonsport. Turn right on any village road toward the river. The inn is along the bank.

◦❀◦

B: *Don't miss the copper-lined "Murphy" bathtub that unfolds from the Keeping Room wall cabinet. The innkeepers claim it's the only one of its kind in Iowa.*

The Hancock House
Dubuque, Iowa
52001-4644

Innkeepers: Jim and Julie Gross
Address/Telephone: 1105 Grove Terrace; (319) 557–8989
Rooms: 7, with 1 suite; 5 with private bath, all with air conditioning, TV
   and phone on request. No smoking inn.
Rates: $55 to $150, single or double, EPB.
Open: All year.
Facilities and activities: Located in the heart of historic Mississippi River
   town, with magnificent river views. Near restaurants, cable-car
   elevator, riverboat rides, Woodward Riverboat Museum, Ham House
   Museum. Brilliant fall colors, hiking, biking, cross-country and
   downhill skiing.

Here is a triple treat: a magnificent bluff-top setting, exquisite
Queen Anne mansion, and spectacular views of the Mississippi
River.

I know those are many superlatives, but it would take a
thesaurus-full of adjectives to do justice to the Hancock House.

"You can see sixteen church steeples from any guest room,"
Jim told me. "I challenge guests to find them all. Of course, I think
you have to be a native Dubuquer to get the tough one."

Jim and Julie have meticulously restored this twenty-seven-room mansion built in 1891 by namesake Charles, owner of the largest wholesale grocery in the Midwest at that time. Everything is larger than life. You must experience the 28- x 18-foot dining room to really appreciate it—completely done in quarter-sawn oak, with coffered and beamed ceiling and elegant fireplace.

Speaking of fireplaces, the one in the sitting room, with its elaborate gingerbread detailing, took first place in design competition at the 1894 World's Columbian Exposition in Chicago.

Guest rooms are fabulous. I like the North Bedroom, with its huge brass bed, original marble bath with handsome mosaic floor, marble coal-burning fireplace (that includes a coal-powered foot-warmer), and Bradley & Howard–signed table lamp.

Maybe you'd rather try the East Bedroom. It has a white iron-rail bed, marble sink, claw-footed tub, and four huge windows.

"You get spectacular views of the Mississippi," Julie said. "At night you can see the yellow running lights of double-decked river paddleboats. In the summer you see scores of sailboats."

Jim added: "Then there are the church bells that ring on Sunday mornings. The sound is heavenly. But one day a guest asked me which church played 'Blue Moon.' Those are the bank chimes."

For a real touch of elegance, sample the inn's huge suite. Its 900 square feet boasts a large living/sitting room brightened by the light from seven windows; a wet bar located in the old nursemaid's pantry; an inviting whirlpool for two; and a bedroom with brass bed and handsome stained-glass window.

How to get there: From Illinois, take the Julien Dubuque Bridge to Locust Street, turn north on Locust, and continue. At Twelfth Street, turn left, and then take another left on Grove Terrace to the inn.

❀

B: *In a spectacular sitting room with incredible views, you can see three states at once—Iowa, Illinois, and Wisconsin.*

L'Auberge Mandolin
Dubuque, Iowa
52001

Innkeeper: Judi Sinclair
Address/Telephone: 199 Loras; (319) 556–0069
Rooms: 5; 3 with private bath, all with air conditioning. No smoking inn.
Rates: $65 to $80, single or double, EPB. Two-night minimum on holiday weekends.
Open: All year.
Facilities and activities: Sitting room, music room. Wraparound veranda. Nearby: restaurants, riverboat rides on the Mississippi, museums, Cable Car Square, Fenelon Place Elevator, skiing, hiking, dog racing.

One glance inside, and I saw the home had been built for someone special—and incredibly wealthy. Imagine stained-glass windows, parquet floors, hand-painted canvas wall coverings. You get the idea.

In fact, this 1908 Queen Anne mansion was the home of Nicholas Schrup, Dubuque's leading financial figure at the turn of the century. Apparently he spared no expense, and luckily most of his special touches have survived through the years.

The foyer is massive, graced with tall oak columns and an inlaid wood parquet floor. I immediately noticed the stained-glass window on a stairway landing, fashioned with the likeness of St.

Cecilia, patron saint of musicians. She's clutching a mandolin, hence the name of the inn. (*L'Auberge* means "inn" in French.)

Imagine cypress woodwork in the parlor, probably brought up the Mississippi in a riverboat. "The usual sheen of the wood changes with movement," Judi said. It has an almost iridescent color to it.

The Music Room boasts original hand-painted murals on the north wall. And the dining room! It's engulfed by oak paneling, a floor-to-ceiling beveled-glass china cupboard, and an Italian fireplace. My favorite touch: the original hand-painted canvas mural covering walls that makes it appear as if you're lurking in a dark Victorian forest.

Rooms are equally impressive. My favorite, the Grand Tour room, boasts a trunk stuffed with Victorian clothes, 1910 travel guides on the bed table, antique postcards and maps, and a beautiful Italian antique bedroom set.

Judi says several Schrups still live in the Dubuque area. "They consider this their house of humble beginnings," she said. Humble beginnings? This is a palace.

How to get there: From Galena, take U.S. 20 west across the bridge into Dubuque, turn right on Locust Street, then right on Bluff, and left on Iowa to Loras (Fourteenth Street). Then turn left and continue to Main Street and the inn.

✸

B: *A Midwestern showplace.*

The Redstone Inn
Dubuque, Iowa
52001

Innkeeper: Mary Moody
Address/Telephone: 504 Bluff Street; (319) 582–1894
Rooms: 15, with 6 suites; all with private bath, air conditioning, phone, and TV.
Rates: Rooms: $65 to $88, single or double, EP. Suites: $110 to $165, single or double, continental breakfast.
Open: All year.
Facilities and activities: Afternoon teas (Tuesday through Sunday, 2:00–6:00 P.M.). Walk to restaurants. Dubuque attractions include downhill skiing, Mississippi riverboat cruises, riverboat museum, Cable Car Square (specialty shops in a historic location), scenic railcar climbing 189-foot bluff with view of three states.

If you ever had dreams of piloting a paddle wheeler down the mighty Mississippi, you can get the next best thing in Dubuque. In this historic river town, you can ply the waters on the stern-wheeler *Spirit of Dubuque*, walk the decks of the side-wheeler *William M. Black*, and immerse yourself in the exhibits of the F. W. Woodward Riverboat Museum.

And there's no better way of continuing a "living history" visit than by staying at the Redstone Inn, an 1894 Victorian mansion restored to all its original splendor.

94

I registered in a rich, oak-paneled hallway on a first floor that retains much of the home's original ambience. The mauve, deep blue, green, and burgundy colors are used to complement the Redstone's many original stained-glass windows.

Because no two guest rooms are alike, you can select your favorite from a color-photo portfolio kept at the reception area.

I'm in good shape, so the almost forty steps it takes to get to the third-floor rooms were no problem. (In fact, I enjoyed the exercise.) My room was like many offered at the inn—antique furnishings with walnut beds, balloon curtains, period lighting fixtures, muted floral wallpapers, and bed quilts. Mine also had a whirlpool, which I headed for immediately; some also have fireplaces, with free logs.

Breakfast for those overnighting in junior and deluxe suites is served downstairs in the small dining room. Starched white table linens and fresh flowers adorn the tables. I munched on chewy homemade caramel rolls, croissants, and bagels.

Afternoon teas feature a variety of English teas, dainty finger sandwiches, tarts, biscuits, and—maybe gingerbread cherry pie, an inn specialty. Count on English truffles, too. I recommend The New French Cafe and its *nouvelle cuisine* delights for romantic dinners; it's just a short drive away.

Be sure to peek at the inn's parlor, an exquisite example of Victorian elegance. It took me a few minutes to get comfortable in this very formal room with its ornate furniture, oriental-style rugs and tile fireplace with an elaborate mantel. The gas chandelier is original to the home. So are the cherub figurines that gaze down from the plaster-cast ceiling; yes, they are gold leaf.

How to get there: Whether entering Dubuque from the west via U.S. 151 or east on U.S. 20, pick up Locust Street at the bridge and proceed to University. Turn left and drive to Bluff; then turn left again. The inn is on the street's left side.

❀

B: *Victorian elegance, rivertown style.*

Stone Cliff Manor
Dubuque, Iowa
52001

Innkeepers: Tc and Alice Ersepke
Address/Telephone: 195 West Seventeenth Street; (319) 588–2856
Rooms: 4; all with private bath, air conditioning, and TV. No smoking inn.
Rates: $75, single or double, EPB. Special off-season and midweek discounts. No credit cards.
Open: All year.
Facilities and activities: High Victorian parlor, sitting room, library. Screened porches, Victorian gardens. Nearby: restaurants, riverboat rides on the Mississippi, Fenelon Place Elevator, Cable Car Square, Old Shot Tower, Eagle Point Park, historic homes, Greyhound Park (dog races), skiing, hiking.

Walking into Stone Cliff Manor can send your head spinning. Every room is stuffed with exquisite antique furniture, country primitives, art, and collectibles. There's even a suit of armor in the library.

But rest assured, this fabulous house can be your home for a night or two.

Located at the foot of Seminary Hill, this stately Queen Anne was built in 1889 by Charles Stampher, a prominent Dubuque department-store owner. Now it's been transformed into a haven of old-fashioned hospitality by Tc and Alice.

I visited during the city's annual DubuqueFest celebration. Tours of Stone Cliff were part of the festival's Historic House Tour. Visitors reactions? Flabbergasted. Transfixed. Overwhelmed. Disbelieving.

"How did you find all these fabulous antiques?" several people asked Alice.

"Actually we had most of them back in our old home [in suburban Chicago]," she answered. "When we moved here, everything just seemed to find its place."

Among the highlights:

the column-framed library with roaring fireplace and hand-carved wood paneling, which has the feel of a baronial European castle.

the formal day room, which boasts an 8-foot-high, 130-year-old Seth Thomas grandfather's clock with full-sized doll figures that dance on the stroke of the hour.

a winding staircase, graced with original post-mounted bronze lamps, which leads guests past a stained-glass turret window to their rooms.

Guest rooms are treasure troves of Victoriana. Among my favorites: a huge French armoire resting in the Doll Room (there must be at least 30 antique dolls in here) purchased by the innkeepers in Paris. Tc told me that it had to be hoisted on a pulley up to the roof, then brought inside only after disassembling a large window.

Breakfast (served on Limoges china in the formal dining room) might include steak and eggs, French toast or pancakes with fruit topping and cream.

How to get there: From Galena, take U.S. 20 west to Dubuque and turn right on Locust Street. Turn right on Ninth Street, then left on Iowa, and another left on Seventeenth to Main Street and the inn.

The Stout House
Dubuque, Iowa
52001

Innkeepers: Roland and Judy Emond
Address/Telephone: 1105 Locust Street. (Register at The Redstone Inn, 504 Bluff Street; (319) 582–1894.)
Rooms: 6; 2 with private bath, all with air conditioning, some with TV.
Rates: $65 to $100, single or double, continental breakfast.
Open: All year.
Facilities and activities: Main-floor library, TV lounge, dining room. Near Mississippi River; riverboat excursions, water activities. City has many architecturally interesting and restored buildings. Riverboat museum. Scenic railway to top of high bluffs and panorama of 3 states and river; Cable Car Square specialty shops. Near ski areas.

This is one of the most fabulous mansions I have ever seen—where architecture is *the* attraction.

An 1891 masterpiece built by a local lumber baron at the then-fantastic cost of $300,000, The Stout House boasts massive red sandstone blocks, a squared turret, and huge rounded arches among its notable architectural details.

Inside are treasures far beyond words: heavy lead-glass doors; rosewood, maple, oak, and sycamore woodwork; ornate stained-glass windows; fireplace hearths of beautiful mosaic tiles; beamed ceilings; Italian marble bathrooms; and lots more.

Purchased in 1909 by the Archdiocese of Dubuque for its archbishop's residence, the house has remained in its almost original condition. Recently bought by a restoration company, it's now open for the public's enjoyment.

The reception hall has a baronial feel, with ornate stained-glass windows, a huge marble fireplace, and intricately carved, magnificent rosewood woodwork. The tall grandfather's clock encased in rosewood was especially hand-carved to set into the woodwork.

I counted five fireplaces on the main floor; all hearths are made of imported mosaic tile. The original dining room has a huge quarter-sawn oak table that seats eighteen.

The most impressive room is the main-floor library. There's wonderful oak paneling, and a heavy-beamed ceiling is supported by four magnificent green onyx columns, which themselves are trimmed in decorative mosaics.

I particularly like the second-floor guest rooms. Colorful stained-glass windows threw rainbow light onto my bed. Imported Italian-marble bathrooms (the marble sinks have German-silver legs) made me feel like a visiting dignitary. The inn's largest bath has a beautiful mosaic tile floor with a center medallion. Some rooms have fireplaces.

There's also a "mystery" room, which is done in light colors, French Provincial style—very feminine. It is totally out of character with the rest of the mansion.

Guests must go to the nearby Redstone Inn for a breakfast of egg dishes and quiches, fresh fruits of the season, beverages, and baked goodies like morning glories, caramel and cinnamon rolls, and fresh croissants. For one of Dubuque's finest dining experiences, try the Ryan Mansion.

How to get there: Enter Dubuque from the west via U.S. 151 or from the east on U.S. 20. Pick up Locust Street at the bridge and proceed to the Stout House.

The Travelling Companion
Elk Horn, Iowa
51531

Innkeepers: Karolyn and Duane Ortgies
Address/Telephone: 4314 Main Street; (712) 764–8932
Rooms: 3, with 1 suite, share 2 baths.
Rates: $40, single or double, EPB. No credit cards.
Open: All year.
Facilities and activities: Authentic 1848 working Danish windmill downtown, General Store Museum, historic Bestemor's House, Hans Christian Andersen statue, and Danish ethnic foods in area restaurants. New National Danish Museum.

I never expected to see an authentic Danish windmill in the middle of an Iowa cornfield. But there it was.

When I found out that the town was basically a Danish ethnic community, some of the surprise wore off. In fact, at The Travelling Companion, the innkeepers have named each room for a fable of the town's celebrated champion, Hans Christian Andersen.

The Ugly Duckling Room has antique walnut furniture, with a high Victorian bedstead and handmade quilts. The fainting couch in the corner of the room's small sitting area belonged to

Duane's grandfather. Karolyn showed me his name stamped on the bottom.

The Thumbelina Room is cozy, with pressed-back oak furniture. The bed is so high that you might have to step onto a stool to reach it. Karolyn said a guest once told her the higher the bed off a floor, the more prominent the family. At least, that was the rule of thumb in olden days.

Another room is dusted in warm rose colors, with two full-sized white iron-rail beds.

I asked about the teddy bears sitting on the stairs leading to the guest rooms. These charming fellas were made by Karolyn's sister, who fashioned most of the inn's many country crafts.

A parlor sitting-room is done in quaint Victorian fashion, with especially attractive period love seats.

Karolyn prepares a hearty Danish breakfast for her guests. A special treat is her *strata* (egg-soaked bread stuffed with cheese, baked to a puffy delight). She also offers Danish pastries (of course) and fruit cups.

The Danish Inn restaurant just down the street is Karolyn's favorite going-out-to-dinner spot. Some of her menu suggestions are *aebelskiver* (crispy browned pancake served in spheres), *rullepolse* (onions and spiced beef), and *medisterpolse* (browned pork shoulder sausage).

How to get there: Take I–80 to the Elk Horn exit (#54), and go north 7 miles on Iowa 173 into town. Iowa 173 turns into Main Street, and the home is just a short drive past the windmill, on the left side of the street.

B: *Take a peek behind the home's front door to see a beautiful antique Danish corner wardrobe made of pine. It's one of the finest of its kind I've ever seen.*

Die Heimat Country Inn
Homestead, Iowa
52236

Innkeepers: Don and Sheila Janda
Address/Telephone: Main Street; (319) 622–3937
Rooms: 19, including 8 deluxe; all with private bath, air conditioning, and
  TV. Well-behaved pets OK.
Rates: $28.95, single; $34.95 to $44.95, double; $49.95 to $54.95, deluxe;
  continental breakfast April 15–November 15. Special weekday winter
  rates.
Open: All year.
Facilities and activities: Sitting room. Shaded yard with Amana wooden
  gliders. Walk to restaurant, nature trail. Short drive to 7 historic
  Amana Colonies villages, with antiques, craft, and specialty stores,
  museums, bakeries, Amana furniture shops. Also nearby: winery,
  summer theater, golf, biking, cross-country skiing.

  Homestead is a peaceful little village off a busy interstate in
the historic Amana Colonies, settled in the 1840s by German
immigrants seeking religious freedom and a communal life-style.
And as soon as I turned off the highway to reach Die Heimat
Country Inn, I became absorbed in the quiet of this century-old
agricultural community.
  Whatever pressures might have been building inside me

during the long drive to Iowa disappeared once I stepped inside. Sheila greeted me at the desk, full of good cheer and chatter. She's generously decorated her charming lobby with nationally famous Amana furniture (the sofas are original to the 1854 inn) and a large walnut Amana grandfather's clock ticking softly in the corner of the room.

Soothing German zither music wafted through the inn, and I immediately began to feel at home. (*Die Heimat* is German for "the homestead" or "the home place.") On the way to my room, Sheila pointed out the cross-stitchings hanging on many of the walls; they're German house blessings, many brought from the old country.

My room was small and cozy, with sturdy Amana furniture, an electric kerosene lamp, writing desk, rocking chair, and brass-lantern ceiling lamp. It's so quiet that you'll probably wake up in the morning to the sound of chirping birds, as I did.

Other rooms might feature handsome Amana four-poster beds graced with lace canopies, handmade quilts, Colonies-handmade crafts, and rocking chairs.

I also woke up to a breakfast of Oma and Opa (German for grandmother and grandfather) rolls with frosting and fruit toppings, fresh fruit, juice, and coffee. Then I started the day by swaying on the unique Amana platform swings out in the yard.

Later I explored the thrumming communities of the seven Amana Colonies' villages, with all kinds of historical and commercial attractions, including fabulous bakery goods and meat shops. Sheila can point out the "can't miss" stops.

Bill Zuber's restaurant, just down the street from the inn, was one of her recommendations. Zuber was a pitcher for the New York Yankees, a hometown boy discovered by scouts when he was seen tossing cabbages during a local harvest. I liked the menus in the shapes of baseballs, and the home-style cooking was scrumptious. My baked chicken with fried potatoes, veggies, and green peas in thick gravy would be hard to beat. Also served are Amana ham, pork, and baked steaks.

How to get there: Take I–80 to exit 225 (151 north), and go about 5 miles. At the intersection of Highways 6 and 49, turn left past Bill Zuber's restaurant to the inn just down the block.

Strawtown Inn
Pella, Iowa
50219

Innkeepers: Roger Olson, general manager; Marcia Pothoven, inn manager
Address/Telephone: 1111 Washington Street; (515) 628–2681
Rooms: 17, with 4 suites; all with private bath. Wheelchair access.
Rates: $60 to $70, rooms; $85, suites; EPB.
Open: All year.
Facilities and activities: Full-service restaurant with 5 dining rooms, a third-story barroom. Also hot-tub area with sun room. Gift, antiques, and country-store shops next door. Surrounding town has many old-world Dutch-front buildings; thousands of planted tulip beds. Massive *klokkenspel* (several Dutch figures performing to the accompaniment of a carillon) at Franklin Place. Annual Tulip Time festival in May. A 45-minute drive to Des Moines.

I visited the Strawtown Inn during the spring, when thousands of blooming tulips planted along walkways and in gardens create swirls of rainbow colors and fragrant scents for lucky guests. (They're replaced by bright red geraniums in summer.)

This is just one way the inn honors its ethnic heritage. Another is the inn's name: Mid-1800s Dutch settlers built huts on this corner of the then-tiny village from long slough grass and covered them with straw woven into a stick frame.

The guest rooms are delightful. Each *kamer* (room) is artfully decorated and has its own personality. The *Bedstee kamer*, with Dutch prints, pastel floral wallpaper, and Dutch beds built into the wall, is one of my favorites. Stenciling fans will love the *Pannigen kamer*, with its Dutch border stencils on walls and ceilings.

And the *Juliana kamer* is a long room with a slanted ceiling, skylight windows, walnut antique reproductions, and a photograph of former Netherlands Queen Juliana hanging on the wall. It was named for the queen to commemorate her May 1942 visit to Pella. The Queen, however, didn't get to enjoy the Jacuzzi tub that now beckons guests.

I cannot think of a better place to enjoy a Dutch breakfast than in the inn's bright morning room. Ladder-back chairs, rich oak woodwork, cheery pastel colors, and scatter rugs covering plank floors add to the old-world ambience. A cold-meat tray is a real treat, along with Dutch cheeses, breads, rolls, beverages, and a hard-boiled egg.

Five antiques-laden rooms host inn lunches and dinners; one even has double Dutch ovens. The food is celebrated, having received recommendations from diverse publications like the *Des Moines Register*, *The New Yorker*, *Travel Holiday*, and *The Saturday Evening Post*. I was especially intrigued by stuffed pork chops with apple-walnut dressing and mushroom sauce, Dutch spiced beef, and pheasant under glass carved tableside.

The inn also holds special international gourmet-dinner weekends in April and November.

How to get there: Pella is reached off Iowa 163. Follow that to Washington Street. The inn is on the west side of town.

☙

B: *Many of Pella's stores have Dutch fronts; you can see wooden shoes being carved at the Historical Village; and authentic Dutch street organs pipe happy tunes for visitors.*

Hannah Marie Country Inn
Spencer, Iowa
51301

Innkeeper: Mary Nichols
Address/Telephone: U.S. 71 (mailing address: R.R. 1); (712) 262–1286
Rooms: 3; all with private bath and air conditioning. No smoking inn.
Rates: $50 to $60, single or double, EPB and afternoon hors d'oeuvres.
  Children $10 each extra.
Open: April through December.
Facilities and activities: Located on 200-acre corn-and-soybean farm;
  hammock, rocking chairs, and country swing on porch; rope swing
  on old farm tree; croquet. Short drive to restaurants. Boating, fishing,
  and swimming in Iowa's great lakes 20 miles away. Lots of antiques
  shops, arts and crafts nearby.

Mary might be the most cheerful innkeeper I've ever met.

"I want you to feel right at home, so it's okay to open the door
and shout, 'I'm here, Mom.' "

Mary's historic farmhouse, built in 1910, sits on her 200-acre
corn-and-soybean farm. "It took talented craftsmen two years to
restore the building," she said. A San Francisco expert on Victorian
paints was called in to custom-mix turn-of-the-century colors for
the inn. "That accounts for our special glow," Mary added.

106

Everything is special about the Hannah Marie, named for Mary's mother. Consider the guest rooms. Beda, named for her aunt, is the "tomboy" room. It has walnut furniture, soft apricot and forest green colors, queen bed, and whirlpool. "It's delightfully cuddly," Mary said. "You get a great feeling of being wrapped in a cocoon."

Elisabeth, the "genteel woman" room, boasts lots of bird's-eye maple and has an antique white iron tub. "I tell people to relax here," Mary said. "That's why all baths come with yellow rubber duckies. We also have the best bubbles around. So many guests just soak in their tub immersed in their bubble baths. Even lots of the men."

The Louella room is the inn's smallest but features a red-acrylic claw-footed tub. "When the sun shines through the lace curtains and falls on the tub, it's really beautiful," Mary said.

Elegant breakfasts include fresh fruit and juice, strata, home-made scones and muffins, strudel, and tortes. Afternoon-tea luncheons (also served to the public) can be three-course affairs. Special "Tea with the Mad Hatter" takes its theme from *Alice's Adventures in Wonderland*, with guidelines provided by the Alice Shops of Oxford, England, and the Lewis Carroll Society. "Near the afternoon's end, everyone gets to celebrate their un-birthday," Mary said, "complete with un-birthday candles."

Her top-hat scones are also special, receiving rave reviews from veteran England vacationers. And hors d'oeuvres are served daily between 5:00 and 7:00 P.M.

"I also provide parasols and walking sticks for farm strolls," Mary said. And she can't wait for her croquet course to be constructed on her "farm lawns."

How to get there: From Minnesota, take U.S. 71 south to Spencer (in northwest Iowa), then continue south 4 miles; the inn sits on the east side of the road.

⊱✣⊰

B: *Mary moved a country Victorian-vintage home 6 miles from the middle of town to her property. In the planning stage are Carl Gustav dining rooms, more guest rooms, and, in between the two houses—a Monet garden.*

Old World Inn
Spillville, Iowa
52168

Innkeeper: Cheryl Novak
Address/Telephone: 331 South Main Street; (319) 562–3739 or 562–3186
Rooms: 4; all with private bath.
Rates: $30, single; $35, double; EP.
Open: All year.
Facilities and activities: Renowned Czech restaurant downstairs, featuring home cooking and daily specials. Walk to the Bily Clocks museum and the Antonin Dvořák exhibit.

All the food is homemade, from scratch. It's Czech-style, with Pilsner Urquell Czech beer to go along with the meal. Need I say more?

This 1871 general store, a two-story limestone building just a stone's throw from the Turkey River, was restored in 1987 and transformed into this specialty restaurant and lodging. If you're wondering about the Czech influence, let me add a little more history.

The quiet village is where famed composer Antonin Dvořák stayed during the summer of 1893. Its landscape so reminded him of the Czechoslovakian countryside that he was inspired to write the *New World Symphony* here.

Now Cheryl features hearty Czech food in her restaurant, in a dining room that offers huge merchant's windows, red-checked tablecloths, and country and Old World crafts, all of which provide a homey decor.

During my last visit, I just missed a Czech film crew that stayed at the inn while filming a documentary about Dvořák's time here.

I checked the menu, filled with dishes like Czech ham, kraut and dumplings, braised Viennese pork roast, beef cabbage soup, and desserts featuring prune and apricot *kolaches*, poppyseed cake, and *bublania* (sponge cake base with baked-in fruit, served in warm whipped cream). It was tough to make a decision.

Country-charming guest rooms include Victorian dressing tables, quilt wall hangings, wall borders, high back chairs, and old merchant globe ceiling-lamps.

How to get there: From Dubuque, take U.S. 52 north to Iowa 325. Turn west and follow into Spillville. This road leads right to a T and the inn.

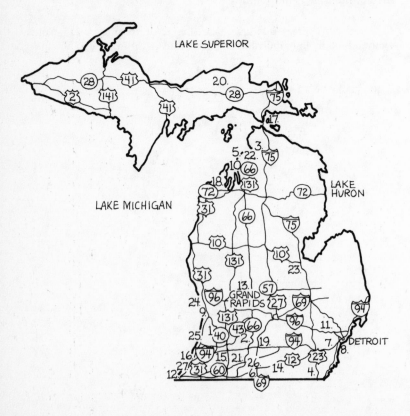

LAKE SUPERIOR

LAKE MICHIGAN

LAKE HURON

GRAND
RAPIDS

DETROIT

Michigan

Numbers on map refer to towns numbered below.

DeLano Inn
Allegan, Michigan
49010

Innkeepers: Robert and Jean Ashley
Address/Telephone: 302 Cutler Street; (616) 673–2609
Rooms: 5 share separate men's and women's baths down the hall; all with air conditioning.
Rates: $45 to $85, single or double, EPB. Special winter rates available.
Open: All year.
Facilities and activities: Walk to antiques shops, museums, riverfront. Near historic-home tours, water sports, winter sports, dinner cruises, train rides, snowmobiling, cross-country and downhill skiing, Todd Farm. Specialty shops of Saugatuck beach community about 20 miles northwest.

Bob and Jean are former Chicagoans, so we got along famously. Their handsome inn, built between 1863 and 1865 by a Civil War veteran, is an ornate Italian Provincial mansion that is the crown jewel of this quiet historical neighborhood.

I asked Bob how Chicagoans got their hands on one of the most renowned buildings in Allegan. "We have family in town, and we always drove by the house when we came up here on visits," Bob explained. "Then one time we saw a FOR SALE sign. We bought the house in one day."

However, it took seven months to restore the home, which was in remarkably good condition for its age. "That's because only four families had owned it previously," Bob said. "In fact, it was in one family's hands for more than one hundred years."

I really like bright homes, and three huge 9-foot-tall windows in the common room illuminate the inn from dawn to dusk. The house also boasts fine Italian marble fireplaces, ornate ceiling crowns and moldings, original lead-glass windows, and more.

Guest rooms do not lack their own attractions. My favorite is the Ashley Room, offering a huge four-poster bed with Dutch eyelet-lace canopy. There is a three-step stool to reach the bed's topside; that's because at least four mattresses are required to fill the Victorian bedframe and reach the base of its tall headboard.

The Doyle Room contains a large brass bed that one can get lost in—because it's a European feather bed. Other rooms offer period furnishings, like stenciled beds and Victorian marble-topped dressers, and boast original plank floors.

All guest quarters boast scenic views.

The silver service used to serve breakfast is original to the house. Antique lovers should also like the dining room's 8-by-9-foot oak sideboard that displays the innkeepers' beautiful china and crystal collection.

The large front porch boasting antique wicker furniture and rockers is delightful for relaxing. DeLano Inn evenings also include complimentary cheesecake (it's made in Chicago and is delicious) and coffee, as well as time to talk with new friends.

How to get there: Allegan is located just off I–94 from the Paw Paw exit 60. Then take Michigan 40 north into town.

The Old Lamp-Lighter's Homestay

Battle Creek, Michigan
49017

Innkeeper: Roberta Stewart
Address/Telephone: 276 Capital Avenue, Northeast; (616) 963–2603
Rooms: 8; all with private bath, air conditioning, and TV. No smoking inn.
Rates: $48.50 to $70, single or double, EPB. Cross-country ski and golfing
    packages available.
Open: All year.
Facilities and activities: Sitting room, parlor, dining room, library, antiques
    shop. Nearby: fitness center, parks, McCamly Place (Saturday night
    concerts), Civic Theater, shops, restaurants, jogging, biking.

A local architect once called this 1912 mansion "flagrantly
medieval." It has also been cited by a national architectural
association as "one of the purest Arts and Crafts–style houses"
existing today.

Whatever they call it, I say The Old Lamp-Lighter's is quite
special.

Let me list a few of the home's outstanding features: The
dining room is a showplace. You enter by walking through
intricate stained-glass French doors that depict a Victorian forest,

and you are confronted by four hand-painted, original canvas wall murals boasting another forested landscape—an almost mythological depiction that quickly grabs your attention. That's not all. Over a long dining-room table where guests eat breakfast hangs a massive Steuben chandelier so breathtaking that it looks as if it belongs in the Metropolitan Museum of Art. In the living room, a large stone fireplace is flanked by two of the thirteen stained-glass windows that grace the home. Add a French Aubusson rug and fine Victorian furnishings to the tally. Honduran mahogany and oak woodwork is everywhere.

Originally the home of Seirn Cole, a prominent Battle Creek builder, it's now home to Roberta, her sister-in-law, Evelyn, and their lucky guests.

Guest rooms boast their own antique finery. Consider the Kellogg Room, with its 1912 Sir Cassian walnut bedroom set; the Rich Room, with its heirloom hand-hooked rug; or the McCamly Room, which is great for families—it sleeps six and offers period tables and chairs for fun and games.

The atmosphere remains very Gothic here. The inn is private and quiet, and even on sunny days it can be quite dark due to its stylings. But the opportunity to enjoy these one-of-a-kind surroundings makes it a sunny day for travelers.

How to get there: From east or west, take I–94 to Battle Creek, exit north on Michigan 66. Follow Michigan 66, which turns into Division and the Capital Avenue Northeast, to the inn.

The Terrace Inn
Bay View, Michigan
49770

Innkeepers: Patrick and Mary Lou Barbour, Frank Schumway
Address/Telephone: 216 Fairview; (616) 347–2410
Rooms: 44, with 6 suites; all with private bath, 8 with air conditioning.
Rates: $42 to $89, single or double, continental breakfast. Winter ski
    packages and several weekend-long event packages available.
Open: All year.
Facilities and activities: BYOB. Dining and sitting rooms, ice-cream parlor,
    porch. Within walking distance of weekly chamber music concerts,
    Sunday-evening vespers program, drama and musical theater pro-
    ductions. Nearby hiking trails on 165 acres of virgin forest; tennis;
    swimming at private beach; Saturday-evening movies at the Audito-
    rium. Gaslight Shopping District 5 minutes away. Near town of
    Harbor Springs with boutiques, golf, horseback riding, sailing, fishing.
    Mackinac Island about 45-minute drive north of Bay View.

    Entering The Terrace Inn is like walking into the past. That's
because the 1911 inn, located on a quiet street among tall beech,
oak, and maple trees, is part of the historic Bay View community.
    The entire town is listed on the National Register of Historic
Places. There are more than four hundred Victorian summer
homes here built between 1875 and the turn of the century. If

you're a fan of Victorian homes and like lots of gingerbread, you'll go crazy.

I spent lots of time walking along gently curving streets lined with buildings graced with intricate gingerbread finery. It's as if the entire town is a frozen snapshot, stopped still in the 1890s.

The inn, built by W. J. DeVol in 1910, sits high on a terrace off Little Traverse Bay. It's one of the last buildings constructed by a group of Methodists who established the Bay View Association in 1875 as part of its traveling Chautauqua arts series. That dedication to the arts continues here today.

There's a great fireplace in the parlor that warms guests on chilly summer nights. And rocking chairs are everywhere.

Guest rooms have iron-rail beds, cheery, bright quilts, oak dressers, and high ceilings. I especially like the transom windows; I could relax on my bed while gazing out at the sky.

In the off-season, Mary Lou serves guests a continental breakfast next to that great inn fireplace. Dinners in the turn-of-the-century eating hall feature scrumptious feasts. An inn specialty is planked whitefish served with duchesse potatoes and freshly baked bread.

How to get there: From the south, take U.S. 31 east through Petoskey. Upon leaving the city limits and entering Bay View, the road jogs to the right and crosses a railroad track. Turn right at the first road after the track (the main entrance to Bay View). Turn right again at the first street (Lakeview) and turn left at the Glendale Street stop sign. The rear entrance to the inn is ¼ mile down Glendale on the left. From the north, take U.S. 31 south. The main entrance to Bay View is the second street past the pedestrian overpass. Then follow the above directions.

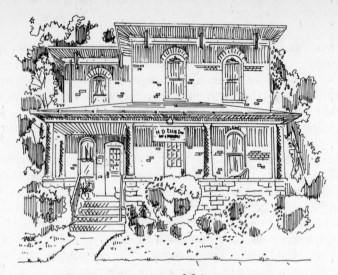

H. D. Ellis Inn
Blissfield, Michigan
49228

Innkeepers: The DeSotos
Address/Telephone: 415 West Adrian Street; (517) 486–3155
Rooms: 4; 2 with private bath, all with air conditioning, TV, and phone.
Rates: $40 to $55, single; $50 to $65, double; continental breakfast.
Open: All year.
Facilities and activities: Two sitting rooms. Part of the Hathaway House "village" of restaurants and specialty shops. Near Main Street Stable and Tavern, Crosswell Opera House, Lenawee Historical Museum, Michigan International Speedway. Seventy minutes southwest of Detroit, 20 minutes northwest of Toledo.

One of the first things I noticed was a sign hanging in the bathroom. It simply said, "Enjoy the soft water." A typically quaint touch to this comfortable inn.

The fine red-brick home was built in 1883 by its namesake, a Scots-Irish harness-and-hardware store operator. Walk around the northwest side of the home and you'll see the cornerstone confirming that date.

I tinkered with the melodeon that rests in the downstairs sitting room. Made in 1749, it's operated by bellows and produces a sound somewhere between that of a harpsichord and an organ.

All rooms are tastefully furnished with period antiques and reproductions. I especially liked the Hervey Bliss Room, named after the village's founder. Its Victorian headboard stands at least 6 feet high. Soft wildflower-print wallpaper adds a soothing touch, as do Dutch lace curtains that hang on the room's three tall windows.

The continental breakfast is a simple one: freshly baked breads, muffins, homemade jellies and jams, juices, and beverage.

Be sure you save some tummy space for the daily buffets offered by the Hathaway House, just across the street. This is an 1851, eighteen-room Greek Revival–style mansion that was once called the finest home between Buffalo and Toledo; you can see the architect's 1850 charcoal sketch of the home in the foyer. The Sunday buffet includes roast round of beef, baked ham carved at the board, country-fried chicken and shrimp, potatoes, vegetables, and a choice of six homemade dressings for your salad.

How to get there: From Detroit, take I–75 south to U.S. 223. Then go west into Blissfield. U.S. 223 is called Adrian Street in Blissfield.

The Bridge Street Inn
Charlevoix, Michigan
49720

Innkeepers: John and Vera McKown
Address/Telephone: 113 Michigan Avenue; (616) 547–6606
Rooms: 9; 3 with private bath. No smoking inn.
Rates: $72 to $105, single or double, continental breakfast. Two-night
   minimum stay July 1 through Labor Day weekends. Off-season rates
   available.
Open: All year.
Facilities and activities: Charlevoix is a colorful harbor town on Lake
   Michigan. Huge marina, fleet, pleasure boating, and charter fishing.
   Restaurants, specialty and antiques shops. Swimming and picnicking
   on Lake Michigan and Lake Charlevoix beaches. Ferry boats to
   Beaver Island. July Venetian Festival; August Art Fair; Fall Color
   Cruises.

Vera has created a whimsical world of antique attractions
inside this magnificent building that boasts spiky gables, lead- and
stained-glass windows, and a long wraparound porch. The decor
reflects a gentle English cottage look, with original maple floors
covered with oriental area rugs, Waverly print fabrics on loveseats,
and blue-checked wing chairs.

Both living and dining rooms are graced with English,

120

German, and Chinese antiques and a baby grand piano invites guests to play some of the old tunes charted on scores of sheet music.

The nine guest rooms are warm and friendly, with hardwood plank floors dashed with antique floral rugs. Vera adds a special touch with fresh flowers in each room, individually decorated with more antiques.

In the Autumn Leaves Room, I found a quarter-sized cigar-store Indian and a genuine humpback steamer trunk. The Harbor Rose Room has oak and cherry furnishings and a view of the lake. But I'll take Evening Glow, where I had a spectacular view of Charlevoix's great sunsets.

Breakfast is served in the dining room, with its handsome woodwork and rose-colored, Victorian print carpeting, or you might open the French doors and take your meal to a cozy sitting area. Vera's choices include homemade Belgian waffles with fresh fruit, home-baked scones with fresh marmalade, strawberry bread with cream cheese, plum and apple tarts, sour cream coffeecake, and more.

I like the nearby Grey Gables Inn for dinners, especially their Lake Superior whitefish. The innkeepers also recommend Tapawingo and Rowe Inne, gourmet restaurants that are among the most highly-rated in Michigan. Or just stroll to the channel; there the Weathervane restaurant features fine food—and you can sit at a window table and watch the boats go by.

How to get there: From Chicago, take I–94 north to I–196 and continue north. At U.S. 131, go north; then at Michigan 66, turn northwest. At U.S. 31, go north into downtown Charlevoix. Here the road also is called Michigan Avenue. Take 31 one block north of the drawbridge to Dixon and the inn.

B: *The home (once called the Baker Cottage and intended as the personal residence of the namesake family who built the grand Beach Hotel—long since demolished) has a terrific view of Lake Michigan, Lake Charlevoix, and the downtown drawbridge.*

Chicago Pike Inn
Coldwater, Michigan
49036

Innkeeper: Rebecca A. Schultz
Address/Telephone: 215 East Chicago Street; (517) 279–8744
Rooms: 6, with 1 suite; all with private bath, TV and phone on request.
Rates: $75 to $130, single or double, EPB. Two-night minimum on special
   weekends.
Open: All year.
Facilities and activities: Parlor, library, dining room, wraparound front
   porch, gardens, gazebo. Walk to downtown shops. Nearby: antiquing, golfing, boating, fishing, swimming, cross-country skiing, orchards, nature trails, lake activities, Turkeyville Dinner Theatre,
   museums, wineries, historic architecture.

   One glance at the Chicago Pike Inn, and my pa and I realized
we were about to experience something special.
   Built in 1903 by Morris Clarke, owners Jane and Harold
Schultz, along with daughters Becky and Jody, have carefully
restored this spectacular house to reflect early 1900s grandeur. I
admired the magnificent reception room, with its double-manteled
cherrywood fireplace adorned by Staffordshire dogs, and with a
sweeping cherry staircase that leads to upstairs guest rooms.
   "Local legend says that the wood came from Morris Clarke's
own cherry orchard," Jane said.

The rest of the inn reflects Jane's impeccable taste in antiques and fine fabrics. Leaded Bradley and Hubbard lamps, Schumacher and Waverly wall coverings, fluted cherrywood columns, hand-carved antique furniture, stained-glass windows, parquet floors—the list is seemingly endless.

What results from all this attention to the smallest details (guests are supplied with thick terrycloth robes, and Jane's Victorian candy stand in the library is always stocked with fine goodies) is a feeling of luxury and comfort that's difficult to match.

We headed to the library, with its unusual whitewood woodwork. My pa settled in a wing chair next to a roaring fire and immersed himself in his reading. I complimented Jane on a spectacular restoration. "It's such a grand old house," she said. "Restoring it is kind of our legacy to the community."

Guest quarters are exquisite. I stayed in Ned's Room, its bold red-and-paisley wall coverings, huge brass bed, and green leather wing chair giving it the feel of an exclusive gentlemen's club. My pa opted for Charles' Room, reflecting the Victorians' fascination for period Chinese and boasting a handsome sleigh bed framed by a wall canopy.

My little girls would love the Grandchildren's Room, all pink with two twin iron-and-brass beds, white Victorian wicker, and eleven antique portraits of darling little girls.

Then there's Miss Sophia's Suite, two rooms fully bursting with a hand-carved antique bed, an oak-manteled fireplace, a velvet-covered period sofa, a Martha Washington chair—and even its own private balcony.

Include Becky's scrumptious breakfasts and her delightful hospitality, and you have all the ingredients for one of the best Midwest inns.

How to get there: The inn is located on U.S. 12 (the old Chicago Pike), midway between Detroit and Chicago, just minutes south of I–94.

The Dearborn Inn
Dearborn, Michigan
48124

Innkeeper: Peter Steger, general manager
Address/Telephone: 20301 Oakwood Boulevard; (313) 271–2700 or (800) 228–9290
Rooms: 234, with 20 suites and 5 reproduced historic homes; all with private bath, air conditioning, TV, radio, and phone.
Rates: $130 to $175, single; $145 to $190, double; EP. Special weekend packages available.
Open: All year.
Facilities and activities: Two full-service restaurants, lounge, sitting room, concierge, room service, gift shop, newsstand, baby-sitting service on request. Also gardens, patio, outdoor swimming pool, tennis courts, fitness center. Nearby: Henry Ford Museum, Greenfield Village, professional sports, Fairlane Town Shopping Center, Dearborn Historical Museum, Henry Ford Estate, Northville Downs, golfing, Windsor, Ontario.

My wife, Debbie, and I drove up the sweeping circular driveway that leads to the graceful porticoed entrance of the Dearborn Inn. It reminded me of a grand mansion of a wealthy Colonial landowner.

Listed on the National Trust (recognized for its stately Geor-

124

gian architecture), the hotel was built in 1931 by Henry Ford. It served as the nation's first "airport hotel" (a small landing field was located across the street) and housed visitors to the Henry Ford Museum and Greenfield Village just down the road.

It has become an elegant showplace, showered with opulent appointments. I easily recognized Ford's love for early America carried out in the hotel's decor. Our suite in the main building exhibited handsome Colonial fashions, with four-poster beds, wing and Windsor chairs, polished wooden chests, and brass lamps. We easily surrendered to this kind of luxury.

Particularly fun is a small Colonial "village on the green," with five historic-home replicas of famous Americans; you'll feel like a houseguest of Edgar Allan Poe, Patrick Henry, Barbara Fritchie, Walt Whitman, and Revolutionary War hero Oliver Wolcott.

My favorite remains the Poe Cottage, a little white clapboard house that often serves as a honeymoon suite. A delightfully devilish touch: the black, iron raven hovering above the doorway.

Dining here is a gustatory delight. The Early American Room, romantic with glittery chandeliers, crisp white linen, and fresh flowers on tables, pampers food lovers. We dined on Rock Cornish Game Hen Madeira and Country Pork Loin Applejack while a three-piece, tuxedo-clad combo provided music for evening dancing.

After a delightful meal, we headed to the Snug, a lounge where liquor bottles are still kept out of sight, underneath the copper-topped bar, in deference to Ford's lifelong opposition to alcohol.

How to get there: From Detroit Metro Airport: Go north on Merriman Road to I–94 East. Follow I–94 about 5 miles to Southfield Freeway; then go north 3 miles to Oakwood Boulevard. Finally, go west 2 miles to the inn.

River Place Inn
Detroit, Michigan
48207

Innkeeper: Ian Rumsey, manager
Address/Telephone: 1000 Stroh River Place; (313) 259–2500
Rooms: 107; all with private bath, air conditioning, TV, phone, refreshment
bar, and refrigerator.
Rates: $135 to $165, single; $155 to $165, double; $200 to $300, suites;
EP.
Open: All year.
Facilities and activities: Sitting area, 2 restaurants with room service,
concierge, indoor swimming pool, spa, sauna, weight room and
exercise pavilion, croquet lawn. Walk to shops, restaurants, bou-
tiques. Short drive to Renaissance Center, Greektown, and historic
sites.

Someone once wrote that for a hostelry in the heart of the
Motor City, River Place Inn is everything you would never expect.
That is an understatement.

Imagine the sophistication of a weekend in the city with the
charm of a stay in the country. Ambience more reminiscent of an
elegant estate rather than a hotel. European-style service that
would be hard to duplicate anywhere.

The River Place Inn is simply a gem, unmined gold yet to be

discovered by large numbers of travelers to Detroit. It is part of a $250 million project called Stroh River Place (it's located next to Stroh Brewery's corporate headquarters), one of the most architecturally ambitious redevelopment project in the city's history.

Sitting on thirty acres of green fields next to the banks of the Detroit River, the project will eventually include shops, restaurants, apartments, and offices in a wonderful setting.

But let's get back to the hotel. It sits so close to the Detroit River that from some rooms the only land you see is Canada, on the opposite shore. Other rooms afford views of the graceful Belle Isle Bridge upstream and the world's tallest hotel downstream.

All have been ingeniously fitted into the historic 1902 Parke, Davis & Co. pharmaceutical laboratory. As a result, no two rooms are exactly alike. But all are washed with natural light from huge windows and are furnished in distinctive period stylings, including lush woods, handsome wall coverings, special fabrics, fluffy bed quilts, original artwork, marble and brass bathroom fixtures; some also have a sitting area and a writing desk.

Several rooms even occupy more than one level—a few scale three floors! My view from Room 117 brought the Canadian shore within arm's length. I also watched pleasure boats and commercial river traffic slip quietly by.

Dining at River Place can be a marvelous experience (with great river views); but if you feel like a short walk, stroll down to The Rattlesnake Club, named by *Esquire* magazine as "one of the best new restaurants in America."

How to get there: From Chicago and the west, take I–94 east to the Chrysler Freeway (I–75) south; as it becomes I–375, take the Jefferson Avenue East exit and continue until reaching Joseph Campau Boulevard; turn right into Stroh River Place, left at the gatehouse; then go 1 block east to the inn.

∽

B: *After motoring up the long circular drive leading to the inn, I expected to find the parking area. Not here. Instead, this elegant hotel has fashioned a championship-sized croquet court.*

The Kirby House
Douglas, Michigan
49453

Innkeepers: Marsha and Loren Konto
Address/Telephone: Center Street and Blue Star Highway (mailing address: P.O. Box 1174, Saugatuck, Michigan 49453); (616) 857–2904
Rooms: 10; 6 with private bath, 5 with air conditioning.
Rates: $80, shared baths; $90, hall baths; $100, private baths; EPB. Deduct $15 on weekdays.
Open: All year.
Facilities and activities: BYOB. Common room, swimming pool, hot tub. Walk to Lake Michigan beach. Near restaurants, art colony in Saugatuck; Allegan Forest; Grand Rapids antiques markets; Holland's ethnic Dutch villages, museums, specialty shops. Cross-country skiing close by.

The grand Kirby House is an irresistible Victorian pleasure. It just "jumped out" at me with its turrets, gables, lead- and stained-glass windows, and a quaint peach-colored picket fence surrounding the grounds.

Marsha and Loren have preserved elegant Victorian interiors that really impressed me. Especially fetching are leaded-prism windows that fling shards of sunlight on original hardwood floors. I was particularly taken with the parlor fireplace (one of four in the house). Marsha told me that it was of an unusual cast-iron design.

The home was built in 1890 by Sarah Kirby, who made her considerable fortune from farming ginseng. She wanted to be rid of troublesome pitchers and wash basins, so she replaced them with corner sinks in the bedrooms; some remain to this day.

In 1932 the home became a community hospital and operated in that capacity for thirty years. In fact, the old hospital operating room is now named for Jackie Onassis. Ask Marsha to explain that one.

I almost lost my head over the Anne Boleyn Room. Marsha surmised that it was the maid's room in older times because a dumbwaiter was located in the corner. Now it's bright and airy, with a fabulous oak sleigh bed and pleasant period pieces.

Breakfast means croissants, cheese Danish, old-fashioned sticky buns, fresh fruit, sausage, bacon, eggs, quiches, and juices— all served buffet-style. By early morning, many of Marsha's guests were already enjoying the inn's backyard deck, where lounge chairs, hot tub, and swimming pool await.

A new town sensation is Checquers, an English-flavored restaurant boasting Shepherd's Pie, Chicken Cornu with curried yogurt sauce, and Bubble and Squeak (sirloin chucks wrapped in cabbage with hot brown sauce).

How to get there: From Chicago, take I–94 north to I–196 north and go to exit 36. Go north on Blue Star Highway into Douglas. Turn left at the only traffic light and you're there.

☀

B: *Most curious inn addition: Percy the Peacock, who ''just dropped in two years ago—from where we don't know,'' said Loren. So the innkeepers bought him a lady friend named Prissy, and they proudly strut about the grounds.*

The Rosemont Inn
Douglas, Michigan
49406

Innkeepers: Mike and Shelly Sajdak
Address/Telephone: 83 Lakeshore Drive (mailing address: P.O. Box 541);
    (616) 857–2637
Rooms: 14; all with private bath and air conditioning. Wheelchair access.
Rates: $40 to $65, single; $50 to $85, double; continental breakfast.
Open: All year.
Facilities and activities: BYOB. Garden room, swimming pool, screened
    front porch. Located across road from beach. Nearby: charter fishing,
    boating, scenic supper cruises; golf; hiking the Lake Michigan dunes;
    summer theater; cross-country skiing in winter. Close to fine restau-
    rants, unique shops.

On a cool late-spring day, I drove to The Rosemont Inn.
Foghorns sounded off Lake Michigan, which is just across the tiny
road and down a steep bluff. Winds rustled tall trees that shade the
inn's landscaped acre. A touch of sun peeked through the clouds.

If there's a more perfect location for an inn, I'd like to know
about it.

The inn stands like an inviting friend, a turn-of-the-century
Queen Anne–Victorian that got its start as an 1886 tourist hotel.
French doors open onto a small formal sitting room, with an
elegant hardwood column fireplace as the focal point.

I walked out back to the Garden Room, perhaps my favorite spot. It's bright and sunny, with cathedral ceilings, and a ceiling-to-floor glass wall that looks out onto the swimming pool. This is where Mike and Shelly serve a buffet-style continental breakfast of juice, croissants, muffins, interesting quiches, bagels, cereal, and more. They can also suggest some fine dinner spots in nearby Saugatuck.

Country antiques fill the comfortable guest rooms; nine have gas fireplaces that add a cozy touch. Brass beds adorned with charming bed quilts of rich country prints supply a pinch of colorful pizzazz. Some rooms boast a view of the lake through the tall maples that ring the grounds.

Two of three common areas also boast "wet bars," great conveniences for families with constantly thirsty little ones.

This is a terrific inn for family-style vacations. One summer, my family and my brother-in-law, his wife, and toddler, spent a glorious, long weekend at the inn. Especially inviting was that swimming pool, where the kids splashed and played endlessly. It made for good memories.

How to get there: From Chicago, take I–94 north to I–196 north. At exit 36, near Douglas, take Ferry Street north to Center Street. Turn west on Center Street and go to Lakeshore Drive; then turn north to the inn.

*

B: *One of my favorite pastimes is reading a good book on the long veranda.*

The House on the Hill
Ellsworth, Michigan
49729

Innkeepers: Buster and Julie Arnim
Address/Telephone: Box 206, Lake Street; (616) 588–6304
Rooms: 3 share 2 baths; all with air conditioning.
Rates: $65, single or double, EPB.
Open: April to January.
Facilities and activities: Turreted veranda overlooking St. Clair Lake. Nearby: golfing, boating, fishing, swimming, two gourmet restaurants. Lake Michigan is 5 miles away.

Magnolia Blossom greeted me first. That's the inn's low-to-the-ground basset hound, who's equipped with a foghorn instead of a bark.

Buster and Julie are from Texas. Didn't take a genius to figure that one out, what with their delightful Texas twang and the Lone Star State flag flying high from a pole in the back yard.

Buster grabbed my hand and gave me a welcoming whomp on the back. "We specialize in old-time Southern hospitality," he told me. I soon discovered there couldn't be two more gracious hosts around.

Their one-hundred-year-old renovated farmhouse is perched atop a high hill, overlooking St. Clair Lake like an imposing

132

sentinel. "It's part of a chain of lakes," Buster said. "You can hop from one to another all day."

The Arnims decided to become innkeepers after touring a number of inns during a swing through New England. A relative in Indiana told them about this home. After doing research on the area (while still in Texas), the Houston natives put a down payment on the house without ever setting foot in Michigan!

The guest rooms are full of country charm, with antique furnishings and country crafts set about in lively combinations. The Blue Room has a thick Texas Star quilt, fanciful draped curtains, a rocking chair, and charming wall borders.

My favorite is the Rose Room, bright and cheery, with a view of the lake. And the Wicker Room exhibits some of the innkeepers' collection of Southwestern art.

"We serve a good Texas breakfast," Buster said. "I don't let anyone go away hungry." Get ready for fresh fruit, ham, sausage, eggs, homemade breads, and Julie's delicious strudels.

"One of the reasons we decided on this location is because we're right between two gourmet restaurants that may be the finest the state has to offer," Buster said. The Rowe Inn and Tapawingo are landmarks that draw crowds from miles away. Gourmet delights include rhubarb-strawberry soup, spinach-and-Montrachet tart, breast of pheasant *chasseur*, and white-chocolate mousse with raspberry sauce.

How to get there: From Grand Rapids, take U.S. 131 north to Michigan 66. Turn west, and near East Jordan, go west on County 48 to the inn. Or take I–75 north to Michigan 32, go west to County 48, and then west again to the inn.

❋

B: *The long gingerbread-laced wraparound porch, from which you can view the lake far down the hill, has comfy wicker rockers.*

Botsford Inn
Farmington Hills, Michigan
48024

Innkeeper: John W. Anhut
Address/Telephone: 28000 Grand River Avenue; (313) 474–4800
Rooms: 75, plus 3 suites; all with private bath, air conditioning, TV and phone. Wheelchair access.
Rates: $45 and $55, single; $60 to $70, double; $110 to $125, suites; EP. Special "Historic Weekend" packages.
Open: All year except Christmas Day and New Year's Day.
Facilities and activities: Coach House restaurant with 5 private dining rooms; serves breakfast, lunch, and dinner daily, except Christmas Day and New Year's Day; ballroom. Henry Ford Museum and Greenfield Village nearby. Also Henry Ford Fairlane Estate, Franklin Village, Northville, historic specialty shopping areas. Shopping at Hunter's Square and Twelve Oaks Mall 10-minute-drive away. "Blitz Strip," elegant and sophisticated shops along Northwestern Highway, close by.

I swung open the heavy oak door in one of Michigan's oldest inns. My heels clicked on plank flooring that stretches to a huge hearth crackling with a warming fire, with two Windsor chairs huddled around the blaze. A massive oak desk runs almost the length of the room, and in an office behind it is a table said to have been used by Abe Lincoln. History is everywhere.

The 1836 white clapboard house, converted into a tavern five years later, quickly became a popular stagecoach stop on the Grand River plank road, about 16 miles from the then-young city of Detroit.

Known as the Sixteen Mile House, it was a resting spot for farmers and drovers heading toward the city. But only traveling "gentlemen and ladies" could sleep in rooms; rougher elements had to stretch out on the taproom floor.

The inn became a favorite courting spot in the 1920s for Henry Ford and his future wife, Clara, who attended country dances in the inn's ballroom.

The inn owes many of its antiques to Ford's restoration efforts: Original Hitchcock chairs grace the parlor; a turn-of-the-century Chickering square piano is said to have belonged to *the* General Custer's sister; and there's a buffet from General Robert E. Lee's home.

John purchased the inn in 1951, adding rooms to the original structure while preserving its pioneer roots in a number of historic suites. I was especially fascinated by the suite created for and used by Thomas Edison, filled with oversized carved-oak furnishings.

Make sure to get a room in the restored historic wing. The hallway is long and narrow, dotted with sitting benches, velvet couches, and antique prints. My room had stenciled Victorian wallpaper, a huge walnut bed, a "pie safe" used as a chest of drawers, and more. John's pampering touches include fresh flowers and bright calico bed quilts.

The Coach House taproom and restaurant serves good Midwestern staples. These include pan-fried chicken, Veal Supreme, honey-baked ham, and roast duck with wild rice. I was delighted with a house specialty, Botsford chicken pie. Hot cherry cobbler with vanilla ice cream topped off my tasty dinner.

How to get there: Follow I–96 from Detroit and get off at the Farmington Hills exit. From Chicago, follow I–94 to Michigan 39 and continue north to I–96; then go west. The inn is located at the intersection of Eight Mile Road and Grand River Avenue.

Tall Oaks Inn
Grand Beach, Michigan
49117

Innkeepers: Sherman and Mary Ann Atkinson
Address/Telephone: Station and Crescent roads; (616) 469–0097
Rooms: 11, with 8 suites; all with private bath and air conditioning.
   Wheelchair access.
Rates: $65 to $140, single or double, EPB. Reduced rates on off-season
   weekdays. Two-night minimum on weekends June through October.
Open: All year.
Facilities and activities: Living room, garden room. BYOB. Five acres of
   heavily wooded grounds. Private beach, cross-country ski trails. Inn
   has 12 pairs of cross-country skis for guest use; also 8 bicycles, 1 golf
   cart. Short drive to restaurants, New Buffalo's antiques and specialty
   shops; Lake Michigan dunes, state parks, orchards, wineries.

My wife pointed out that the welcoming goose statues
flanking the inn door were sporting red-vinyl rainhats. It is a
whimsical touch at an inn that is quiet and comfortable—but
above all, elegant.

Sherman told me it was built in 1914 as a summer retreat for
employees of a Midwest box-making company. Later it became
part of a complex that included the largest frame hotel ever seen in
these parts; yes, bigger than the Grand Hotel on Mackinac Island,

Sherman said. That hotel, with its own 70-meter ski jump, cross-country trails, huge pier, and 27-hole golf course (that still is part of Grand Beach), burned down during the winter of 1939.

Enough history. Tall Oaks is the story today, and it is fabulous. Guest rooms are named for North American wildflowers and are so attractive you'll have a hard time deciding on a favorite.

Suites are huge. Typical is the Prairie Clover, which I like very much. Its spindle bed, tall Victorian dresser, 8-foot armoire, and wood-burning fireplace would seem to be enough to entice any traveler. But there are also a sitting room, two-person whirlpool, and private deck that looks out over the handsome grounds, which were blooming in trillium and dogwood during my visit.

I'll bet you never saw a single room as gracious as the Wild Rose. It boasts a full-sized German antique bed that's split in the middle so that it might be divided if the occupants are not married, a traditional Old World touch. It also has its own whirlpool, solid pine plank floors, and a private deck.

Guest common rooms are uncommonly elegant. The living room is dominated by a 10-foot-wide fieldstone fireplace that crackles with a fire on most summer nights (it can get nippy by the lake) and throughout the day during winters. I counted thirty-nine windows in the Garden Room; they make up three entire walls. It's a great place to relax, play games, read a book by the potbellied stove, or watch the inn's only television—a big-screen giant.

Sherman said the inn's commercial kitchen allows it to make all kinds of breakfast goodies; in fact, it supplies local bakeries with cakes and pastries. That's where I found Mary Ann preparing some of the treats for this weekend's guests: chocolate pound cake, strawberry pie, nut bread, and more. A full breakfast might include all of the above, plus dishes like English-style eggs, tea rings (giant ring pastries stuffed with fruit filling), freshly baked breads, and muffins, juice, and beverages. You can even have these goodies delivered to your room for a romantic "breakfast in bed."

How to get there: From Chicago, take I–94 to U.S. 12 (second New Buffalo exit). Go south to Grand Beach sign, cross the railroad tracks, turn left through arches, and continue to the Y in the road. Bear left (on Station Road) and continue to Crescent Road and the inn.

Winter Inn
Greenville, Michigan
48838

Innkeepers: Robert King and Nancy Badge
Address/Telephone: 100 North Lafayette Street; (616) 754–3132 or 754–7108
Rooms: 14; all with private bath, air conditioning, phone, and TV.
Rates: $43, single; $48 to $50, double; continental breakfast.
Open: All year.
Facilities and activities: Full-service restaurant and bar. Short drive to several ski areas, Grand Rapids historical district, and Gerald R. Ford Presidential Museum.

The Winter Inn is an unusual find, tucked on a busy commercial street of this small town. It seems that lumbermen who worked the Big Woods would come to the "city" for some rest and relaxation. They'd take stagecoaches from the city train station to the hotel on "Main Street."

The 1902 inn was one of Greenville's two first-class hotels. I could see lots of evidence toward that claim. For example, the lounge contains one of my favorite inn antiques: an immense Brunswick oak-and-mahogany bar made in the 1880s, complete with a long brass foot rail. With the lounge's pressed-tin ceiling, solid oak floor, and a collection of antique prints, oil lamps, and memorabilia, it made me feel as though I had just stepped into an authentic Victorian pub.

The dining room boasts more handsome surroundings. Tables are cast with the warm glow of light filtered through stained-glass windows, and there's lots of greenery. A light breakfast of fresh fruit, danish, and coffee comes with your stay. And dinner fare is all-American, small-town good, featuring seafood, home-baked chicken, and tasty steaks.

The lobby is filled with more antiques. Handsome nineteenth-century Victorian couches and chairs, cut and stained glass, magnificent tapestries, and ceiling-high hallway mirrors celebrate the inn's heritage.

Guest rooms are furnished in contemporary style and remain comfortable and cozy. All have extra-long beds, especially attractive to someone like me who stands 6'2''.

How to get there: From Chicago, take I–94 north to I–196 and continue north to U.S. 131. Go north to Michigan 57 and turn east, continuing to Greenville. The road turns into Lafayette Street in the city.

※

B: *It's fun to browse among the inn's historic photos (located on the second floor), which depict a long-ago era.*

The Munro House
Jonesville, Michigan
49250

Innkeepers: Jerry and Sandy Witt
Address/Telephone: 202 Maumee Street; (517) 849–9292
Rooms: 5; all with private bath.
Rates: $58, single; $63, double; EPB. Lower rates on weekdays.
Open: All year.
Facilities and activities: Gift shop, sitting parlor, gardens. Walk to Grovenor
   House Museum. Mill Race golf course, restaurants, 2 arboretums,
   biking, canoeing, and cross-country skiing nearby. More than 50
   antiques shops located minutes away in Allen, antique capital of the
   state. Professional summer theater in Coldwater.

Sandy said her pre-Civil War home, started in 1832, was the
first brick house built in Hillsdale County. "In fact, it took seven
years to complete, and the bricks were hauled here by ox and cart
from 10 miles away."

The Munro House also was part of the Underground Railroad.
Sandy showed me the hidden room that housed runaway slaves,
located above the ceiling of what is now one of the guest baths.
Slaves were moved at night, along a route through Detroit to
Windsor, Ontario, in Canada—to freedom.

This is a gracious home, with ten Italian marble fireplaces,

12-foot ceilings, and guest rooms furnished with fine period antiques. The Munro Room, named after the Civil War general whose family occupied the home for more than one hundred years, has original poplar plank floors, a handsome American Empire-style sleigh bed, fireplace, crystal chandelier, and its own porch. Sandy also offers vintage period linens on the bed, double stack pillows, and a cozy down comforter.

If you stay in the Sauk Trail Room, you'll be living history. That's because Wild Bill Hickok, who was from Ohio, slept in these antique four-poster cannonball beds.

I also like the Shaker Room, resplendent in its simplicity. More plank floors, with a trundle bed, ladderback chairs, and utilitarian wooden peg rack in true Shaker style. There's also a Shaker "hired man's bed" made especially for this room.

I felt right at home with Sandy. "There's coffee on twenty-four hours a day [herbal tea, lemonade and hot apple cider is available, too], and the cookie jar is always full," she said. During summer, you can take coffee on the porch, or you can walk among Sandy's fragrant perennial and herb gardens. In winter, you might head to the cozy warmth of the library's fireplace.

Breakfast is a treat. Sandy's French toast is her specialty, and she offers morning meats, fresh fruit, juices, freshly baked sweets, and beverages. She'll be happy to recommend a nearby restaurant to suit your dinner tastes.

How to get there: From Detroit, take I–94 west to U.S. 127. Go south to U.S. 12, then turn west and continue into Jonesville. The inn is at the corner of that highway and Maumee Street.

✳

B: *Sandy and Jerry are only the fifth owners of the home since 1832! Get them to show you the original shutters that fold up, hidden in the window frames. They are of the type invented by Thomas Jefferson.*

Bartlett-Upjohn House
Kalamazoo, Michigan
49007

Innkeepers: Carleton and Lucy Casteel
Address/Telephone: 229 Stuart Avenue; (616) 342–0230
Rooms: 8, with 1 suite; all with private bath, air conditioning, phone, and
TV. No smoking inn.
Rates: $45 to $65, single; $55 to $75, double; continental breakfast.
Open: All year.
Facilities and activities: Dinner available; 2 parlors, music room and dining
room. Located in the Stuart Avenue Historic District. Close to
Western Michigan University, Kalamazoo College, and the schools'
many sports facilities, and downtown. Many city-wide festivals,
antiques stores. Less than an hour's drive to Lake Michigan beaches
and water activities.

Carleton and Lucy run this fabulous house for Carleton's
brother, Bill, who, along with wife, Andy, also owns the Chappell
House next door and the James Balch House just down the street.
Built in 1886, it is a magnificent example of Victorian, Queen
Anne, and Eastlake architecture, with several gables and lots of
exterior gingerbread. Bill pointed out the unusual gold roof
ornament that rests high on the home's tower.

Just walking into the home is an experience in Victorian

142

excess. I've never seen a fireplace located in a foyer, which opens onto two parlors, a music room, and the dining room. Those rooms are paneled in oak and cherry, and the hand-painted wall coverings are authentic restorations. The main staircase leading to second-floor guest rooms is itself an elegant touch, with unusual straight spindles.

Then there's a massive stained-glass window on the staircase landing that often washes the foyer in jagged slashes of color.

My guest room had a great view of the historic neighborhood, with floor-to-ceiling windows, Belgian lace curtains, elaborate woodwork, Chippendale sofa, and one of the most comfortable beds I've ever slept in. "We've been restoring old homes for many years," Andy said. "And one thing we've learned is that a good bed is most appreciated by guests."

Carleton serves breakfast in the handsome dining room, which overlooks woods and the McDuffy Garden, an acre of trees, greenery, and flowers where guests may stroll, picnic (in the gazebo), and watch goldfish frolic in the lily-graced pond. "This type of garden is common in England but rare in the United States," Andy said.

Carleton can also arrange dinnertime meals, with advance reservations, cooked on his massive AGA stove. Get him to show you this English contraption, which weighs 1,300 pounds, takes twenty-four hours to preheat, and has four ovens that cook simultaneously at different settings.

How to get there: From Chicago, take I–94 east to northbound U.S. 131 exit. Go north to Michigan 43 (Exit 38A), turn east, and continue for 3 miles to Stuart Avenue. Then turn left to the inn.

Hall House
Kalamazoo, Michigan
49007

Innkeepers: Pamela and Terry O'Connor
Address/Telephone: 106 Thompson Street; (616) 343–2500
Rooms: 4, with 2 suites; all with private bath, air conditioning, and TV. No smoking inn.
Rates: $75, single or double, continental breakfast. Two-night minimum on selected weekends.
Open: All year except December 23 through January 2.
Facilities and activities: Kalamazoo is a city of festivals, with some event virtually every weekend. Nearby: parks, Kalamazoo Museum, Institute of Arts, Air Zoo, Timber Ridge downhill-ski area, tours of General Motors plant, year-round theater, 2 universities with music, sports, and other events. Also antiques stores, winery tours, restaurants, dinner train.

As I walked through the dining room, Terry pulled me to a window. "There's one of our guests you haven't met yet," he said, pointing to a woman walking out front, wearing a down-to-the-ankles English day dress. "That's Lady Wedgwood. She and her secretary are staying here while she's taking part in the Western Michigan Medieval Festival."

While I didn't expect to meet lords and ladies at the Hall

House, I'm not really surprised. This Georgian Revival red-brick home, built in 1923, is fit for a king.

The foyer is graced with Pewabic tile, and common rooms boast handsome ceiling moldings and mahogany woodwork. Pam's English brass rubbings are framed and hang throughout the house. "I never thought we'd find a house that had walls long enough to hang these pieces," Terry joked. They are beautiful.

The innkeepers have named guest rooms for previous owners of the house. The Vander Horst Room, a bow to the home's builder, has a tile fireplace, four-poster canopy bed, custom cedar closets, and a large bath done in tile handmade at Detroit's own Pewabic pottery site. Every piece of tile is still handmade and glazed. "It's enjoying a great renaissance," Pam said. (By the way, *Pewabic* is an Indian word meaning "clay with a copper color." Pewabic's founders used copper ore in many of their glazes, giving them a characteristic verdigris color. The Hall House is the only identified residential building in southwestern Michigan with original Pewabic tile installations.)

Lady Wedgwood stayed in the Borgman Room, with its queen-sized brass bed. "I remember sitting with her at breakfast one morning while she instructed me in the fine art of mating parakeets!" Pam said. And the Rutherford Room boasts an elegant shower that features seven shower heads.

With advance notice, you can enjoy breakfast in your room. Or head down to the sun room for fresh croissants, muffins, fruit breads, juice, and home-baked scones. The innkeepers can match your dinner tastes to several fine area restaurants.

And I challenge you to find two secret hiding places that apparently held the family jewels in earlier times.

How to get there: From Detroit or Chicago, take I–94 to U.S. 131 north (Exit 74). Go north to Michigan 43 east (West Main Street, Exit 38). Turn east and continue for about 3 miles. As you start down a hill, look for the inn almost at the bottom, on the southwest corner of Thompson Street.

B: The telephone booth on the second-floor landing is a real conversation piece.

Stuart Avenue
Inn–Balch House
Kalamazoo, Michigan
49007

Innkeepers: Bill and Andrea Casteel
Address/Telephone: 405 Stuart Avenue; (616) 342–0230
Rooms: 6; all with private bath, air conditioning, phone, and TV. No
  smoking inn.
Rates: $45 to $60, single; $55 to $70, double; continental breakfast.
Open: All year.
Facilities and activities: Parlor, library, dining room. Kalamazoo is a
  festival-crazed city; there's seemingly a celebration each week. About
  an hour's drive to Lake Michigan beaches, resort towns.

I wasn't in the best frame of mind as I drove up to the Stuart
Avenue Inn. I'd come a long way in a powerful thunderstorm. I
was tired and cranky. Then I had to make a long run to the
entrance at the side of the building, and I got soaked. But once
inside, I forgot about all that. This charming retreat was just the
cure for a trying day.

The 1889 Queen Anne–style building is part of the Stuart
Avenue Historic District of prosperous Kalamazoo homes. Bill and
Andy have said many times that their goal is to provide travelers

with a unique and pleasant experience in an elegant, friendly home. They've succeeded, lovingly restoring their Victorian inn with comfortable, well-appointed antique furnishings.

All guest rooms have fun names. The Mayor's Room (named for a former owner who happened to be a three-term mayor of the city) is the largest. I especially liked the antique Eastlake bedroom suite, complete with high headboard and marble-topped dresser.

The Deer and Rabbit Room, less formal, features hand-printed wall coverings and an iron-and-brass bed. Another favorite of mine is the Arboretum, a romantic spot with many windows and a cozy fireplace.

A special gathering spot for guests is the lovely Eastlake Sitting Room, with its handsome beveled-glass window. The breakfast room also is terrific, with ten windows that let you start a clear day with lots of bright sunshine. Here Bill and Andy deliver their special home-baked treats along with fresh fruits.

On my last visit here, our then-infant daughter, Dayne, was the centerpiece of mealtime conversation. Guests buzzed around her, amid clattering dishes, hearty exchanges, and lots of laughter. Dayne, of course, slept through the entire commotion.

The innkeepers can recommend good area restaurants for dinners. For an elegant dining treat, make advance reservations at the Bartlett-Upjohn House with Chef Carleton; he serves fine meals in the grand European tradition.

How to get there: From Detroit, take I–94 west to exit 81. Follow exit 81 (which is Business Loop I–94) to Michigan 43 (Kalamazoo Avenue) and go west to Stuart Avenue and the inn.

The Pebble House
Lakeside, Michigan
49116

Innkeepers: Jean and Ed Lawrence
Address/Telephone: 15093 Lakeshore Road; (616) 469–1416
Rooms: 7, plus 3 suites and 1 house; all with private bath and air conditioning. Wheelchair access.
Rates: $85 single; $90, double; $91 to $130, suites; $190, house; EPB.
Open: All year.
Facilities and activities: Private tennis court, screen house with hammocks. Access to beach across road. Hiking, boating, fishing, charter fishing for chinook and coho, sailing, golf, biking, horseback riding, downhill and cross-country skiing, snowmobiling, tobogganing. Warren Dunes State Park nearby. Short drive to restaurants, antiques shops, art galleries, winery tours, pick-your-own-fruit farms. Hang gliding in Warren Dunes.

I like this inn for its peaceful, laid-back ambience. It's as comfortable as your favorite easy chair, a good place to just wind down and relax. And it's located in the heart of Michigan's dune-swept Harbor Country, with Lake Michigan just across the road.

"We call it a European-style inn," Jean said, "because of our Scandinavian breakfasts." That's a special treat, with European breads, imported cheeses, smoked sausages, herring—and Jean's fresh muffins and home-baked pastries.

There's a daily hot dish, too; it might include anything from Swedish pancakes to Danish brunch eggs.

The main building, constructed in 1912, is located in a tranquil village with rolling countryside noted for its farms, orchards, and vineyards. I could see the lake from the porch and from some of the guest-room windows and decks.

One of my favorite spots is an enclosed porch with a large fireplace, perfect for nighttime reading by a crackling fire. The inn also boasts a large collection of oversized Mission-style furniture, giving it one of the most unique looks around.

Guest rooms have self-descriptive names. The Rose Room boasts lace curtains, rose borders, and an Art Nouveau rocker in front of a floor-to-ceiling etched-glass window that overlooks Lake Michigan.

Trek through the inn grounds on boardwalks that pass among wildflower gardens and manicured lawns to reach the Coach House and Blueberry House, whose suites make guests feel like owners of this lakeside estate. I especially enjoy the Coach House's Garden Room, done in Arts and Crafts style, and boasting a lead-glass window and deck facing the lake.

(Not surprisingly, Jean and Ed are leaders in the Midwest Arts and Crafts movement. They travel extensively to search for antiques and to learn more about the origins of that movement; in fact, the inn offers special weekends for those whose share similar interests.)

Try Miller's for formal *nouvelle cuisine* dining that draws many media types from Chicago; or escape to Beyond the Sea Crab House or Red Arrow Road House for less glitzy surroundings, but great food. I also sugggest the Harbert Swedish Bakery, in Harbert on Red Arrow Highway. The freshly baked Danish butter-pecan sweet rolls, pineapple-bran muffins, pecan brownies, and elephant ears are a delight to anyone with a sweet tooth.

How to get there: Take I–94 to the Union Pier (exit 6). At the bottom of the ramp, turn left if coming from Chicago, or right if coming from Detroit or the west to Lakeside Road. Continue on Lakeside Road, crossing Red Arrow Highway, until you reach the stop sign at Lakeshore Road. Turn left and continue for ½ mile. The Pebble House is on the left.

Grand Hotel
Mackinac Island, Michigan
49757

Innkeeper: R. D. Musser, III, corporation president
Address/Telephone: Mackinac Island; (906) 847–3331
Rooms: 317; all with private bath.
Rates: $120 to $225, per person; children in same room with 2 persons,
$15 to $60 per child; MAP. Special packages available.
Open: Mid-May to early November.
Facilities and activities: Main dining room, Geranium Bar, Grand Stand
(food and drink), Audubon Bar, Carleton's Tea Store, pool grill.
Magnificent swimming pool, private golf course, bike rentals, saddle
horses, tennis courts, exercise trail. Carriage tours, dancing, movies.
Expansive grounds, spectacular veranda with wonderful lake vistas.
Nearby: museums, historic fort, and other sites, guided tours; spe-
cialty shops. There are no motor vehicles allowed on historic
Mackinac Island; visitors walk, or rent horses, horse-drawn carriages
and taxis, and bicycles.

The Grand Hotel, built in 1887, has been called one of the
great hotels of the railroad and Great Lakes steamer era. Its
location high on an island bluff provides magnificent vistas over
the Straits of Mackinac waters.

Its incredible, many-columned veranda is 700 feet long (it

claims to be the longest in the world) and is decorated with huge American flags snapping in the wind, bright yellow awnings that catch the color of the sun, and colorful hanging plants everywhere. Many guests simply sit in generous rockers, sip on a drink, relax, and enjoy cooling lake breezes. I also like to admire the hotel's hundreds of acres of woodland and lawns, finely manicured with exquisite flower gardens and greenery arrangements.

At the Grand Hotel, I feel immersed in a long-ago era of luxury and elegance. Even the attire of hotel attendants is impressive; they're dressed in long red coats and black bow ties. Once I rode the hotel's elegant horse-drawn carriage (the driver wore a black top hat and formal "pink" hunting jacket) from the ferry docks, up the long hill, to the grand portico.

Inside, the hotel is all greens, yellows, and whites, with balloon draperies on the windows, high-back chairs and sofas everywhere in numerous public rooms, and a healthy dash of yesteryear memorabilia hanging on hallway walls. One 1889 breakfast menu especially caught my eye, listing an extraordinary selection of foods, including lamb chops, lake fish, stewed potatoes in cream, and sweetbreads.

Special services are legion and include complimentary morning coffee, concerts during afternoon tea, horse-drawn-carriage island tours, dinner dances, and much more. It seems the pampering never stops.

Many of the guest rooms have spectacular lake views. Rates include breakfast and dinner, with Lake Superior whitefish an evening specialty. A dessert treat—the Grand pecan ball with hot fudge sauce—almost made me melt.

How to get there: From either Mackinaw City from the Lower Peninsula or from St. Ignace on the Upper Peninsula, a 30-minute ferry ride brings you to Mackinac Island. Dock porters will greet your boat. There's an island airstrip for chartered flights and private planes.

❀

B: *Simply one of the "Grand"-est inns imaginable.*

Haan's 1830 Inn
Mackinac Island, Michigan
49757

Innkeepers: Vernon and Joy Haan; Nicholas and Nancy Haan
Address/Telephone: P.O. Box 123; (906) 847–6244 (winter address: 1134 Geneva Street, Lake Geneva, Wisconsin 53147; 414–248–9244).
Rooms: 7, with 1 suite; 5 with private bath.
Rates: $75 to $95, single or double; $105, suite; continental breakfast. Off-season discount of 20 percent. No credit cards.
Open: May 22 to October 16.
Facilities and activities: Located off Front Street, main street of Mackinac Island, one of the Midwest's most famous summer resort communities. Short walk or drive to historic sites, specialty shops, restaurants, golf course, ferry boats, other attractions.

Haan's 1830 Inn is easily one of my favorite Mackinac Island hideaways. A stately Greek Revival design with tall white columns, it dates all the way back to . . . surprise—1830. That's when the island was still operating as a fur-trading center.

The home, listed on the National Register of Historic Places as one of the oldest examples of Greek Revival architecture in the old Northwest Territory, was once owned by Colonel William Preston, the last physician at the historic English settlement of Fort Mackinac and the first mayor of the island. I never pass up a chance to tour this historic fort, which stands sentinel atop the island overlooking the straits.

The exterior is a gem. Once a frontier log cabin (it's actually built on the foundations of a trader cabin brought over from the mainland during the American Revolution), the main house's Greek Revival features date back to 1830, and the west wing was added in 1847. I could see original tongue-and-groove walls and the wavy lead windows made in the early 1800s.

Guest rooms are furnished in striking authentic period antiques, beautiful pieces that call to mind the island's rich legacy. Such historic items as Colonel Preston's original desk and bed grace the premises.

Rooms are named after significant island figures. The Lafayette Davis Room has twin four-poster cannonball beds made in 1790. (Can you guess which bed is filled with horsehair?) It also has fine English prints. Old newspapers, dating from March and April of 1847, were found inside the walls during restoration. They were used as a crude insulation against the frigid winter cold.

The John Jacob Astor Room has a handcrafted antique burled-walnut double bed with English bedspreads, and a rare butternut chest; a screened-in porch offers a view of the garden of neighboring St. Anne's Church. (The church, whose congregation began worship here in 1695, was the first one dedicated in this part of the country.)

Breakfast is taken in the dining room on a handsome 12-foot-long farm harvest table. It includes home-baked spice breads, muffins, coffeecakes, juice, and other beverages. The innkeepers will recommend one of the island's many restaurants for dinner fare.

Did I mention that no cars are allowed on the island? You must walk, rent a horse or horse-drawn carriage, hansom (horse-drawn taxi), or bicycle. There are miles of rugged lakeshore to explore.

How to get there: Catch a ferryboat from the Upper or Lower Peninsula, off I–75, at St. Ignace or Mackinaw City. Once on the island, walk a few blocks east down Huron (Main) Street, around Hennepin Harbor, to the inn.

Hotel Iroquois on the Beach
Mackinac Island, Michigan
49757

Innkeepers: Sam and Margaret McIntire
Address/Telephone: Lake Shore Drive; (906) 847–3321
Rooms: 47; all with private bath.
Rates: Full season: standard, $98 to $168, single or double; deluxe, $200; deluxe suites, $275; EP. Early and late season: $58 to $195, EP. Special packages available.
Open: May to October 20.
Facilities and activities: Full-service restaurant, bar, lounge. Swimming at private beach or public pool. Nearby: golf course, tennis, biking, hiking, island tours, museums, specialty shops, historical sites, horseback riding, boating, charter fishing. Mackinac Island is a historic site—home of a British Revolutionary War fort and former fur-trading center.

Every time I ride the ferry across the Straits of Mackinac to Mackinac Island, the sight of this white, gabled Victorian building shimmering in the mist ahead always sends shivers down my spine. The hotel literally sits on the beach, the lake waters lapping its grounds out on the point.

This marvelous vision of the Hotel Iroquois always stays with me, so I never miss the chance to visit this turn-of-the-century house that offers spectacular guest-room views at the water's edge.

The hotel always seems to be expanding, but it never fails to maintain the charming appeal of an earlier era. And while it's an expensive inn, the location and resulting ambience are unsurpassed. You can hear seagulls crying during sun-drenched summer days and foghorns faintly sounding romantic calls at night. There is a large lakeside veranda and rooms that seem to stretch right out over the water; in fact, some suites with daring alcoves do just that.

The guest rooms are cheerful, decorated in bright floral wallpaper, with wall-to-wall carpeting, and mostly contemporary furnishings. Some rooms have windows on almost every wall, so guests are virtually engulfed by the blue Straits waters.

The hotel's Carriage House dining room is quite spectacular; you can look out over the water, alive with the flickering lights of pleasure boats and the shadows of massive freighters passing far in the distance. A candlelight dinner in this setting is especially romantic.

Lake Superior whitefish, an island specialty, is really a tasty dinner treat. Other items on the varied menu emphasize American home-style cooking. Then there are all the home-baked breads and rolls. The dessert selection can drive you mad.

How to get there: Off I–75, there's ferryboat service from St. Ignace on the Upper Peninsula and from Mackinaw City on the Lower Peninsula. The hotel's dock porter meets all boats and transfers luggage to the hotel. It's only a short walk to the hotel, or you can take a horse-drawn taxi.

Metivier Inn
Mackinac Island, Michigan
49757

Innkeepers: Mike and Jane Bacon, Ken and Diane Neyer, owners; Irma
  Kujat, manager
Address/Telephone: Market Street (mailing address: Box 285); (906) 847–
  6234
Rooms: 15, with 2 efficiencies; all with private bath.
Rates: $88 to $145, rooms and efficiencies ($115 to $165 from July 1
  through August 22), continental breakfast. After September 8, 20
  percent discount Sunday through Thursday. Cribs and cots available.
Open: May through October.
Facilities and activities: Short walk away from main street on Mackinac
  Island, unique summer resort community. No motor vehicles
  allowed—only horses, carriages, bicycles. Restaurants, many specialty shops, historic island sites, horseback riding, swimming, golf,
  tennis nearby.

  This handsome 1877 building, situated on one of the most
history-laden streets on historic Mackinac Island, borrows heavily
from the Colonial English and French influences that saturated the
region in the 1700s and 1800s.
  Irma pointed out that most of the furniture is from the Ethan
Allen English pine collection. It's perfectly suited to the inn's

styling. There also are a number of original antiques gracing both common and guest rooms.

The guest rooms are enchanting, especially if you want to enjoy country-inn ambience without sacrificing modern conveniences. Each room is named for a historic island figure. The John Jacob Astor Room (a building used as one of his historic fur-trading offices is located just down Market Street; it's now a preserved historic home) has a four-poster bed, wicker chairs, and soothing rose-colored wallpaper. A special touch: I could see the bay waters from a romantic turret alcove.

Other rooms have antique headboards and iron-rail beds, marble-topped dressers, tulip lamps, padded rockers, and more.

Four new rooms and an entire tower have been added recently. Owner Jane has decorated in more of a "Victorian, Mackinac Island–style," with antique wicker dominating the rooms warmed by light peach and yellow floral colors.

I enjoyed relaxing in a wicker rocker on the expansive front porch and watching the parade of island visitors pass by. You might want to explore the island's six square miles of unique beauty. Just walk, rent a horse or horse-drawn carriage, or rent a bicycle. There are no motorized vehicles allowed on the island.

Breakfast fare is light: fruit, croissants, coffeecake, juice, and other beverages. For dinner, I put on my best dinner jacket and headed for the famous Grand Hotel. Its luxurious formal dining room offers a wonderful Mackinac whitefish and a score of more traditional gourmet feasts.

How to get there: Take a ferryboat to Mackinac Island. Ferries run from both the Upper and Lower peninsulas, off I–75. From the Sheppler ferry dock, follow the road leading up the hill; turn right on Market Street to the inn.

B: *Staying overnight on Mackinac Island is like stepping into a long-ago world, filled with history and surprises.*

Leelanau Country Inn
Maple City, Michigan
49664

Innkeepers: John and Linda Sisson
Address/Telephone: 149 East Harbor Highway; (616) 228–5060; Fax (616)
    228–5013
Rooms: 6 share 2 baths.
Rates: $35 to $40, single or double, continental breakfast.
Open: All year.
Facilities and activities: Full-service dining room with wheelchair access;
    sitting area, porch. Area winery tours. Near Sleeping Bear Dunes
    National Lakeshore, Glen Lake, Lake Michigan, historic Leland
    "Fishtown" with craft, art, and specialty shops.

If Bob Newhart's television inn ever moved to the Midwest, it
might look just like this.

The gabled clapboard house has all the comforts needed for a
restful stay in the country, including front and side porches that
boast comfy chairs. Tall trees shade the grounds, and seasonal
flowers burst in rainbow colors everywhere. I found Linda in the
garden doing yet more planting.

This house is an old farmstead that was built in 1891. Pictures
of the then newly built structure hang on inn walls. Linda pointed
out photos of all the families that have lived here. And she said

that the granddaughter of the original owners now lives right across the street.

The inn began serving traveling families from Chicago. Linda has an early-1900s guest register. "Some deal," she laughed. "Guests paid $1 per day for a room and three meals."

While the prices may have changed, I found the same kind of warm hospitality that must have welcomed turn-of-the-century guests to this charming country retreat.

Although there are three dining rooms, my favorite is the long enclosed porch that's done in lively colors, offering a view of the flowers and grounds out front. The inn specializes in seafood, which John has flown in fresh from Boston. Another inn specialty is homemade pasta. Favorites like roast duckling with walnut-mint sauce and blackfish Provençal are served regularly.

Linda has fashioned guest rooms that are simple, quaint, and charming. The plank floors made me feel as though I were back at my aunt's Wisconsin farm. Fancy bedspreads and wall wreaths add splashes of color, and the old-fashioned rocking chairs are fun.

Breakfast includes fresh fruit, freshly made croissants, rolls, coffee, and tea.

How to get there: From Chicago, take I–94 north to I–196 north. Continue to U.S. 31 north. Turn north on Michigan 22 and continue north just past County Road 667. Turn right into inn driveway.

*

B: *Maybe I didn't emphasize strongly enough how wonderful the food is here at the inn. Well, in a local newspaper poll, Leelanau Country Inn has been voted the best restaurant in Leelanau County, with the best Sunday brunch, the best country setting, and the best service; it was also voted the best place to go for a drive and have a meal. I get hungry just writing about it!*

McCarthy's Bear Creek Inn
Marshall, Michigan
49068

Innkeepers: Mike and Beth McCarthy
Address/Telephone: 15230 C Drive North; (616) 781–8383
Rooms: 14; all with private bath, air conditioning; some with wheelchair access and balcony.
Rates: $63 to $93, single or double, Sunday night discount available, continental breakfast.
Open: All year.
Facilities and activities: Dining room. Cross-country skiing, hiking, and fishing on grounds. Scores of fine Victorian homes throughout town, with 12 national historic sites and 35 state historic sites. Museums, including Honolulu House, numerous antiques stores. Local theater. Boating, swimming, fishing, natural habitat zoo nearby. Monthly town events and celebrations.

The first things I noticed as I pulled up to this imposing home, perched atop a knoll overlooking Bear Creek, were the fieldstone fences. They were hand-built by the home's original owner in the 1940s and meander about the grounds, surrounding the main house, outbuildings, tall burr oaks more than 100 years old, sugar maples, and stately spruces.

This is country living at its finest, with fourteen acres of farm fields to wander and explore and a twisting creek gurgling outside the windows of inn rooms.

Two children and a dog were cavorting on the creek's edge as I stood and let the beauty of the landscape absorb me. The mutt's yipping and their laughter pretty much characterized good times here.

The handsome Williamsburg-style Cape Cod main house, which resembles an English country estate, is comfortable country. A sitting room boasts a fireplace with a stuffed black teddy bear sitting on the mantel. One first-floor guest room has a four-poster cherry bed, soothing green-and-rose floral wall coverings, wing chairs, and a large bay window overlooking the fields.

Upstairs, rooms feature iron-rail, brass, and Jenny Lind beds, high-back chairs, and private porches that provide great views of the grounds.

Seven new rooms have been fashioned out of a historic outbuilding called the Creek House just behind the main inn. In fact, you'll feel that it's possible to reach out and scoop up chilly creek water in your hands. Here rooms are more elegantly country, and the Sunset Room's large arched window offers spectacular sunset vistas.

French doors open from the sitting room onto an enclosed porch with fieldstone floors and more spectacular views of outbuildings and farm fields. An extensive continental breakfast buffet includes breads for toasting, fresh fruit, cereals, egg dishes, home-baked goodies, and beverages. (Hard to believe this feast is called "continental," isn't it?) I'd recommend Win Schuler's restaurant for good family-style dinnertime meals. The innkeepers will arrange dinner reservations for you there or at any other of Marshall's eating establishments.

How to get there: From Lansing, take I–69 south to Michigan Avenue, and turn west. Then turn south on 15 Mile Road, then a quick right (west) on C Drive North to the inn.

❀

B: Note the handsome cupola; like much of the inn's elegant furniture, it was designed and built by Mike and Beth.

The National House Inn
Marshall, Michigan
49068

Innkeepers: Sharlene and Jack Anderson; Barbara Bradley, manager
Address/Telephone: 102 South Parkview; (616) 781–7374
Rooms: 16, with 2 suites; 14 with private bath, all with air conditioning.
   Wheelchair access.
Rates: $53 to $89, single; $59 to $95, double; continental breakfast.
Open: All year except Christmas Eve and Christmas Day.
Facilities and activities: Sitting room, dining room, The Tin Whistle Gift
   Shoppe. Many fine examples of historic Victorian homes throughout
   town, with 12 national historic sites and 35 state historic sites.
   Museums, including the Honolulu House. Antiques stores. Stage
   productions at local theaters. Boating, fishing, swimming at nearby
   lakes. Winter cross-country skiing. Monthly town events and annual
   celebrations.

   Stepping into The National House Inn is like entering a way
station on nineteenth-century frontier back roads: Rough plank
wood floors, hand-hewn timbers, and a massive brick open-hearth
fireplace with a 13-foot single timber mantelpiece bring back
visions of the frontier.
   And why not? The house was built in 1835 as a stagecoach
stop. As it stands, it's the oldest operating inn in Michigan.

More history? Barbara told me that the inn is reputed to have been part of the Underground Railroad and once also functioned as a wagon factory. Now it provides a glimpse into the past for travelers and is furnished with antiques and Victorian finery.

The rooms are named after local historical figures. "Color schemes are authentic to the early 1800s," Barbara said. So you'll see muted salmons, blues, and greens—all copied "from original milk-paint colors that were made from wild berries to achieve their hue."

The elegant Ketchum Suite is formal Victorian, with a high bedstead and a tall, marble-topped dresser. Other rooms reveal iron- and brass-rail beds, elaborate rockers, and balloon period curtains.

I was overwhelmed by the huge armoire in the Charles Gorham Room; it must stand 9 feet high. Still more rooms evoke pure country charm, with bright quilts that complement pine, maple, and oak furniture, and folk art portraits that grace the walls.

Continental deluxe breakfast in the nineteenth-century–styled dining room features five different home-baked pastries (including bran muffins, bundt cake, and nut breads), boiled eggs, fruit, cereal, applesauce, juice, and other beverages. Ask the innkeepers to suggest an area restaurant; there are several good ones nearby.

How to get there: From Detroit, take I–94 west to Marshall (Exit 110). At the Fountain Circle, jog right and follow the road around to the inn.

B: *I love touring the town, which is teeming with all sorts of Victorian-era homes, histories, and legends.*

TAYLOR

The Helmer House Inn
McMillan, Michigan
49853

Innkeeper: Kathy Plefscher, manager
Address/Telephone: County Road 417, "on the creek"; (906) 586–3204
Rooms: 5 share 2 baths; 2 with air conditioning, cordless phone on
  request.
Rates: $29 to $36, single; $34 to $45, double; EPB.
Open: May through October.
Facilities and activities: Full-service dining room. Near Upper Peninsula
  attractions: Tahquamenon Falls, Devil's Slide, agate beaches of Grand
  Marais, sand beaches of Lake Michigan, Pictured Rocks, mouth of
  Two Hearted River. Also swimming, fishing, sailing, biking, hiking,
  backpacking.

Deep in the Upper Peninsula's spectacular Hiawatha National
Forest on Manistique Lake, The Helmer House harkens back to a
time of simple country comforts.

It's a rather ordinary-looking white clapboard house built in
the late 1800s by a Presbyterian minister. (It has been a mission
house for early Michigan settlers, a general store, a U.S. Post
Office, and a resort hotel.)

But there's nothing ordinary about the inn's hospitality,
friendliness, and terrific home-style meals.

164

A unique inn feature is called the "Salesman's Room." There is a tiny space for a white iron-rail bed and oak dresser. Salesmen traveling on business ask specially for the room. Why not—it's one of the Midwest's best country-inn bargains at $29 per night. And that includes a full breakfast of bacon, eggs, toast, fruit, and coffee!

Other upstairs guest rooms feature more antique furnishings. There are big black-iron beds and brass beds, oval reading tables, cane chairs, and writing desks.

The inn has an amenity that's just perfect for me—a room with a lovely antique brass shaving stand. It's one of my favorite pieces and helps me keep my bushy mustache well trimmed.

A common room with original inn furniture (red velvet covered couches and deeply cushioned chairs) is a nice place for an evening chat with other guests.

An enclosed porch serves as the inn's dining room, crowded with antique oak tables and chairs and cheered by lacy curtains. Dinner choices include hearty country fare like Helmer's old-fashioned flame-broiled chicken, 10-ounce steaks, pork ribs, and Flamed-grilled Whitefish (an inn specialty) at hard-to-beat prices.

Make sure you try the homemade desserts, too; a guest favorite is bread pudding laced with rum sauce and topped with a mountain of whipped cream.

How to get there: From Chicago, take I–94 north to I–196 and continue north to U.S. 131. Go north to U.S. 31 and continue north to I–75. Go north to Michigan 28 and turn west, heading toward McMillan. Turn south on County H–33; then turn right on County 417 to the inn.

B: *Michigan's Upper Peninsula is pure, magnificent wilderness— some of the Midwest's most unspoiled acres. Be ready for a startling starlight sky show and unbelievable quiet.*

The 1873 Mendon Country Inn
Mendon, Michigan
49072

Innkeepers: Dick and Dolly Buerkle
Address/Telephone: 440 West Main Street; (616) 496–8132
Rooms: 18; all with private bath, 16 with air conditioning, 7 with whirlpool and fireplace. Wheelchair access.
Rates: $45 to $72, single or double, continental breakfast.
Open: All year.
Facilities and activities: Rooftop garden with view of creek; antiques shop. Continuous special inn weekend events like Country Fair, featuring more than 30 craftspeople; Halloween nights, with spooky magic, ghost stories, and goblin's brew; and family Christmas weekend, an old-fashioned celebration. Near antique market and Shipshewana, Indiana, Auction and Flea Market; local Amish settlement. Restaurants, golf, tennis, fishing, boating, museums, winery tours also nearby.

The 1873 Mendon Country Inn is everything I imagine a country inn should be. Others must feel the same way: It was featured in the January 1986 issue of *Country Living* magazine and in the February 1989 issue of *Country Home.*

Like all newcomers, I was welcomed in the Indian Room, a gathering place on the first floor with Native American artifacts strewn about. Here Dick provides guests with area maps that identify local points of interest—restaurants, specialty stores, historical attractions—just about everything needed to enjoy a stay in this quaint town.

He told me that the inn was built as a frontier hotel in the 1840s, then rebuilt with locally kilned St. Joseph River clay bricks in 1873. It was called The Wakeman House, a name the locals still use for the inn today.

Guest rooms are decorated thematically, though several exhibit interiors done in the grand style so popular after the Civil War. The Amish Room has a beautiful antique Amish quilt. The Nautical Room features country-pine furnishings, with a swag of fishermen's netting used for the bed canopy; it also has a creekside porch. But my favorite is The Wakeman Room, of elegant post–Civil War design—including 8-foot-tall windows, a 12-foot-high ceiling, and fine oversized country Empire furnishings.

The best bargain is the Hired Man Room, a small space in country-style decor with a three-quarter bed and a shower across the hall—for only $45. That includes a breakfast of juice, rolls, and coffee.

The inn's Roof Top Garden affords another view of the creek and is great for sunbathing or private late-night moon gazing. "We're the only country inn around with its own treehouse," Dick told me. Not to mention the stage out back that serves as a centerpiece for classical music concerts and other special entertainment.

Dick and Dolly's most recent inn addition, the Creekside Lodge, is fashioned in Native American stylings; but I doubt if early Indian inhabitants of the area enjoyed whirlpool suites with fireplaces, full cedar sauna, and a covered deck that overlooks water and wildlife areas.

There's lots more. But I think you've already got the idea.

How to get there: From Chicago, take the Dan Ryan expressway south to the Indiana toll road (I–80/90), and go west past Elkhart to US 131. Then go north to Michigan 60/66. Head east into Mendon. M–60/66 is called Main Street once in town; follow it to the inn.

TAYLOR

Stafford's Bay View Inn
Petoskey, Michigan
49770

Innkeepers: Stafford and Janice Smith; Judy Honor, manager
Address/Telephone: U.S. 31 (mailing address: P.O. Box 3); (616) 347–2771
Rooms: 30, with 5 suites; all with private bath and air conditioning. Wheelchair access.
Rates: $46 to $88, single; $56 to $128, double; EPB except low season (winter), when continental breakfast included. Weekday, weekend, seasonal rates and special packages available.
Open: May 15 through October; December 25 through March. Inn restaurant open all year; weekends-only schedule during winter.
Facilities and activities: Full-service restaurant, sitting rooms, sun porch. Located outside Bay View, a city whose Victorian architecture qualifies it as a National Historic Site. Near Petoskey's Gaslight Shopping District and ritzy Harbor Springs boutiques. Bay View chautauqua programs feature concerts and lectures throughout summer. Biking in summer; cross-country skiing, ice boating, snowmobiling in winter. Sailboat charters on lake; golfing nearby.

Stafford's Bay View Inn, overlooking Little Traverse Bay, calls itself a "Grand Old Dame of the Victorian resort era." It's certainly steeped in rich Victorian traditions; in fact, it sits next to a village whose treasure of Victorian gingerbread architecture might be unmatched anywhere.

168

Built in 1886, this elegant white clapboard inn has served North Country hospitality to four generations of discerning travelers. It's a classic summer house, in the sense that it offers cool breezes due to its bayside location, all kinds of outdoor activities, and an ambitious community program of music, drama, and art. Did I forget great shopping nearby, too?

A long sun porch overlooks the bay, furnished with oversized wicker pieces. Guest rooms filled with antiques and reproductions from several famous Michigan furniture makers reflect the styles of the Victorian era. Room 3 has a four-poster bed so high that even I had to use a stepstool to climb atop it—and I'm 6'2". You'll also find brass beds and sleigh beds, and inviting flower wreaths on room doors.

Several dining rooms serve food with a fine reputation, including fresh Great Lakes whitefish and local specialties such as honey-mustard shrimp and Veal Louisiana in creole-mustard sauce, which have been featured in *Gourmet* magazine.

A full breakfast ordered from the regular menu is included in the price of the rooms. That means choices like malted waffles or whole-wheat pancakes with Michigan maple syrup, and biscuits with sausage gravy or even eggs Benedict and red-flannel hash.

Stafford's also offers food at three other nearby locations: One Water Street, on Lake Charlevoix in Boyne City, offers specialties like Trout Hemingway and cold black-cherry soup, as well as various game selections; Stafford's Pier Restaurant is in Harbor Springs, near one of Michigan's most scenic drives along Michigan 119, north from the village; another is the Weathervane, in Charlevoix.

One of the inn's newest acquisitions—the 81-room Stafford's Perry Hotel—is also in Petoskey. This historic 1899 hostelry, boasting its own full-service restaurant, is decorated with turn-of-the-century stylings.

How to get there: From any direction, the inn is right on U.S. 31, just outside Bay View.

❋

B: *Chic boutiques in nearby Harbor Springs are a hot spot just a short drive away.*

Montague Inn
Saginaw, Michigan
48601

Innkeeper: William Schipper
Address/Telephone: 1581 South Washington Avenue; (517) 752–3939
Rooms: 18, with 1 suite; 16 with private bath, all with air conditioning, TV, and phone.
Rates: $55 to $125, single; $60 to $130, double; continental breakfast. Add $5 for third person or child in room.
Open: All year.
Facilities and activities: Full-service restaurant (lunch, dinner Tuesday through Saturday by reservation). Nestled on 8 beautifully landscaped acres, formal flower gardens, herb garden, cooking classes in summer, elegant picnic lunches provided guests for afternoons spent at Lake Linton, just behind inn. Walk to Japanese Garden and Teahouse, children's zoo, Hoyt Park, Old West Side business district. Health club, summer and winter sports activities available to guests.

After driving nearly sixteen hours with my wife and baby Dayne, then six months old, I made an evening call to the Montague Inn, searching for a room. It was answered by one of the owners, Norm Kinney, who told me he had had a cancellation, so he'd be expecting us. Turns out we got the final room.

We were lucky in several ways, since the Montague Inn

quickly became one of our favorite stopovers. It's an elegant Georgian mansion, built in 1929 by its namesake, a prosperous businessman who made products from Saginaw's sugar-beet crop.

The inn has the ambience of a fine, intimate European hotel, with elegant classical Georgian antiques, oriental and Persian rugs, formal flower and herb gardens, private "park," and lakeside location all adding to its clublike atmosphere.

It also boasts six fireplaces, a dining room overlooking Lake Linton, and a library that contains a swinging shelf to reveal a small hidden room.

Our quarters, the third-floor Goodridge Room, was a cozy bedchamber tucked beneath a gable, with three alcove windows overlooking the grounds, two twin beds, and a cedar-lined bath.

Most inn rooms are far more spacious; some offer marble fireplaces, Art Deco–tiled baths, pegged oak floors, and views of the lake or park.

Dining is also a treat. Formal servers wear what closely resembles butlers' uniforms. Entrees include shrimp sautéed in hazelnut oil and finished with strawberry puree and ground hazelnuts; Norwegian salmon served with leek-and-pink-peppercorn cream sauce; and grilled medallions of tenderloin sauced with Dijon and demi-glace. Even lunch offers selections like grilled tenderloin tips and smoked turkey salad.

Norm's wife, Kathryn, conducts tours and offers samples of the inn's herb garden, relating the history and myths of herbs; later, a special luncheon featuring herb-rich delicacies.

How to get there: From Detroit, take I–75 north into Saginaw. Exit on Michigan 46 and go west to Remington. Follow Remington northwest to Washington and turn left. Continue to the inn.

Kemah Guest House
Saugatuck, Michigan
49453

Innkeepers: Terry and Cindi Tatsch
Address/Telephone: 633 Pleasant Street; (616) 857–2919
Rooms: 6, plus 1 suite, share 3 baths.
Rates: $75 to $95, single or double, continental breakfast.
Open: All year.
Facilities and activities: Rathskeller (for guests only). Located on a quiet hill, high above the hustle of this lakeside Midwest art-colony village. Short drive to restaurants, antiques and specialty shops, art galleries, beaches, swimming, boating, dune exploring, and more.

The Kemah Guest House is one of the most intriguing residences in the lakeside village of Saugatuck. It reminds me of traditional European homes and combines an old-world German flair with touches of Art Deco—and Frank Lloyd Wright!

Built by a German sea captain, the home is named for its site on a breezy hill. (*Kemah* is a Potawatomi Indian word meaning "teeth of the wind.") Cindi said that the captain, ever a superstitious seaman, wanted to ensure that his sails would always billow with the winds, so he graced his home with a good-luck moniker.

It was remodeled in 1926 by William Springer, a Chicago Board of Trade member. You can see his initials carved everywhere—from wood panels in the rathskeller to the massive wrought-iron arched doorway.

There are so many highlights:

Stained- and lead-glass windows depict sailing scenes.

Hand-carved wooden landscapes on the solarium paneling recount the house's various appearances through the decades.

A bricked, semicircular solarium with a running fountain was designed by T. E. Tallmadge, a disciple of Frank Lloyd Wright, and captures the master's Prairie School architectural style.

Beamed ceilings, cornice boards, and a fireplace (of Pewabic tile) recall the Art Deco era.

Have a drink in a genuine rathskeller, boasting the home's original wine casks, wall stencils, and leather-strap and wood-frame chairs hand-carved in Colorado in the 1930s.

Can you find the secret panel that hid whiskey and spirits during Prohibition days? A hint: Look at the windows near the arched door and kitchen.

There's a cave on the grounds and an Indian grave on the side of the hill.

Cindi has fashioned charming guest rooms in rich individual styles. One is done in fine lace; another recalls a gentleman's room, filled with oak furniture and a 6-foot-tall Victorian headboard on the bed.

My favorite room features an eleven-piece bedroom set made in 1918, one of only two like it ever made. It's all walnut, of gorgeous craftsmanship. Can you find the secret jewelry drawer in the dresser?

There are rolls, danish, fresh fruit, juices, and coffee for breakfast. If you wish, the innkeepers will recommend one of many good area restaurants, too.

How to get there: From Chicago, take I–94 north to I–196. Exit at Saugatuck on Blue Star Highway and go south to Pleasant. Turn right and continue to the inn.

Maplewood Hotel
Saugatuck, Michigan
49453

Innkeepers: Donald Mitchell, owner; David Cofield, manager
Address/Telephone: 428 Butler Street (mailing address: P.O. Box 1059); (616) 857–1771
Rooms: 13, with 4 suites; all with private bath.
Rates: $75 to $159, single or double, May through October, continental breakfast. Rates lower rest of year.
Open: All year.
Facilities and activities: Sitting room with fireplace and bar, screened porch, full-lap swimming pool. Walk to art galleries, specialty and antiques shops, restaurants, lake, swimming, yachting, historic houses. Nearby: sightseeing cruises aboard old sternwheeler down Kalamazoo River, tours of area vineyards and cellars.

I have some great news for admirers of this landmark Greek Revival building prominently located on the village green of the lively art-colony, lakeshore village. Major restoration and refurbishing have been completed and have transformed the Maplewood Hotel into an elegant and fanciful guest house.

Upon entering, I was surprised to observe the extent of the renovation. Downstairs common rooms boast wonderful, warm fabrics, shiny chandeliers, fireplaces, and more.

Three of the four new suites offer attractive floral wallpapers, comfy beds, antiques, and whirlpool baths. The other features a cozy fireplace that transforms cold, blustery Michigan winters into warm, cuddly nights.

I was especially fond of all the Baker furniture fashioned in Grand Rapids; though locally made, it's nationally renowned. Handsome Greek Revival stylings are a perfect complement to the inn's white-columned exterior.

Other surprises are a full-lap swimming pool, a screened-porch sun room, and a lounge with fireplace, bar, and player piano.

I could understand why the Maplewood Hotel is once again receiving lots of attention from weekenders. But then, it's always been in the limelight. Built in 1860, its downtown location makes it an ideal spot for shopping, and it's close to restaurants, art galleries, and the chain ferry on the Kalamazoo River that goes to famed Oval Beach.

Breakfast usually includes freshly baked muffins, croissants, and pastries, as well as beverages. Then take a walk through the inn green, which has the feeling of a small private park.

How to get there: From Chicago, take I–94 north to I–196 north and exit at Blue Star Highway. Go south to Allegan Road, then west to Butler and the hotel.

The Park House
Saugatuck, Michigan
49453

Innkeepers: Lynda and Joe Petty
Address/Telephone: 888 Holland; (616) 857–4535
Rooms: 8, with 1 suite; all with private bath and air conditioning. Wheelchair access.
Rates: $65 to $95, single or double, continental breakfast.
Open: All year.
Facilities and activities: Gathering room, porch. Short drive to restaurants, Lake Michigan beaches, swimming, boating, charter fishing, cross-country skiing, specialty stores, antiques shops, art galleries, and other lakeside attractions including sand-dune schooner rides, golf, hiking, biking, lake cruises.

When I arrived at The Park House, Lynda and Joe were muscling up railroad ties and timbers, landscaping their garden and grounds. Nobody else was working that hard on a hot Sunday afternoon in this fun-filled Lake Michigan resort town.

So it's not suprising that The Park House is a treasure. Built in 1857 by a local lumberman, the two-story clapboard home is Saugatuck's oldest historic residence. The innkeepers recently restored the historic wing of this handsome inn, which had been removed in the 1940s. Now the porch wraps around the house, is screened in, and overlooks pretty gardens.

176

Lynda told me a great story of how the inn got its name. Seems a former owner fenced the home's almost eight acres and stocked the pasture with deer. Their grazing cropped the grass, giving the grounds a manicured look. People started calling it the "park" house.

Want more history? Susan B. Anthony stayed here for two weeks in the 1870s and helped form the county's first temperance society. In fact, Joe laughingly said that Anthony was responsible for closing down half the bars in Allegan County!

The house is built from original timbers that once stood on the property. Some special touches include the original wide-plank pine-wood floors, pretty wall stencils done by Lynda, a wide fireplace, and antique furnishings throughout the home. French doors in the parlor open onto an herb garden. All in all, it's a real country charmer.

Each cozy guest room is distinctly decorated, and all have queen-sized iron-rail beds and warm oak furniture.

Lynda serves breakfast at an antique oak table in a gathering room dotted with country crafts and antiques. Get ready for freshly baked muffins, granola, fruit, homemade jams, and the Pettys' own blend of coffee. They'll also suggest a few "can't miss" dinner spots.

The Park House is usually part of a spectacular Elizabethan Christmas feast and a February progressive dinner in which guests partake of each meal course at a historic Saugatuck inn; the holiday decorating ideas alone are worth the price of the meal.

How to get there: From Chicago, take I–94 north to I–196 and continue north to exit 41 (Blue Star Highway). Turn west and continue on Washington (where Blue Star turns left) to the inn. (Washington changes to Holland at the city limits.)

Twin Gables Country Inn
Saugatuck, Michigan
49453

Innkeepers: Mike and Denise Simcik
Address/Telephone: 900 Lake Street (mailing address: P.O. Box 88); (616) 857–4346
Rooms: 14, with 1 suite; all with private bath and air conditioning, some with wheelchair access; 3 cottages.
Rates: May 1 to October 31: $49 to $59, weekdays; $69 to $89, weekends; continental breakfast. Weekly and weekend rates for cottages. Off-season rates available. Two-night minimum on weekends during summer season.
Open: All year.
Facilities and activities: Sitting, dining rooms. Garden terrace with pond. Short walk or drive to art galleries, specialty shops, antiques stores, beaches, swimming, boating, and more.

Denise explained that her inn originally stood on a hill across the Kalamazoo River. One winter it was moved across the frozen waters by mule team and log sled to Saugatuck.

She laughed. "After all that trouble, the owners thought they'd put it too close to a road. So they moved it again to its present location."

178

The inn is all that's left of a genuine Midwest ghost town. The old logging town of Singapore hugged a spot on the dune-filled eastern shores of Lake Michigan that is now occupied by Saugatuck. But when the trees had been cut down, lumber interests left, and the town was abandoned. Eventually the crumbling buildings were buried under tons of ever-shifting sand dunes. Now the old town is just a historical footnote.

The 1865 inn is built from timbers cut in the old Singapore sawmill. And it was designed by the same architect who built the magnificent Grand Hotel on Mackinac Island.

It has a fascinating history, including a stint as an ice house for an 1860s brewery, a tanning factory, and boat building works. Denise said tugboats were constructed under this roof.

It's now named for the historic hotel that was established here in 1922.

I love the old pressed-tin ceilings, walls, and wainscoting. Add to that a common-room fireplace surrounded by comfy chairs, sofas and rockers, and the atmosphere is just right for lazing away a weekend.

The guest rooms are lovingly furnished, each distinctive and warm. The Wicker Room, of course, has wicker chairs, and is brightly decorated in shades of yellow—quite a sight on a sun-drenched morning—while the Cape Cod Room features beautifully crafted pine furniture made by Mike. (He also handcrafted the four-poster yellow pine bed in the Captain's Quarters.) But my favorite is the Dutch Room, all tulips and royal blue colors, with 1914 furniture made in Gettysburg, Pennsylvania.

A continental breakfast of fresh fruit, granola, sweet rolls, juice, and a privately blended coffee that's famous with guests is served buffet-style in the dining room. Or you can eat out on the long porch and watch boats sail out of the village harbor. Good hearty dinners are served up in area restaurants; Denise can recommend the spot for you.

How to get there: From Chicago, take I–94 north to I–196. Continue north to exit 36 and go north on Blue Star Highway. Turn left on Lake Street and continue to the inn.

✳

B: *The inn's heated outdoor pool is a great haven—or you can take a dip in the large indoor hot tub.*

Wickwood Inn
Saugatuck, Michigan
49453

Innkeepers: Sue and Stub Louis
Address/Telephone: 510 Butler Street; (616) 857–1097
Rooms: 11, with 2 suites; all with private bath and air conditioning. Wheelchair access.
Rates: $65 to $100, January 2 through April; $80 to $115, May 1 through January 1; continental breakfast, afternoon hors d'oeuvres.
Open: All year.
Facilities and activities: Sunken garden room, library/bar. Located in resort town of Saugatuck, with beaches of Lake Michigan nearby, as well as specialty stores, antiques shops, restaurants, golfing, boating, fishing, cross-country skiing.

Staying at the Wickwood Inn is almost like taking a mini–European vacation. That's because it was inspired by a visit to the grand Duke's Hotel in London. Sue and Stub vowed to open an equally exquisite inn back home in the United States.

The result is outstanding. All linens, wallpapers, and fabrics are from British designer Laura Ashley's collections. There are elegant pieces from Baker Furniture's "Historic Charleston" line. Complimentary soaps and shampoos by Crabtree & Evelyn of London are provided in every bathroom.

180

I discovered more British influences. The library/bar calls to mind an English gentlemen's club. And Stub sometimes whisks away visitors in his authentic London taxicab for tours of this lively and colorful coastal village. It's usually parked right in front of the inn.

These are some of the finest guest rooms I have ever seen. Exquisite walnut, pine, and cherry antique furnishings are outstanding. The Carrie Wicks Suite features a magnificent four-poster Rice bed. In the Master Suite, I found a cherry-wood canopy bed with an antique white eyelet spread and hand-crocheted canopy. Its sitting room contains an Empire-style couch, with finely carved swan heads gracing the arms.

Other rooms feature scalloped wallpaper borders, brass and hand-painted headboards, hand-rubbed paneling, primitive sailing-ship prints, braided rugs, and more.

One of my favorite gathering rooms is the sunken garden, with its vaulted beamed ceiling and greenery everywhere; and the toy room holds Stub's antique toy-train collection.

Continental breakfast includes homemade coffeecakes, bran muffins, juice, and other beverages. There's also a special Sunday brunch of ham and cheese soufflé, fresh fruits, muffins, juice, and more. The innkeepers will find a dinner spot perfect for you.

How to get there: From Chicago, take I–94 north to I–196. Continue north to exit 41; turn southwest on Blue Star Highway, just outside Saugatuck. At the fork in the road, take Holland Street (to the right) into town. Turn right at Lucy; then left at Butler to the inn.

క్రిం

B: *The inn's screened gazebo demands nothing of you except to relax in oversized California redwood furniture and enjoy the evening's cool breezes.*

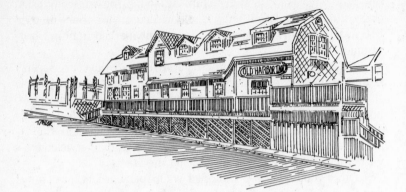

Old Harbor Inn
South Haven, Michigan
49090

Innkeeper: Gwen DeBruyn, owner
Address/Telephone: 515 Williams Street; (616) 637–8480
Rooms: 31, with 4 suites; all with private bath and air conditioning. Wheelchair access. Some with whirlpool and kitchenette.
Rates: $50 to $115, single; $60 to $125, double; suites, $120 to $175; EP. Children free when sharing same suite with adults.
Open: All year.
Facilities and activities: Indoor pool, hot tub, 22 quaint shops and eateries in village. Nearby: beaches, sailing, sailboarding, spectacular sunsets, U-pick farms, windswept sand dunes, biking, hiking, horseback riding, cross-country skiing, boutiques, art galleries.

The Old Harbor Inn sits on the banks of the Black River, in what resembles a re-created, New England fishing village. I strolled along cobblestoned walkways, on boardwalks that skirt the water, and through quaint shops that had names like Bahama Mama's and Flying Colors—both specializing in splashy beachwear.

I also walked to the village docks where charter fishing boats offer Coho challenges on Lake Michigan; or you can take up more sedate pursuits, like leisurely sailboat cruises.

This is all part of the charm of South Haven, a lakeside village boasting an atmosphere that closely resembles that of a California beach town.

If you don't believe me, just go to North Beach during the height of the summer season. It literally teems with Hawaiian shirts, outrageous bikinis, volleyball games, frisbee players, and remarkable tans.

I'd like to make the inn my headquarters for all the above fun. That's because guests relax in high South Haven style, enjoying the luxury of their elegant Old Harbor Inn hideaway.

By far my favorite room is Number 6. It's huge, with a handsome sitting area, a fine mix of antique reproductions and contemporary furnishings, queen-sized bed, white-wicker settee, and a mini-kitchen.

It also has magnificent views of the Black River from a long bank of windows on two walls; you can soak up river views while relaxing in a massive indoor hot tub that seems to assure romance.

There's even more: A blue-and-white ceramic-tile fireplace sits in the corner of the room; and French doors open to a walkout balcony facing the river.

Dinner is just a short walk away, aboard the *Idler*, an authentic Mississippi riverboat that offers fine cuisine on the lower decks while a complete delicatessen and cocktail lounge occupy the upper deck.

Visit during the Labor Day weekend, and you'll be treated to the Venetian Festival's lighted-boat parade, with miles of brightly-illuminated boats floating down the Black River.

How to get there: Exit I–196 at Phoenix Street. Continue for three stop lights, then turn right to the inn.

❋

B: *Try your luck aboard the famous* Captain Nichols Perch Fleet *sailing daily in season for one of the best-eating fish in the world.*

Yelton Manor
South Haven, Michigan
49090

Innkeepers: Jay and Joyce Yelton
Address/Telephone: 140 North Shore Drive; (616) 637–5220
Rooms: 11, with 1 suite; all with private bath and air conditioning.
Rates: $74.20 to $132.50, single or double, continental breakfast. Two-
night minimum on weekends in high season. Special rates and
packages available.
Open: All year.
Facilities and activities: Sitting rooms, enclosed porch-dining area. Walk to
beach, specialty shops, Lake Michigan water activities including
salmon and trout charters, restaurants. Nearby: U-pick fruit farms,
winery tours, cider mills, golfing, nature trails, biking, hiking,
cross-country skiing, Todd Farm Goose Sanctuary.

My wife, Debbie, and I consider South Haven's North Beach
among the finest in the Midwest. In fact, a summer never passes
without bringing our daughters, Kate and Dayne, up to South
Haven for a little sand-castle construction and a dip in the water.

Now that Jay and Joyce have lavishly restored the historic
"chalet de la mer" (house of the sea), we might have to invent even
more excuses for trips up this way.

Originally built in 1873 for two Chicago sisters, the handsome home is a delightful mix of country Victorian and luxury. Jay told me many of the furnishings were handcrafted–in fact, the pencil-post beds found in many guest rooms were fashioned by Amish craftsmen.

We stayed in the elegant Honeymoon Suite—a special treat— with slanted walls tucked under the house's gables, Dutch-lace curtains, and window views of the lake.

Snuggling is easy in the huge king-sized bed adorned with eight pillows and a down comforter, and a large Jacuzzi can be adventurous—without the kids. There's also a sitting room with television, but I've got the feeling it's not often used.

Other rooms offer their own delicate Victorian country stylings, fancy wall coverings, walnut chests, four-poster beds, and more.

A cozy common sitting room warmed by a fireplace is a good spot for conversation during winter months. In summer, I especially like to breakfast on the enclosed porch. Joyce's meal might include ham soufflés with salsa; stuffed French toast with cream cheese; apple tortes with cheese filling; and homemade poppyseed cake.

And an open "refrigerator room" is always stocked with beverages, freshly baked goodies, and other treats.

How to get there: From the north or south, take I–196 to I–196 Business Loop (Phoenix Street), then turn right on Broadway; at the drawbridge, Broadway turns onto Dyckman; take Dyckman to the stop sign. The inn is located on the left corner of Dyckman and North Shore Drive.

❀

B: *One of the finest inns around.*

The Victorian Villa
Guest House
Union City, Michigan
49094

Innkeepers: Ronald and Susan Gibson
Address/Telephone: 601 North Broadway Street; (517) 741–7383
Rooms: 11, with 3 suites; all with private bath, 7 with air conditioning. No smoking inn.
Rates: $70 to $80, single; $75 to $85, double; $110 to $125, suites; EPB on weekends, continental breakfast on weekdays.
Open: All year.
Facilities and activities: Sitting room, parlor, dining room, Christmas & Sherlock Holmes gift shop. Six-course nineteenth-century dinners available Friday and Saturday by reservation for $45 per couple; seven-course picnic basket lunches available by reservation at $22.50 per couple; afternoon teas, too. Gazebo boasts classical music concerts. Specialty weekends include Victorian Summer Days, murder mysteries, Sherlock Holmes Days, and more. About 500 quality antiques dealers within 25 miles. Six Victorian homes/museums, nineteenth-century historical walking tours, 3 summer stock theaters, country auctions, fishing, summer festivals, golfing, cross-country skiing, biking (free tandems to guests).

186

Steady yourself before entering The Victorian Villa for the first time. The grandeur of its elegant Victorian appointments is overwhelming. I could manage only a silly "Wow!"

This Italianate mansion, built in 1876 at the then-whopping cost of $12,000, is nestled in the quaint river village of Union City. Its formal Victorian decor makes it an absolutely perfect romantic hideaway.

The formal entrance hallway, with a winding staircase, is all dark woodwork, highlighted with hurricane lamps, red-velvet curtains, and gingerbread transoms. The "informal" parlor is absolutely elegant. Heavy red-velvet high-back chairs are placed around a marble fireplace. Tall hurricane lamps and tulip-shaped chandeliers cast a warm glow over the room. One of my favorite touches is a massive gingerbread arch over the doorway.

Guest rooms are equally impressive. The 1890s Edwardian Bedchamber has a headboard almost 8 feet high, with antique quilts and pillows, dark rose wallpaper, a marble-topped dresser, and more. The 1860s Rococo Bedchamber has a working fireplace, Tiffany-style lamps, an antique armoire, and a tall Victorian rocker.

Tower suites are decorated in country Victorian and separated by a small sitting room. I like the rough-hewn country feel, with iron-rail beds, exposed brick walls, and round tower windows. And the inn's Carriage House bedchambers are equally impressive. Try the Sherlock Holmes bedchamber, very English with its grand library. (The inn is becoming renowned for its Holmes and Dr. Watson weekends.)

Breakfast in a magnificent formal dining room includes Susan's special treats: breakfast meats; special concoctions that offer heaping helpings of sausage, cheddar cheese, eggs, and onions; muffins; homemade preserves; Amish pastries; fresh fruits; imported teas; and more. Afternoon English high tea also is part of Villa tradition with scones, tea cookies, fresh pastries, and lots of other extras. And you'll find fancy chocolates on your bed pillows at turn-down time.

How to get there: From east or west, take I–94 to I–69 and go south. Turn west on Michigan 60 (exit 25) and continue 7 miles to Union City. There Broadway Street is the town's main street.

The Inn at Union Pier
Union Pier, Michigan
49129

Innkeepers: Madeleine and Bill Reinke
Address/Telephone: 9708 Berrien (mailing address: P.O. Box 222); (616) 469–4700
Rooms: 15; all with private bath and air conditioning, 11 with wood-burning stove.
Rates: $85 to $125, single or double, EPB.
Open: All year.
Facilities and activities: Sitting rooms, enclosed porch, deck and dining area; decktop hot tub. Located in southwestern Michigan's Harbor Country, where lakeshore communities hug Lake Michigan. Walk to breathtaking beaches; drive to antiques shops, U-pick fruit farms. Inn will arrange sailboarding, bicycling, fishing, canoeing, horseback riding, winery tours, cross-country skiing in winter.

I cannot put out of my mind those circular, ceiling-high, wood-burning Swedish stoves that grace most guest rooms. These colorful tile masterpieces are so difficult to assemble that the inn "imported" experts from Sweden to ensure that they were installed correctly.

But that's only one of the highlights of this elegant inn, located on the eastern shore of Lake Michigan. Just a walk from the sand castles and sweeps of the lake's beaches—two hundred steps from the front door—I enjoyed refined hospitality with all the comforts of a well-appointed country home.

The seventy-year-old beach-resort house has been completely redone in spectacular finery by Madeleine and Bill. Especially elegant touches are the huge terra-cotta-and-iron chandeliers in the gathering room. There are also beveled-glass windows casting prisms of sunlight on the pretty pastel colors used to decorate the inn. That massive pagoda-style oriental stove in the gathering room is another Swedish design.

Madeleine's guest rooms, located in the main building, Four Seasons quarters, and Pier House, are pictures of country elegance. From the polished hardwood floors and comfy country furnishings to those wonderful Swedish stoves and lacy window curtains, I felt like a country squire.

A long wood deck connects the main house with the Four Seasons; just between them is an outdoor hot tub, a favorite gathering spot for guests.

Breakfast is served out on the enclosed porch at tables adorned with white linen and fresh flowers, some more of Madeleine's attentive touches. There are two courses: first comes fresh fruit, juices, and home-baked breads; then hearty entrees like blueberry pancakes, cinnamon bread—maybe even a Finnish Florentine, Madeleine's blend of eggs with spinach, cheeses, and sausage. In winter you might enjoy some old-fashioned baked apples, or "egg bakes" with fried tomatoes and all the trimmings, including homemade biscuits and muffins. The innkeepers can recommend many fine area restaurants for dinners to suit your taste.

How to get there: From Chicago, take I–94 north to exit 6. Go north on Townline Road less than a mile to Red Arrow Highway. Turn right; then go a little more than ½ mile and turn left on Berrien. The inn is about 2 blocks ahead on the left side of the road.

∽

B: *Snacks like iced coffee, tea, lemonade, and cookies are treats for summer guests. Potato soup and chili often are offered at afternoon snacktimes during the cold season.*

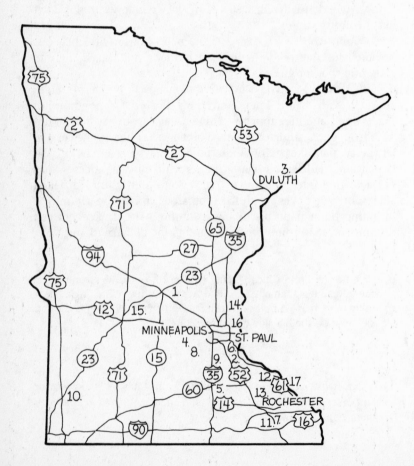

Minnesota

Numbers on map refer to towns numbered below.

Thayer Hotel
Annandale, Minnesota
55302

Innkeeper: June Pannhoff
Address/Telephone: Downtown on Highway 55; (612) 274–3371
Rooms: 14, with 6 suites; all with private bath and air conditioning, some
with TV. Wheelchair access.
Rates: $35 to $65, single or double; $55 to $75, suites; EPB Saturday and
Sunday only. Special winter cross-country ski package rates.
Open: All year.
Facilities and activities: Full-service restaurant, lounge, sauna. Very good
antiquing area. Twenty-five lakes within 5 miles. Snowmobiling and
skiing nearby.

There's something about pioneer hotels and country-Victorian
charm that brings to mind tales of the Old West—probably
because, like most little kids, I always wanted to be a cowboy.

This 1888 building was built to accommodate overnight
passengers and crew of the Soo Line railroad at this turn-of-the-
century resort town. (There are scores of lakes within an hour's
drive of the hotel.)

Now I know why all the handsome glass transoms above the
guest-room doors are etched with Soo Line themes—everything
from massive locomotives to the line's attractive logo.

Guest rooms ooze country charm. Spotless and cheery, they're decorated to convey a turn-of-the-century feel. Some have canopy, four-poster, or iron-rail beds. Others boast fancy Dutch lace curtains on windows that stretch almost from ceiling to floor. I love the brass clothes hooks and handmade quilts.

One bow to the twentieth century: There's a sauna on the third floor.

I think you'll agree that the dining room looks much like a real frontier restaurant. The woodwork here is rare. It is made from tamarack—swamp trees. You don't find many swamps around here any more.

Sample the hotel's Chicken Oscar (grilled chicken breast stuffed with shrimp and crab and smothered in a secret recipe sauce) for a real treat. Another mouth-watering delight is stuffed pork chops with Burgundy sauce. Or try the prime rib; it's the hotel's specialty.

How to get there: From Minneapolis, take Minnesota 55 northwest to Annandale. The hotel is located on 55, in the heart of the downtown area.

Quill and Quilt
Cannon Falls, Minnesota
55009

Innkeepers: Denise Anderson and David Karpinski
Address/Telephone: 615 West Hoffman Street; (507) 263–5507
Rooms: 4, with 1 suite; all with private bath and air conditioning.
Rates: $45 to $85, single; $55 to $95, double; EPB. Midweek and holiday
   packages available.
Open: All year.
Facilities and activities: Social hour, sitting room, library, dining room,
   basement recreation room, porches. Nearby: Cannon Valley trail
   (biking, hiking, cross-country skiing); antiques shops, boutiques,
   historic river towns; golfing, tennis, swimming, boating canoeing,
   tubing, downhill skiing.

   The first thing I noticed was the oak and Italian marble
fireplace in the parlor. It had a double mantel, and on display were
the innkeepers' collection of glass candlesticks and tiny cottages
depicting a European village.
   Then I wandered into the library—and found a haven that
was difficult to leave. The reason: a huge collection of Agatha
Christie novels, along with O. Henry short stories and a dollop of
Sherlock Holmes.
   I decided that the Quill and Quilt began to feel more like
home with each passing minute.

The 1897 house, a delicate Colonial Revival, is country elegant. From its gracious daily social hour to dainty chocolates set on your pillow during evening's turn-down time, you'll discover that Denise and David have lots of pampering in mind.

The guest rooms are charming. The first-floor Quilter's Room has a classic gingerbread panel overhanging the pocket door transom. Inside you'll enjoy a brass bed, a handmade Log Cabin quilt and a wall hanging that closely matches it, and wood-planked floors. You'll also discover fluffy, color-coordinated bath-robes in your private bath down the hall.

Grandmother's Fan boasts early American hand-stenciling on ceiling borders, around windows—the pattern even carries onto curtains. A four-poster bed also looks mighty inviting.

The Covill Suite is bright and dramatic, with seven windows, a four-poster lace-canopied bed, and double whirlpool. Relax on the private porch, and you might catch action on the baseball field out back.

Tracy's Room offers a queen-sized iron-and-brass bed, a handmade quilt, and an antique rocking chair.

And after a long day of bike riding, hiking, or just plain wandering around picturesque Cannon Falls, settle down in the Keystone Room for a classic movie.

How to get there: From the Twin Cities or Rochester, take U.S. 52 to the Cannon Falls exit (Minnesota 19); then turn east on Minnesota 19 to Seventh Street (about ½ mile), turn north on Seventh to Hoffman, and go east a half-block to the inn.

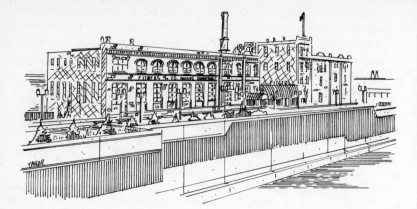

Fitger's Inn
Duluth, Minnesota
55802

Innkeeper: George Hovland, general manager
Address/Telephone: 600 East Superior Street; (218) 722–8826 and Minnesota toll-free (800) 726–2982
Rooms: 48, including 6 suites; all with private bath, air conditioning, TV, and phone. Wheelchair access.
Rates: $84.95 to $104.95, single or double; $135 to $260, suites; EP.
Open: All year.
Facilities and activities: Three restaurants, two lounges, and a nightclub. Expansive patio courtyard facing Lake Superior. Near boat excursions, charter fishing, Lake Superior Zoological Gardens, Glensheen historic estate, sailboat rentals, The Depot (art museum), and more.

I sat on a chair in the courtyard on a sweltering summer day and toasted my good fortune. Lake Superior was throwing some cooling breezes over its cold waters. Colorful sailing boats crisscrossed choppy waves. In the distance, a large tanker slowly passed across the horizon.

Fitger's Inn surely comes in handy during the dog days of August.

Actually, any time is the right time to visit this handsome hotel. It's located in a ten-building brick complex overlooking

Lake Superior that housed the Fitger Brewing Company for 115 years until it closed its doors in 1972.

In 1984, major renovation and restoration began, and the results were so appealing that the inn won historical renovation awards. Now the elegance of the ninenteenth century blends with brewery lore and modern amenities to create fashionable lodgings that are fun, too.

You can obtain walking-tour pamphlets that explain some of the secrets of Fitger's, so I'll only mention a few of the "shouldn't misses":

Start in the lobby. Imagine that exquisite lead-glass skylight, dating to 1884, in a brewery!

The elegantly crafted, hand-wrought-iron registration desk is also original to the inn. This 1884 masterpiece used to be the brewery's cashier's cage.

Notice all the original oak woodwork, oak stairway, and the charcoal drawing of Gambrinus (mythical Flemish king and inventor of beer, naturally) done by a member of the Fitger family in Bremen, Germany.

That shiny copper planter used to be a tasting pot for the brewmaster.

There's lot more brew lore, but let's head to the guest rooms. They're handsome and tasteful, with antique and reproduction furnishings, elegant wallpaper, and brass lamps.

My favorites are those with floor-to-ceiling windows overlooking the lake that afford great views of the sunrise.

How to get there: From Minneapolis, take I–35 north to Duluth and follow the Superior Street exit to the inn.

The Mansion
Duluth, Minnesota
55804

Innkeepers: Warren and Susan Monson
Address/Telephone: 3600 London Road; (218) 724–0739
Rooms: 10, with 1 suite; 6 with private bath. Wheelchair access.
Rates: $75 to $145, single or double; suite, $195; EPB.
Open: May 15 to end of October; weekends throughout other times of the
   year.
Facilities and activities: Sitting and dining rooms, library, screened porch.
   Six acres of grounds with 525 feet of gorgeous Lake Superior
   shoreline; includes lawns, woods, and gardens. An hour's drive from
   Apostle Islands National Lakeshore.

"It's kind of like a medieval castle," Susan said.

Sure is. The entryway Gallery is all massive plaster-cast walls
sand-finished to resemble blocks in a great baronial hall, with
heavy exposed beams adding to the Middle Ages styling. With its
spiky, iron wall sconces and floor-to-ceiling torchlights, I expected
Sir Lancelot to clank down the hall in his shiny suit of armor.

Warren said that the majestic 1932 Tudor home took four
years to build; it has twenty-five rooms, with ten guest rooms. This
is a house that made me feel special. An exquisite touch is the
library, crafted in English hand-hewn white pine, with a 5-foot-

wide fireplace and a tremendous selection of classic books. A cozy spot is a Swedish pine–paneled living room with another fireplace, brass chandeliers, and lead-glass windows. Just down the hallway is a large screened porch with arched windows.

Seven guest rooms have a view of Lake Superior. One of my favorites is the South Room, with its high walnut Victorian headboard and matching furnishings that are at least 150 years old. There's also a working fireplace. Even from here, I could hear the sound of crashing waves pound the beach.

Would you like to have an entire floor of the fabulous mansion to yourself? The master suite offers windows overlooking the lake, including a big bay that's the setting for a king-sized bed, two dressing rooms, and an 18-foot-long black-and-white marble bath with an overhanging crystal chandelier.

Nobody goes hungry here. Susan whips up a handsome country breakfast of French toast, bacon, eggs, and sausage—and her special home-baked caramel rolls. Best bets for a Duluth dinner are at the Pickwick and Fitger's.

French doors off the Gallery lead to magnificent grounds fronting the lake. I walked down to the beach and skipped stones off the water.

How to get there: In Duluth, follow U.S. 61 (also called North Shore Drive and London Road). Follow this north and turn into the driveway leading to the mansion.

☀

B: *A privacy-filled lakeside retreat.*

Christopher Inn
Excelsior, Minnesota
55331

Innkeepers: Joan and Howard Johnson
Address/Telephone: 201 Mill Street; (612) 474–6816
Rooms: 8; 6 with private bath, air conditioning, and phone jacks, 1 with wheelchair access. No smoking inn.
Rates: $70 to $120, single or double, EPB. Midweek discounts up to 20 percent.
Open: All year.
Facilities and activities: Wimbledon-style grass tennis court. Complimentary bicycles. Horse-drawn carriage can take guests to dinner at area restaurants in all but winter months. Nearby is Old Log Theater, paddle-wheel-boat cruises, antiques stores, cross-country skiing, ice-house fishing.

A huge, white-and-yellow tent covered the expansive, sloping front lawn of the Christopher Inn. Chairs sat under the tent's shade, lined in crisp rows. Howard busily explained to helpers what else was needed to prepare for a wedding, which was to take place on the front porch of the inn in just a few hours.

Still, amid all the frenetic hubbub, the Christopher Inn was a nice place to be.

It's a palace of Victorian gingerbread gone wild, built in 1887, whose front lawn once stretched two blocks to the scenic shore of Lake Minnetonka.

Guest rooms are named after Johnson family members. Peter (who had been helping his dad in the yard with last-second wedding chores), boasts a huge mahogany headboard that almost touches the ceiling. Ann has two Victorian Eastlake double beds and hardwood floors and is decorated in cheery country Victorian.

Chris is an explosion of all things blue—wallpaper, rug, curtains, even down to the stripes on chair fabrics.

Third-floor rooms are the largest (also the most modern) with ceilings sloping under the eaves.

The parlor, a favorite gathering spot for guests, is bright and cheerful; it would have to be with seven huge windows washing the room with sunlight. Victorian couches and chairs are comfy, and there's a piano for ivory ticklers.

Breakfast may mean Joan's eggs Benedict, a fruit goblet (that day's featured melon, strawberries, kiwi, and grapes), peaches and cream, French toast, seafood *strata*, coffeecake, and rolls. You may have to drag your body from the table.

The innkeepers can recommend an in-town restaurant to suit your dinner tastes.

P.S.: Howard was last seen hosing down the front steps just hours before the wedding—not surprising, since the Christopher Inn hosts nearly fifty weddings annually for up to three hundred guests. This just might make it the "wedding receptions king" of Midwest country inns.

How to get there: From Minneapolis, take Minnesota 7 west to Excelsior exit. Go to Mill Street (just past bridge), and turn left to inn.

❋

B: *"I always dreamed of having my own private, grass tennis court,"*
says Howard, a teaching tennis pro. Lucky for him the inn has
one, an original feature of the 1887 home.

The Hutchinson House
Faribault, Minnesota
55021

Innkeeper: Marilyn Coughlin
Address/Telephone: 305 Northwest Second Street; (507) 332–7519
Rooms: 6, with 1 suite; all with private bath and air conditioning. No smoking inn.
Rates: $60, single; $65 to $115, double; EPB. No credit cards.
Open: All year.
Facilities and activities: Two sitting rooms, porch. Walk to Faribault woolen mills, stores. Nearby: restaurants, lake and water activities, River Bend Nature Center, biking, golfing, cross-country skiing, apple orchards, berry farms, Cannon River canoeing, Borbeleta Gardens, state parks, historic architecture, museums.

Marilyn is an ebullient artist who has fashioned a unique room. Winged-cupid cherubs float upon the wall of the John Hutchinson Suite, part of Marilyn's hand-painted mural that includes winging doves, a blossoming hillside, and other ethereal delights.

"I love showing off my baby," she proudly said of this guest room.

If that isn't enought, the ever-entertaining innkeeper will regale you with tales of her ten-week "self-discovery" trip to

India. She took more than one thousand photographs of her epic journey to self-realization, and she often plays sitar-tinged ethnic music that she recorded during her travels. She even told me of plans to conduct "self-discovery" Indian tours for other women, with the Hutchinson House as a sort of Bombay-esque headquarters.

"Since I am an artist, I have put my signature on the house," said Marilyn. That's an understatement. The handsome Queen Anne home, built by woolen king John Hutchinson in 1892, is strewn with Victorian, Art Deco, and Art Nouveau pieces.

"Pay particular attention to my light fixtures," she instructed me while pointing out a unique grape-cluster shade in one of the rooms.

Besides the cherub-graced suite, I especially liked the Violin Room, which houses a like-named instrument inlaid with mother-of-pearl that was handmade by her Norwegian father.

Guests are treated to Marilyn's home-cooked breakfasts ("everything's made from scratch") served on Royal Doulton and Rosenthal china. You might be offered delicacies like wild-rice banana crepes and seafood and asparagus quiches as well as granola and yogurt—along with upside-down rhubarb coffeecake.

How to get there: From Minneapolis, take I–35 south to Country Road 21, drive to Fourth Street, turn east to Third Avenue, then turn right to the inn.

Rosewood Inn
Hastings, Minnesota
55033

Innkeepers: Pam and Dick Thorsen, owners; Joan Mathison, manager
Address/Telephone: Seventh and Ramsey; (612) 437–3297
Rooms: 8, with 1 suite; all with private bath and air conditioning, TV and
 phone upon request. No smoking inn.
Rates: $60 to $185, single; $75 to $200, double; EPB. Two-night
 minimum on weekends. Special packages available.
Open: All year.
Facilities and activities: Dinner by reservation. Sitting room, parlor, library,
 porch. Nearby: Historic river town architecture, arts and crafts, stores,
 antiques shops, specialty boutiques, Mississippi River water activities,
 bluff touring on bikes and hikes, St. Croix Valley Nature Center,
 Alexis Bailly vineyard winery, downhill and cross-country skiing,
 snowshoeing, golfing.

This handsome Queen Anne, built in 1878, now houses one
of the most romantic getaways imaginable. That's not really
surprising, since Pam and Dick's other Hastings hideaway (the
Thorwood Inn) reflects similar pampering-inspired luxuries.

As soon as you see Rebecca's Room, you'll get the idea. This
is a stirring romantic retreat, with a marvelous all-marble bathroom highlighted by a double whirlpool resting in front of its own

fireplace. There's also a second fireplace opposite an inviting four-poster antique bed. And a four-season porch offers views of the inn's rose garden.

Or consider the Vermillion Room, with a see-through fireplace that warms both an ornate brass bed and a sunken double whirlpool.

If you want shameful opulence, try the Mississippi Room. As large as an apartment, it offers skylights over a sleigh bed, its own fireplace, baby grand piano, bathroom with both a copper tub and double whirlpool—and a meditation room where "people can either relax or be creative," said Joan. "We've even had several guest do paintings here." A collection of some of those works are hanging about the room.

Joan's breakfasts are added treats. And her mealtime flexibility is unusual. "I'll serve whenever guests are hungry, between 6:00 A.M. and 11:00 A.M." Eat in one of the dining areas, on the porch, in your room, or in bed—the choice is yours.

The feast might include homemade breads and blueberry muffins, cheese *strata*, wild rice gratiné, cherry strudel, raspberry coffeecake. . . . Aren't you hungry just thinking about all this food?

Joan is also happy to arrange an in-room "hat box" supper, or to package a delightful evening with dinner at one of the town's fine restaurants that includes limousine service. And she occasionally arranges dinner at the inn featuring Minnesota-accented recipes accompanied by live chamber music.

How to get there: From the Twin Cities, take U.S. 61 south into Hastings and exit at Seventh Street; then turn left and proceed 1½ blocks to the inn.

Thorwood Inn
Hastings, Minnesota
55033

Innkeepers: Pam and Dick Thorsen
Address/Telephone: Fourth and Pine; (612) 437–3297
Rooms: 7; all with private bath and air conditioning. Wheelchair access.
   No smoking inn.
Rates: $69 to $144, single; $75 to $150, double; EPB. Can arrange for pet
   sitters. Special package rates available.
Open: All year.
Facilities and activities: Walking tour of historical area just blocks away.
   Quaint Mississippi River town with specialty and antique shops,
   several good restaurants. Parks and nature trails nearby; also river,
   streams, lakes, and all sorts of summer and winter sports.

"People seem to enjoy the morning breakfast baskets more
than anything else," Pam told me as we sat in the parlor of her
gracious inn. "It has grown into quite a tradition."

Once when she mentioned to a repeat couple that she'd been
thinking of changing that practice, "They immediately spun
around, with dismayed looks on their faces, and said, 'You
wouldn't.' I knew right then we could never change."

Lucky for us. The breakfast basket, delivered to the door of
your room, is stuffed with platters of fresh fruits, omelets or

quiches, pull-apart pastries and rolls, home-baked breads, coffee, juice, and more. As Dick says, "Pace yourself."

It's all part of the pampering the innkeepers lavish on guests.

The home, fashioned in ornate Second Empire style and completed in 1880, is a testament to the innkeepers' restoration prowess. When I saw the marble fireplaces, ornate rosettes and plaster moldings on the ceilings, and elegant antiques and sur-roundings, it was difficult to imagine that the house had once been cut up into several apartments.

For fine detail, just look to the music room. Pam said maple instead of oak was used for flooring because it provided better resonance for live piano concerts, popular with society crowds at the turn of the century.

One of my favorite guest rooms is Captain Anthony's, named for the original owner's son-in-law, who operated a line of steamboats on the Mississippi. It boasts a canopied four-poster brass bed and Victorian rose-teal-and-blue Laura Ashley fabrics. The Lullaby Room (the house's historic nursery) has a double whirlpool. "Guests in this room feel like they're in the tree tops," Pam said, as she looked out a tall window.

Maureen's Room is another popular choice, with its unusual rag-rug headboard, fireplace, country-quilted bed, and double whirlpool.

Or try Sarah's Room, with its bedroom-sized loft, window views of the Mississippi River Valley, and skylight over a queen-sized brass bed.

But perhaps the ultimate retreat is the Steeple Room, with a see-through fireplace and a double whirlpool—set in the house's steeple. The steeple rises 23 feet above the tub and boasts a ball chandelier hanging from the pinnacle.

How to get there: From LaCrosse, take U.S. 61 north to Hastings; then turn left on Fourth Street and proceed to inn.

☀

B: *A complimentary bottle of wine from the local Alexis Bailly vineyards and snacks of fruits and pastries continue the Thorwood notion of pampering.*

Mrs. B's Historic Lanesboro Inn
Lanesboro, Minnesota
55949

Innkeepers: Jack and Nancy Bratrud
Address/Telephone: 101 Parkway; (507) 467–2154
Rooms: 9; all with private bath and air conditioning. Wheelchair access. TV and phone on request.
Rates: $48 to $58, single or double, weekdays; $80 to $90, single or double, weekends; EPB. Lodging, MAP package available Thursday and Friday nights for $180 to $200. No credit cards.
Open: All year.
Facilities and activities: Gourmet dinners; sitting room, porches. Near bike and cross-country ski trails, antiques shops, bluffs, golf, tennis, fishing. In heart of state hardwood forest.

Kirk, the innkeepers' son, is the chef. "I love to cook for guests," he said, as we walked to the inn's cozy dining room. "People come in here at first, frazzled, with little to say, and sit down at the table. But by the time dinner is almost finished, it's great to listen to all the laughter and noise. Sometimes they even burst into song."

You might, too, after sampling some of Kirk's five-course

country dinners. Imagine boned chicken stuffed with forest mush-rooms, succotash, asparagus spears, cranberry-and-orange sauce—and lemon meringue pie or bananas *Blagsvedt*.

In fact, Kirk's gustatory creations have been critically ac-claimed in the media. No small wonder. Consider some of his imaginative, sophisticated dishes: shrimp, escargot, and spinach tarts; Chicken Valentine (stuffed with spiced sausage, smoked chicken breast, and gourmet cheeses); grilled smoked pork loin served on a bed of tomatoes and leeks; a salad of fresh greens boasting black raspberries and topped with a hot, wild mushroom custard; and much more.

Historic Lanesboro is surrounded by high bluffs covered with tall hardwood trees. In fact, a 500-foot bluff, looming just beyond the inn, almost blocks the town's main street.

The 1872 inn has a big canopy shading tall arched merchant windows facing the street. Anyone is welcome to play a tune on the sitting room's baby grand piano; there's also a big brick fireplace with comfy high-back chairs and sofa nearby.

The guest rooms are comfortable and cozy, with pine head-boards and canopy beds, quilts, rose floral print wallpaper, writing desks, and other antique pine reproductions. One room has a headboard with two hand-carved dragon's heads on its posts. "Only those with impure hearts would be frightened," Nancy joked. Some of them have outside balconies, and it's fun to sit out on a ladder-back rocking chair and look out over the Root River behind the inn to the high bluffs beyond.

Kirk recommends a walk along a hiking trail that crosses the old bridge and faces the bluff. "You really get a feel for the bluff country," he said. It's probably also a good way to work off his breakfasts, which include eggs, ham, bacon, oatmeals, fruit soups, hot breads, and delicious coffee.

How to get there: Take Minnesota 16 to Lanesboro. In town, turn north on Parkway and proceed to the inn.

Schumacher's New Prague Hotel
New Prague, Minnesota
56071

Innkeepers: John and Kathleen Schumacher
Address/Telephone: 212 West Main Street; (612) 758–2133
Rooms: 11; all with private bath, double whirlpool, air conditioning, and phone, some with gas fireplace and hairdryer.
Rates: $99.50 to $113.50, single or double, Sunday through Thursday; $127.50 to $141.50, single or double, Friday through Saturday; EP. Special packages and senior citizens' rates available. Personal checks from Minnesota only.
Open: All year except Christmas Eve and Christmas Day.
Facilities and activities: Full-service restaurant with wheelchair access. Bavarian bar, European gift shop, travel agency. Drive to cross-country and downhill skiing, swimming, golfing, boating, fishing, biking, hiking, orchard, museums, racetrack, amusement park.

I stepped into Schumacher's New Prague Hotel through a hand-stenciled door and thought I'd somehow been caught in a time warp, ending up in old-world Bavaria.

John and Kathleen are very proud of their beautiful inn, and rightly so. It looks similar to many European country hotels I've stayed at. A peaceful air of rich handiwork, fine craftsmanship, wonderful imported old-world antiques, and a deep commitment to dining excellence are what make Schumacher's one of the best there is.

Built in 1898, the hotel boasts an ornate European-style lobby, with pressed-tin ceilings, rich floral wallpaper, fine European antiques, and oriental rugs that cover original maple hardwood floors. A wonderful front desk is original, too.

John commissioned renowned Bavarian folk artist Pipka to design the graceful stenciled scenes that enliven guest, lobby, and restaurant rooms.

Upstairs are eleven individually decorated guest rooms, named in German for the months of the year, and furnished with old-world trunks, chairs, beds, and wardrobes; several have fireplaces, and all boast double whirlpools. More authentic touches include eiderdown-filled pillows and comforters, and 100-percent-cotton bedding and tablecloths, which were purchased in Austria, Czechoslovakia, and West Germany.

August is my favorite, with its king-sized bed, primitive Bavarian folk art, and a red wildflower theme carried out in stenciled hearts on the pine floor and on an ornately decorated wardrobe. You'll feel as if you've been transported to southern Germany.

And *Mai* has a high-canopied double bed reached by a small ladder; the design inside the canopy features storybook-style figures from newlyweds to senior couples. John thoughtfully places a complimentary bottle of imported German wine and two glasses in each room, just one of the many thoughtful touches.

Guess who's the chef? John is a classically trained cooking school graduate who specializes in excellent old-world cuisine—with a Czech flair. His extensive menu features more than fifty-five dinner entrees.

"What's your pleasure? I'll cook you a feast!" he said. A typical Central-European meal includes *romacka* (cream of bean soup with dill) and Czech Roast Duck served with red cabbage, potato dumplings, and dressing, with apple strudel for dessert. Then you're ready to browse in the hotel's gift shop, which offers handmade gifts and glassware from Central Europe.

How to get there: From Minneapolis, take 35 W south; exit on County Road 2. Continue to Minnesota 13 and turn south; proceed directly into New Prague; the hotel is on the left.

The Archer House
Northfield, Minnesota
55057

Innkeepers: Dallas and Sandy Haas
Address/Telephone: 212 Division Street; (507) 645–5661, Minnesota toll-
free (800) 247–2235
Rooms: 38, with 19 suites; all with private bath, air conditioning, TV, and
phone.
Rates: $40 to $135, single or double, EP.
Open: All year.
Facilities and activities: Tavern restaurant, deli, ice-cream and coffee shop,
bookstore, specialty stores. Nearby, Carleton and St. Olaf colleges and
Northfield Arts Guild offer programs of theater, art, concerts, films,
and lectures. Hiking, biking, canoeing on Cannon River, tennis,
swimming, cross-country skiing, ice skating (in season).

Though we hadn't seen each other for more than a year,
Dallas pumped my hand, whacked me on the back, and welcomed
me on my return to the Archer House. He also invests some of that
amazing exuberance in his charming hotel; ten luxury suites, with
elegant antique reproductions, have recently been added to the
historic building.

First let me tell you that the Archer House is just a short walk
from the local bank that the Jesse James gang attempted to rob in

1876. Yep, the "Great Northfield Raid" was a desperado disaster that virtually ended Jesse's reign of terror on the frontier.

Dallas has done a terrific restoration job. He leaves doors to unoccupied rooms open so browsers can appreciate the rooms' turn-of-the-century charm. Sandy is the interior designer, and each room reflects a personality of its own, with ruggedly elegant country warmth. I loved the handcrafted pine furniture, some boasting rosemaling, brass beds, handmade quilts done by local artisans, and embroidered samplers.

I stayed in the Manawa Room, done in a Dutch country style, with blue floors, stencils on walls, a pine bed with blue-and-white-point star quilt, and a needlepoint sampler. I'm sure my room's Dutch hex sign has brought me good luck.

New suites all feature inviting whirlpools, and some have a lovely view of the Cannon River, which is sporting a new river walk.

The pace here is unhurried and casual, making it an ideal place to relax amid the homespun graciousness of this interesting and pretty Minnesota town.

How to get there: From the Twin Cities, take I–35 south to the Northfield exit. Follow Highway 19 east to the first stoplight. Go east for 2 blocks. Turn left onto Division Street and go 2 blocks. The Archer House is on the left.

From Rochester, take Highway 52 north to Cannon Falls. Then take Highway 19 west 11 miles to Northfield. Go straight onto Division Street. The Archer House is on the right.

༇

B: *Jesse's gang "robs" the local bank every September in a colorful festival celebrating "The Town That Defeated Jesse James."*

The Calumet
Pipestone, Minnesota
56164

Innkeepers: Edward and Colleen Carducci
Address/Telephone: Corner of Main and Hiawatha; (507) 825–5871 or (800) 535–7610
Rooms: 38 (16 antique, 22 modern); all with private bath and air conditioning. Wheelchair access.
Rates: $49, single; $60, double; EP.
Open: All year.
Facilities and activities: Full-service dining room, lounge, pub, ice-cream parlor, gift shop featuring Native American crafts. In Pipestone historic district; walk to other historic structures. Short drive to Pipestone National Monument, Upper Midwest Indian Cultural Center, Pipestone County Museum, health club, Hole-in-the-Wall ski area.

The Calumet Hotel is located in the historic district of tiny Pipestone, a wisp of a town located in the heart of traditional lands home to the Dakota Yankton–Sioux nation. I drove just outside of town and stood gazing over the "grass prairies," still a massively empty, windy landscape—the beginning of the Great Plains.

Native Americans mined pipestone at ancient quarries nearby. The "sacred" soft stone still is used for ceremonial pipes. Visitors

214

can view the quarries and local Indians mining the stone as their ancestors did before them.

This pioneer legacy continues at the inn, a massive pink-and-red quartzite building made of hand-chiseled, locally quarried stone, completed in 1888. Easily its most outstanding feature is a four-story exposed red-stone wall that overpowers the lobby.

Everything here seems larger than life. I walked up a magnificent four-story staircase of oak and maple to reach my room. A high skylight washed the stairs in warm sunlight. (I counted ninety-two steps. Don't worry, there's an elevator, too.)

My room was classically restored to Victorian elegance, with marble-topped dressers, a velvet-covered rocking chair, and two walnut beds sporting high headboards. Later, I found out that antiques brokers were commissioned to seek out the nineteenth-century pieces. They searched old British estates, Colorado-gold-rush mansions, Carolina plantations, and historic New England homes to uncover the splendid period pieces.

All the rooms have names like Paradise Regained and Abigail's Dream. My favorite is the Choctaw Indian Walk, with a wall of exposed brick and Native American artifacts and designs.

Throughout the restored rooms I found fainting couches, chairs of golden oak built extra wide to accommodate ladies' Victorian-era bustles, claw-footed dressers, and antique prints and photos. The hotel quickly became one of my favorites. A photo album at the front desk helps you choose what style room most appeals to you.

The inn is enjoying a highly rated renaissance through its restoration efforts. And its restaurant was named one of the top fifty dining establishments in Minnesota.

How to get there: I–75 and Minnesota 30 and 23 lead into Pipestone, located in extreme southwestern Minnesota. Once in town, make way to East Main Street and continue to the corner of Hiawatha and the hotel.

B: *Pipestone National Monument (ancient Indian pipestone quarries a short drive away) is fascinating. I stayed there for hours.*

The Jail House
Preston, Minnesota
55965

Innkeepers: Deb and Steven Niefeldt
Address/Telephone: 109 Houston 3 Northwest; (507) 765–2504
Rooms: 12, with 1 suite; all with private bath and air conditioning, TV and
   phone on request.
Rates: $35 to $75, single or double, weekdays; $58 to $125, single or
   double, weekends; EPB.
Facilities and activities: Two common areas with stone fireplaces, parlor,
   basement dining room. Nearby: state parks, biking, hiking, cross-
   country skiing, Amish country tours, trout fishing, antiques and
   Amish crafts stores, cave tours, golfing, historic sites, museums,
   canoeing, tubing, bird-watching, local summer theater.

"Slumber in Our Slammer."

That's how "wardens" Deb and Steve invite guests to enjoy
their handsome inn whose not yet fully restored exterior should in
no way inhibit guests from luxuriating in lavish surroundings
inside.

Steven told me that this was once the Fillmore County Jail,
built in 1869 and housing unwilling guests until 1971. Get him to
tell you the story about prisoners who chiseled their way to
freedom by using dinner spoons.

Once modern-day guests step inside, they won't want to leave. The innkeepers have done a magnificent job of transforming this historic building into one of the more ornate Minnesota inns, complete with authentic period antiques dating from 1860 to 1890.

Of course, Deb and Steve couldn't resist keeping one guest room looking much as it might have during its jail heyday. The Cell Block is all steel doors and iron bars—you even sleep behind bars. One big difference—you have the keys. And I doubt that prisoners had a walk-through shower leading to a double whirlpool tub, fluffy quilted beds, rocking chairs, and other decidedly "un-convict" niceties.

"What's ironic is that this room looks like we've done the least to it," Steve said, "but it caused the most backbreaking work."

Guest rooms are named for former sheriffs who served at the jail. Among my favorites: the original courtroom now fashioned into a huge suite with a sitting room and double whirlpool; and the Drunk Tank, boasting Eastlake antiques and original wide-plank pine flooring.

Back to inn antiques: Consider an old china tub weighing nearly one thousand pounds; an 1880s, spoon-carved, three-piece bedroom set; and an antique copper bath made in Chicago.

Breakfast is served in the skylit basement and might include baked egg casseroles, home-baked breads and muffins, and more— the "Cook's Choice" doesn't allow any "convict" to go away hungry.

How to get there: From the north, take Minnesota 52 south into Preston; turn right on County Road 12 and continue to Houston Street; then turn right to the inn.

✸

B: *One problem with this "jail house." As soon as "prisoners" are "paroled" and sent home, they begin to plot another caper that will land them back in the slammer!*

Pratt-Taber Inn
Red Wing, Minnesota
55066

Innkeepers: Darrel Molander and Jane Walker
Address/Telephone: 706 West Fourth; (612) 388–5945
Rooms: 6, with 1 suite; 2 with private bath.
Rates: $69 to $89, single or double, weekends; less $10 on Sunday through Thursday; continental-plus breakfast. Special midweek and business rates.
Open: All year.
Facilities and activities: Parlors, front porch, screened side porch, bikes for guests. Nearby: riverboat dinner excursions on Mississippi River, trolley-car rides, horse-and-buggy rides, cross-country and downhill skiing at Frontenac Ski Area and Welch Village, 5 golf courses, bingo on Prairie Island Indian Reservation. Also, Red Wing antiques shops, specialty shops, art galleries, T. B. Sheldon Auditorium, bluffs to drive and climb.

Garrison Keillor wrote, "When I search for a peaceful moment, I will think of sitting on the porch of the Pratt-Taber Inn." I couldn't agree more.

I opened the door of this elaborate Italianate mansion and walked into a world of old-time elegance. The thirteen-room mansion, built in 1876 by one of Red Wing's first bankers, has been restored to a special magnificence in this historic river town crested by high bluffs of the Mississippi River. I was impressed by the immense lead-glass doors that open into a sitting room full of Victorian finery. Heavy floor-length balloon draperies cascade down tall windows, a handsome secretary almost reaches the high ceiling, and a high-back settee sits on an elegant oriental carpet.

I admired fine details like feather-painted slate fireplaces and fancy gingerbread woodwork. Rich woods of butternut and walnut provide a graceful backdrop for early Renaissance Revival and country-Victorian furnishings that the innkeepers have spent years collecting. In fact, guests are encouraged to take a hands-on approach: Play the Victrola, tour the world in stereographic cards, or simply daydream on the porches or in front of a roaring fire.

One guest room has an antique Victorian dresser that stretches almost to the ceiling. Rich antique wall coverings, which have been historically documented, also add to the period charm. Some rooms even have fireplaces.

Breakfast might include the inn's specialty—homemade blueberry coffeecake—and peaches-and-cream French toast, sausage-and-ham roll-ups, and more. It's usually taken in the Victorian dining room, but just a note on the kitchen table the night before will fetch you breakfast in bed or on the inn's screened porch. Don't pass up the sumptuous seafood or steak dinners served in the elegant Victorian dining room at the St. James Hotel in the heart of town.

I want you to try and spot the hidden Murphy bed in the library. No fair asking Darrel or Jane for hints.

How to get there: Take U.S. 61 into Red Wing and proceed to Dakota. Turn west; then turn north on West Fourth to the home located at the corner of Fourth and Dakota.

*

B: *The inn makes a great first impression—and later surpasses it.*

St. James Hotel
Red Wing, Minnesota
55066

Innkeeper: E. F. Foster
Address/Telephone: 406 Main Street; (612) 388–2846
Rooms: 60; all with private bath, air conditioning, TV, and phone. Wheelchair access.
Rates: $65 to $120, single or double, EP.
Open: All year.
Facilities and activities: Two dining areas, 13 specialty shops. Walking and driving tours of historic river-front town. Antiques and specialty shops. Mississippi River water sports and activities nearby.

E. F. told me that the St. James Hotel was one of the first fine Victorian hotels in the Midwest. It was built in 1875, and its elegance reflected Red Wing's prosperity as the world's largest wheat market at the time.

Now Red Wing is just a historic Mississippi river town. But the St. James's tradition of refined Victorian tastes continues.

"Quiet elegance" is the phrase that best describes the guest rooms. Each is uniquely decorated; I especially like the fancily scrolled wall borders, so popular back in the hotel's heyday. In fact, they set the color tones for coordinated wallpapers and handmade quilts.

220

Authentic antiques and fine reproductions re-create a long-ago era of luxury. E. F. has a great collection of beds; massive four-poster beds, Jenny Lind spindles, shiny brass beds, and more. Unique gingerbread window treatments splash spiky shafts of sunlight into rooms.

In some rooms, a view of the Mississippi River and surrounding high bluffs is a big treat.

Of course, you'll be spoiled after just one day at the St. James. A complimentary chilled bottle of wine welcomes you to your room, and there'll be a steaming pot of coffee and morning paper delivered to your door.

I like all the choices for dining because there is something for every mood and taste: a light snack at the Veranda Café, with al fresco dining on a porch overlooking the Mississippi; or dinners featuring filet of Canadian walleye and other gustatory delights at the Port of Red Wing, decorated to recapture the adventure of the riverboat era.

Then it's up to Jimmy's, the hotel's English-style pub—a great way to end the day.

(*Note:* Ask for a historic room if that is your preference; there are several with modern decor.)

How to get there: Take U.S. 61 into Red Wing, where it becomes Main Street; the hotel's address is 406 Main Street.

Canterbury Inn
Rochester, Minnesota
55902

Innkeepers: Mary Martin and Jeffrey Van Sant
Address/Telephone: 723 Second Street Southwest; (507) 289–5553
Rooms: 4; all with private bath, air conditioning, and phone jack (phones
   on request).
Rates: $59, single; $69, double; EPB and "high tea."
Open: All year.
Facilities and activities: Parlor, sitting room. Near restaurants, Mayo Clinic,
   Mayowood, antiques shops, cross-country skiing, golf.

Mary and Jeffrey are great ladies. And so is their Canterbury
Inn, a beautiful 1890 Victorian with its multi-gabled roof, gingerbread adornments, stained glass, and elegant interior—not to
mention the delicious breakfasts and intimate afternoon teas.

"We just love tea time," Jeffrey said. "Then we can be more
than hosts. We take off our serving aprons and join in as one of the
guests."

"That's right," Mary added. "We just love to host people in
our home. After all, we live here. We're proud of it."

As they should be. The home is graced with oak, pine, and
maple hardwoods, as well as magnificent golden-pine woodwork.
A stained-glass window spills colors onto a grand staircase that
leads to the upper-floor rooms.

The rooms are all bright and airy, with king-, queen-, or twin-sized beds, Victorian dressers, hardwood floors, scatter rugs, and rocking chairs by tall windows.

Teatime means late-afternoon sherry, white wine, elegant hors d'oeuvres—and tea, of course. Expect lots of conversation from Mary and Jeffrey. Their outgoing personalities are one of the inn's most engaging touches.

Breakfast is the time Mary and Jeffrey really try to spoil you. When is the last time you had Grand Marnier French Toast? With bacon and baked apples, wild-rice waffles, *huevos rancheros,* baked-apple pancakes, sourdough blueberry pancakes, whatever—it's a real treat.

The innkeepers recommend the Broadstreet Cafe for fine dining. It's housed in a restored warehouse building and features gourmet-style food and desserts in an informal atmosphere. My dad tried the beef and onions braised in beer and cleaned his plate. I found the seafood quiche light and tasty.

And the Mississippi pecan pie was a winner, too!

How to get there: Take I–90 to either U.S. 52 or directly to U.S. 63, which goes into Rochester. Turn left on Second Street and go about 8 blocks to the inn. From the north, take U.S. 52 south to Rochester and exit at Second Street Southwest. Turn left and go about 10 blocks to the inn.

Country Bed & Breakfast
Shafer, Minnesota
55074

Innkeepers: Lois and Budd Barott
Address/Telephone: 32030 Ranch Trail Road; (612) 257–4773
Rooms: 3; 2 with private bath, all with air conditioning. No smoking inn.
Rates: $50, single; $85, double; EPB. No credit cards.
Open: All year.
Facilities and activities: Porch. Spacious tree-shaded lawn. Maple groves. Walking in surrounding fields. Near restaurants, Ki-Chi-Saga Lake, the Sunrise and St. Croix rivers with riverboat cruises, tubing, canoeing, swimming, fishing. Two downhill ski resorts close by. Cross-country ski and nature trails at Wild River State Park. Also antiques, pottery shops in area. Five miles west of historic Taylors Falls.

"I'm so tired from collecting sap, and I still have to boil it down today. Then I'll just go to sleep."

Poor Budd. I'd stopped midweek by his 35-acre country spread and caught him in the middle of his busy chores. But that didn't stop him or Lois from showcasing their overwhelming country hospitality. After a few minutes with them, I felt as if I'd returned home after a long journey away from this pretty farmstead.

Both Lois and Budd showed me around the place. Lois pointed to the chickens running in frantic circles near their coop. "I'm so proud of my chickens," she said. "I got to have lots of them. You know, fresh eggs for breakfast."

Budd and I laughed. "Yeah, we give you an $18 breakfast here for nothing," he said, "and you can eat as much as you want."

This is no mere boast. Country breakfast features Swedish egg-coffee; omelets with ham, sausage, or bacon—Budd's specialty; Lois's buttermilk pancakes with homemade maple syrup from their groves out back; and raspberries and strawberries from Budd's organic garden. "If you leave here hungry, it's your own fault," he joked. In the evening they suggest that guests take a short drive to Marine on St. Croix for delicious homemade dinners at Crabtree's Kitchen.

Their farmhouse is a quaint 1881 red-brick Victorian. Lois, who grew up here, pointed out original plank floors and a big wood-burning stove in a country kitchen. A comfortable sitting room has a sofa, chair, and television.

Guest rooms upstairs are pictures of farm-country charm. Lois has covered plank floors with scatter rugs; she also uses some white wicker chairs and other country antiques, sheer white curtains on tall windows that flood rooms with sunlight, and pretty print wallpapers.

I lazed part of the day away on the front porch—Budd, my dad, and I just "stirring up the pot" with our stories. There's also a back deck where you can just sit and breathe the fresh country air.

This is the *perfect* place to retreat to country solitude. And you couldn't find two kinder hosts.

How to get there: Enter Shafer on County Road 21. Go through town 1 mile. Then turn left on Ranch Trail and proceed to the inn.

✳

B: *I already missed Budd and Lois five minutes after we left . . . and Pepper the dog and the ducks and the chickens and. . . .*

Spicer Castle
Spicer, Minnesota
56288

Innkeepers: Allen and Marti Latham, owners; Ginger Hanson, manager
Address/Telephone: Off Minnesota 23 on Green Lake (mailing address, P.O.
   Box 307); (612) 796–5870
Rooms: 4, plus 1 cottage and 1 cabin; all with private bath.
Rates: $50 to $80, single; $60 to $90, double; EPB.
Open: All year, but weekends only September 1 through April 1.
Facilities and activities: Afternoon tea, sitting room. Located on beautiful
   Green Lake. Spacious porch and grounds. Nearby: restaurants, sandy
   beach, fishing, hiking, golfing, cross-country skiing.

   "The house was built in 1893 by the grandfather of Allen and
Marti," manager Ginger told me. "It was part of the Medayto
Farm, where he experimented with new agricultural techniques."
   What a goregous piece of country, too. Hugging the shore of
huge Green Lake, Spicer Castle stands sentinel on a craggy bluff
overlooking the blue water. I gazed out at the lake from the inn's
back porch, watching a storm brew far out over the waves.
   I asked Ginger how it got its name. "Fishermen used the
house as a landmark to locate good fishing spots," she said.
"Before long, references to 'Spicer's Castle' began appearing on
fishing maps of the area. The name just stuck."

That's not surprising. It's an imposing house, sitting on five acres with a proud, Tudor-style profile that includes a tall tower resembling those found at ancient castles.

Inside, the parlor has a very masculine feel, with half-timbered ceilings, brick fireplace, tapestry rugs. It's hard to imagine, but all the furnishings are original to the home. Most of the oil paintings, watercolors, and charcoals were done by family members. I browsed through family photo albums. It's even family-member musicians who take up the violin or sit at the piano to provide tunes for dancing.

Guest rooms, comfortable and cozy, have the same, warm family feel to them. Mason's Room has a four-poster bed graced with a paisley quilt, the likes of which I hadn't seen before. Frances's Room boasts an iron-rail bed and a Victorian dresser. Jessie's sports a Jenny Lind spindle bed.

And families might be interested in the log cabin or cottage that rest on the handsome grounds.

Mornings are great fun because they mean breakfast on the dining porch overlooking the lake. You may enjoy Belgian waffles, eggs Benedict, homemade muffins, juice, and coffee. Ginger said that guests sometimes receive morning salutes from captains passing in their boats.

How to get there: From Minneapolis, take U.S. 12 west to Minnesota 23 and turn north into Spicer. Turn right on County 95 (Indian Beach Road, which is the lake road) and follow to sign that tells you where to turn onto access road reaching the castle.

The Lowell Inn
Stillwater, Minnesota
55082

Innkeepers: Arthur and Maureen Palmer
Address/Telephone: 102 North Street; (612) 439–1100
Rooms: 21, with 2 suites: all with private bath, air conditioning, and
phone.
Rates: $94.34 to $168.54, single or double; $164, suites; EP.
Open: All year.
Facilities and activities: Full-service restaurant with wheelchair access.
Many quality antiques, gift, and specialty shops nearby. Good town
bakeries. Cave tours. Not far from the Mississippi River. The inn can
arrange River Run excursions May to September. Winter cross-
country skiing at O'Brien State Park. Downhill skiing at 3 resorts
nearby.

I remember The Lowell Inn for its china cats.

That's right. I walked into my enormous French Provincial–
style room only to find a little "kitty" curled up on the foot of my
bed. Cats and kittens are in every guest room; Arthur and
Maureen believe they add homey warmth to the elegant rooms.

It's not something I expected to find here. The inn, which
opened on Christmas Day 1930, is built in a formal Colonial-
Williamsburg style. The huge veranda is supported by thirteen tall

white pillars that represent the original thirteen colonies, and each bears a pole flying respective state flags.

Stepping inside, I saw an exquisite mixture of Colonial and French Provincial antiques. Many of the inn's gorgeous collectibles are part of the private collection of Nelle Palmer, wife of the original owner.

The dining rooms are handsome, dotted with Dresden china, Capo di Monte porcelain, Sheffield silver, and more. They also exhibit a bit of a classy atmosphere. The George Washington Room is adorned with hand-crested Irish linen, authentic Williamsburg ladder-back chairs, and portraits of George and Martha. Still another surprise is an indoor trout pool in the Garden Room. You can select your dinner by pointing to the fish of your choice. Huge polished agate tables accentuate the earthy quality of the room.

Easily my favorite is the Matterhorn Room, all done in deep, rich woods and authentic Swiss wood carvings. The inn's showpiece, as far as I'm concerned, is a life-sized eagle hand carved by a seventy-eight-year-old Swiss master wood carver.

Dinners here might begin with Swiss *escargots* (pure-white snails picked from vineyards in France and Switzerland), followed by a large chilled green salad with pickled relishes; and for an entree, *fondue Bourguignonne* (beef or shrimp individually seasoned with six different sauces).

Guest rooms are individually decorated in a combination of Colonial and French Provincial styles, with soft colors, frills, mirrors, antiques, and goose-down comforters. A complimentary bottle of wine in my room was a welcome surprise.

How to get there: From Minneapolis–St. Paul, take State Road 36 east. It changes into Stillwater's Main Street. Turn left on Myrtle and go about a block to Second Street.

The Rivertown Inn
Stillwater, Minnesota
55082

Innkeepers: Judy and Chuck Dougherty
Address/Telephone: 306 West Olive; (612) 430–2955 or toll-free (800)
    562–3632
Rooms: 9; all with private bath and air conditioning. No smoking inn.
Rates: $49 to $139, single or double, EPB.
Open: All year.
Facilities and activities: Lunch, afternoon tea, hors d'oeuvres, dinner.
    Sitting room. Gazebo on grounds. Short drive to scenic St. Croix
    riverway; riverboat rides; art galleries, specialty shops, antiques
    stores; golf courses; apple orchards; biking, hiking, cross-country and
    downhill skiing; canoeing; swimming; tours of historic homes;
    restaurants.

I've had my eye on The Rivertown Inn for quite some time.
The stately Victorian home, built in 1882 by a prominent local
lumberman, sits on a hill high above Stillwater, a lovely town
hugging the banks of the scenic St. Croix River.

But it wasn't until Judy and Chuck bought the historic home
and completed much-needed restoration work, that its turn-of-
the-century charm emerged. Now I had to include it in my book.

Judy pointed out original brass chandeliers that were once

illuminated by gas. I marveled at the masterful dining room table that seemed to stretch out forever.

"This table came from a castle in England," she said. "I have four more leaves. It seats eighteen people."

Intricate gingerbread fretwork adorns many inn rooms. "It's all original to the house," Judy told me. "We found it stored in rows out back in the carriage house. It was quite a discovery."

As we talked, lovely violin music played. It was a perfect accompaniment for exploring the guest rooms.

My favorite is John O'Brien's Room, with its huge oak-manteled, tile fireplace; tall, walnut Victorian headboard and dresser; parquet floors; and splash of gingerbread. It has the feel of a room in an exclusive Englishmen's club.

Faith's Room is another gem, with its own fireplace, marble-topped dresser, wash stand, and sitting area. But special features here are an astounding 11-foot-high walnut headboard and a double whirlpool.

More highlights: There's a double whirlpool in Melissa's Room, which also boasts an antique, brass tube bed; Julie's Room has a walnut bed, corner whirlpool, and view of the river; and Patricia's Room is done in golden oaks, has a whirlpool, and looks out over Stillwater's many historic steeples.

Judy and Chuck will serve breakfast in the dining room, on the porch (if weather permits), or, if you prefer, in your room. Count on homemade pastries like caramel rolls, puffs, flans, home-baked breads, fresh fruit, and mouth-watering entrees.

How to get there: From Minneapolis, take Minnesota 36 east to Stillwater. Turn left on Olive Street, go up the hill to Fifth Street, and the inn.

The Anderson House
Wabasha, Minnesota
55981

Innkeepers: John, Jeanne, and Gayla Hall
Address/Telephone: 333 North Main Street; (612) 565–4524, Minnesota
toll-free (800) 862–9702, other states toll-free (800) 325–2270
Rooms: 27, with 4 suites; 17 with private bath, all with air conditioning,
some with TV. Pets OK in certain rooms.
Rates: $40 to $50, shared bath; $49 to $75, private bath; $85 to $99,
suites; EP. Midweek and other packages available.
Open: All year.
Facilities and activities: Full-service dining room with wheelchair access,
ice-cream parlor. In winter, ice fishing, skating, boating. About 30
miles from 3 ski resorts. Across the street from Mississippi River
fishing, boating. Drive to antiques shops.

The Anderson House has the most unusual selection of special
inn services I've ever run across.

Hot bricks wrapped in cotton warm your feet after a long
day's journey.

Shoes will be shined free of charge if you leave them outside
your door before retiring for the evening.

Mustard plasters will be conjured up to treat stuffy congestion
and chest colds.

Sixteen cats are on daily call: You can rent one to help purr you to sleep and make you feel more at home.

Pennsylvania-Dutch specialties like scrapple and *fastnachts*, a meat dish with tasty doughnuts, are served for breakfast.

Now have I got your attention?

It's the oldest operating hotel in Minnesota, never having closed its doors since opening day in 1856. The rambling red-brick inn, which takes up a block of the town's Main Street, traces its roots back to Pennsylvania-Dutch country. In fact, Grandma Ida Anderson, who ran the hotel at the turn of the century, earned her reputation for scrumptious meals conjured up in the hotel's kitchen. The tradition continues under her great-grandson, John.

John has delightfully remodeled all the guest rooms. Most have floral-print wallpaper, antique maple, oak, and walnut beds and dressers—and handmade quilts and bedspreads. John said those were made by two talented ladies from a nearby nursing home. Some rooms that share a bath have a sink. Other rooms will afford you a glimpse of the Mississippi River, just across the street.

A favorite of mine is a room with an enchanting Dutch sleigh bed and matching chest; both are hand-stenciled with flowery patterns and fine handiwork.

Get ready for a real dining treat. Unique inn offerings include cheese soup, chicken with Dutch dumplings, bacon-corn chowder, *kugelhopf, limpa,* pork tenderloin medallions cooked in sauerkraut, and Dutch beer—and if you're very lucky, sometimes sticky-sweet shoo-fly pie for dessert.

How to get there: U.S. 61 and Minnesota 60 go right through town. The inn is located right on North Main Street.

❧

B: *John's family marks the fourth generation of Anderson House ownership. That means a long-standing tradition of warm hospitality that's hard to beat.*

Missouri

Numbers on map refer to towns numbered below.

Borgman's Bed and Breakfast
Arrow Rock, Missouri
65320

Innkeepers: Kathy and Helen Borgman
Address/Telephone: Van Buren Street; (816) 837–3350
Rooms: 4 share 3 baths; all with air conditioning. No smoking inn.
Rates: $35, single; $40 to $45, double; continental breakfast. No credit
    cards.
Open: All year.
Facilities and activities: Sitting room. Porch with rockers. Walk to restau-
    rants, state historical buildings and sites, archeological digs, antiques
    and specialty shops, and The Lyceum Theatre, one of Missouri's
    oldest repertory companies. Guided walking tours of town also
    offered.

    Borgman's Bed and Breakfast has been called "one of the
most enjoyable inns in the state." After my visit to this charming
white clapboard home, I heartily agree.
    Helen greeted me at the door of her little farmhouse, built
between 1855 and 1865 in this tiny historic town. It's filled with
country-style antiques and furnishings that put even the most
harried guests at ease.

Helen's daughter, Kathy, designed the stenciled wall borders that adorn each of the guest-room ceilings. And the beautiful country quilts that add splashes of colors to the beds were handmade by Helen, of course!

Relaxation is the key here. I just sat on the porch, in the shade of tall trees, feeling the cool summer breeze. Helen wound up the old Victrola for a song. It's also fun to stop by the kitchen to visit with Helen when she's making her famous cinnamon buns fresh each morning for breakfast treats.

"It's gotten to the point where guests kind of expect me to serve them," Helen said. "I guess they feel it's a real treat." She also offers homemade breads, cereal, fruits, and beverages.

As Helen and I walked to the upstairs guest rooms, I could feel the country comfort soaking into my city bones, I saw tall Victorian headboards, exposed chimney brick, hurricane-style lamps, lacy window curtains, and rocking chairs in the handsome rooms. The only first-floor guest room has the original plank floor, a four-poster bed adorned with one of Helen's bright quilts, and another antique rocker. All the rooms are bright, cheery, and peaceful.

Kathy works at the Arrow Rock information center and can tell you all about the wonderful history and attractions the village offers. She'll also recommend restaurants that serve wholesome down-home-dinner fare.

Area history is fascinating. Lewis and Clark noted the region during their historic explorations. Indians used local outcroppings of flint to point their arrows—hence the town name. Three forts were once located in the area; one was used during the War of 1812. A portion of the town was burned down during the Civil War.

In town, I toured a wonderful "pioneer" Main Street, lined with historic buildings that still have wooden-board sidewalks and rocky boulders forming crude street gutters. A guided historic walking tour is offered from April through October (sometimes on weekends only, so check ahead).

How to get there: From Kansas City or St. Louis, take I–70 to Route 41. Go north to Arrow Rock and turn right on Van Buren (the first road into Arrow Rock) to the inn about 2 blocks up the street.

The Lamplight Inn
Bed and Breakfast
Guest House
Bonne Terre, Missouri
63628

Innkeepers: Krista and Jorgen Wibskov
Address/Telephone: 207 East School Street; (314) 358–4222 or 358–3332
Rooms: 4; 3 with private bath, all with air conditioning.
Rates: $55 to $75, single or double; $10 per additional child; EPB.
Open: All year.
Facilities and activities: Sitting room. Gourmet dining across the street at
   award-winning The Lamplight Inn Restaurant (which includes a
   bar). Short walk to tours of Bonne Terre mine, a national historic site.
   Nearby: tennis, golf, antiques shops. An hour's drive from Ste.
   Genevieve, a French colonial fur-trading center in the 1700s.

Krista met Jorgen while she was a graduate student in
Denmark. Later, they moved back here (it's Krista's home town)
to take charge of the family restaurant that has gotten rave reviews
and won many awards for dining excellence.

Because so many people travel long distances to enjoy The
Lamplight Inn's delicious food, Krista and Jorgen thought it would

be a good idea to offer travelers an equally charming place to stay overnight.

The result is what they informally call the "Blue House," a charming home that's part of this old lead-mining town's rich legacy. "This home served as a boarding house for the [mining company's] bachelor engineers," Krista said. "So that's probably one of the reasons it's still pretty much in mint shape."

Krista has decorated the home with cozy and comfortable antiques and warm floral wallpapers that add to the inn's friendly feeling. A fire in the parlor's charming brick fireplace is welcome on chilly nights—a terrific place to warm up and read a good book.

The Oak Room is the handsomest of the inn's guest retreats. Soothing shades of soft mauve are offset by the room's attractive antique oak furniture, and six large windows adorned with lace curtains shoot arrows of sunlight into the room.

Inn breakfasts are tasty, with eggs and breakfast meats among the choices. Of course, who can pass up homemade breads with delicious jams? And freshly ground, specially blended coffee. I also dare you to resist Krista's freshly baked sticky buns.

Krista has earned an advanced seminar diploma from the Cordon Bleu cooking school in London and has won cooking awards from the Missouri Restaurant Association. She also recently won a national egg-recipe contest, and that accolade has put the restaurant's "name on the map," said Krista. That's why you cannot pass up a meal at The Lamplight Inn Restaurant, just across the street from the Blue House. The inn specialty is Pepper Steak Flambé (filet mignon flambéed tableside and served with a pepper-mustard sauce). Other gourmet choices include char-broiled marinated shrimp, Cajun-style blackened fish, and orange roughy in parchment.

How to get there: From St. Louis, take I–55 south and continue south on U.S. 67. Turn west on Route 47; then turn left on Allen Street in Bonne Terre. Take a quick right on Main; then an immediate left on East School Street to the inn.

✺

B: *Krista has cooked with French chef Jean-Pierre Auge since 1980. He gives cooking demonstrations during the inn's "Gourmet Weekends" nearly a dozen times per year.*

Mansion Hill Country Inn
Bonne Terre, Missouri
63628

Innkeepers: Doug and Cathy Goergens
Address/Telephone: Mansion Hill Drive; (314) 358–5311
Rooms: 11; 8 with private bath and air conditioning.
Rates: $60 to $80, single or double, continental breakfast. Special packages
    can include scuba diving.
Open: All year; closed Sunday.
Facilities and activities: Full-service inn, bar, gift shop, gardens, deck.
    Situated on 130-acre estate, view of Ozark Mountain foothills;
    cross-country skiing, nature trails, fishing; horse-drawn carriage
    tours of mining town. Short ride to Bonne Terre mine, with land
    tours at this National Historic Site. Also world-class scuba diving at
    mine.

    Cathy always dreamed of owning a country inn. Little did she
imagine that it would be a thirty-two-room mansion on a 130-acre
estate atop the highest point in historic Bonne Terre.
    But first, sit still—you have to know some history. This old
mining town was once the richest lead district in the country.
When mining ceased and water pumps were shut down, the

200-foot-deep mine shafts filled with water. So Cathy and Doug, in a stroke of genius, created a world-class scuba-diving center in the old Bonne Terre mine, with more than 17 miles of dive trails.

Now both divers and dedicated inn hoppers have an equally impressive place to stay overnight. The early-1900s mansion, built as a home for the president of the St. Joe Lead Company, reflects the gracious living and prosperity of those lead-boom days.

I walked into a foyer gleaming with polished hardwood. Wandering into the library, with its massive brick fireplace, heavy-beamed ceiling, stately columns, and decidedly nautical themes (with model sailing ships and other waterabilia), I eavesdropped as a group of divers planned their next mine adventure.

Doug told me that he had done most of the inn's heavy-duty interior restoration, while Cathy spent hundreds of hours coordinating inn decor and searching out special antique items that bring the mansion to life. It shows.

We walked through French doors onto an enclosed porch overlooking an impressive courtyard, garden, and fountain on the first terrace level. The second level was designed for world-class lawn croquet, Doug told me. You also can see miles of surrounding Ozark Mountain foothills.

Guest rooms have a view of the surrounding estate grounds and are decorated in period pieces and reproductions, with four-poster beds among the furnishings. Cathy made many of the inn's floral-styled draperies, valances, and other appointments.

Other inn guest rooms are located in a historic turn-of-the-century railroad depot located at the bottom of the estate driveway (just down the hill).

Dining here is another treat: The plantation-style menu offers staples like baked chicken and thick, juicy steaks; for dessert, the Key lime pie is delicious. Relaxing in the wine and beer garden, surrounded by a white picket fence, is a nice way to wind down an evening. Fitted with a new deck and an outdoor bar, a soothing mint julep is just a few steps away.

How to get there: From St. Louis, take I–55 south to U.S. 67. Continue south to Route 47. Go west into Bonne Terre. At Summit, turn left. At the top of the hill, turn left into a driveway marked by estate posts and inn signs. Proceed up the long road to the inn.

Falicon Inn
Clarksville, Missouri
63336

Innkeepers: Carl and Karen Schulze
Address/Telephone: Rural Route #1, Box 33A; (314) 242–3187 or (314)
    771–1993
Rooms: 2; each with private bath and wheelchair access.
Rates: $80 to $90, single or double, EPB. No credit cards.
Open: All year.
Facilities and activities: Dining room, BYOB. Parlor, library, long veranda,
    estate grounds. Short ride to downtown Clarksville and antiques
    shops. Near Sky Ride, where you can see 80-mile view of Mississippi
    River Valley.

Coming here is like stepping into the Old South—and a real
adventure. I drove up to the old plantation entrance along a
twisting back road, with high bluffs and rolling hills that provide
some of the best views of the Mississippi River Valley. Finally I
reached a dirt path that dives, snakes, and curves past tall trees and
brush.

Then I emerged from the foliage—and the Falicon Inn overwhelmed me. It's the picture of a Southern gentleman's plantation
farm, a massive thirty-room antebellum mansion with tall white
columns and a sweeping veranda.

Karen told me that parts of the home date from before the Civil War; other major renovations took place around the turn of the century. She pointed out the old ice house, playhouse, wash house, cottage for greenhouse workers, and carriage house that still stand on the grounds.

You're in for a treat: Karen and Carl specialize in Old South hospitality in this lavish setting. Some of the huge wall mirrors are from the old historic Clarksville Opera House. The dining room glistens with fine mahogany hardwood everywhere. And that wallpaper I was eyeing? Karen said that it was painted with English gold leaf.

The library is quite handsome, too, done in heavy oak, with tapestry draperies, hardwood floors, and a marble fireplace.

I walked up a long flight of stairs to reach the second-floor guest rooms. My favorite room has a fireplace and a tall canopy bed. Other rooms feature some period antiques; all are comfortable.

Karen serves up a full plantation-style breakfast. Her French toast is light and fluffy; then there's fruit, bacon and sausage, juice, and other beverages. She'll arrange special dinners—intimate feasts in the antique-laden dining room. Stuffed chicken breast, lamb, and a Shrimp *de Jonghe* are some of the inn specialties. It's BYOB for wines and liquors.

How to get there: From St. Louis, take I–70 west to Route 79 north into Clarksville. At County W, turn left and follow it for about 3½ miles until you reach the inn road.

Seven Gables Inn
Clayton, Missouri
63105

Innkeeper: Dennis Fennedy
Address/Telephone: 26 North Meramec; (314) 863–8400
Rooms: 32, including 4 suites; all with private bath, air conditioning, TV, and phone. Wheelchair access.
Rates: $98 to $126, single; $131 to $165, double; $215 to $327, suites; EP.
Open: All year.
Facilities and activities: Two restaurants, bistro, garden court. Just a short drive to all St. Louis attractions: Busch Stadium, Union Station, the Arch, historic river district, and more.

I was surprised to find a luxurious European-style retreat in such surroundings—sleek skyscrapers and modern sculpture dominate the landscape of this tony St. Louis suburb.

The building itself is a masterpiece of sorts. It was built in 1918, and the architect based his design on Hawthorne's House of Seven Gables, which stands in Salem, Massachusetts.

This romantic "continental" getaway also boasts great European-style dining experiences. Chez Louis—intimate, elegant, and serving French classic gourmet cuisine—has received awards and rave reviews from the likes of the *New York Times* and the *St. Louis Post-Dispatch*. Bernard is reluctant to reveal much of the

244

menu, since it changes weekly and sometimes daily. Seafood prepared in classical French style is always a good choice.

The restaurant also boasts a 320-item wine list featuring French, Italian, and Californian products.

Guest rooms are uniquely European, done in handsome, country-French antiques and reproductions, with some boasting brass and white iron-rail beds, writing desks, and comfortable chairs. Fresh flowers give rooms a sweet scent. Fluffy terry-cloth robes are part of a luxurious bath. Even the soap is hand-milled in France.

Head to the inn's other restaurant, Bernard's, for its upbeat, bistro-style tempo. May through September (weather permitting), the Garden Court, an expansive, cobbled patio with the feel of a European sidewalk cafe, is open for "lunch among the flowers or dinner under the stars."

The Seven Gables Inn has been included in the exclusive *Relais et Chateaux*, an organization listing some of the finest hotels in the world. (There is only a handful of United States hotels so honored. To give you an idea of their standards, the list includes the renowned Crillon in Paris.)

How to get there: From the airport, take I–170 south to the Ladue exit and go west into Clayton. This road will take you directly to the hotel.

⤬

B: *Of course, there's turn-down service, with chocolates left on your pillow. You had to wonder?*

Garth Woodside Mansion
Hannibal, Missouri
63401

Innkeepers: Irv and Diane Feinberg
Address/Telephone: R.R. 1; (314) 221–2789
Rooms: 8; all with private bath and air conditioning, phone on request.
Rates: $58 to $80, single or double, EPB.
Open: All year.
Facilities and activities: BYOB. Sitting rooms, parlors, wraparound porch. Acres of gardens, meadows, woodlands. Tours of the mansion given 11:30 A.M. to 3:00 P.M. daily. Short drive to restaurants, Mark Twain's boyhood house, Huckleberry Finn landmarks, Mississippi River paddle-wheel rides, caves, sightseeing tours, Mark Twain Outdoor Theater, specialty shops, and Great River Road that follows the Mississippi.

This is a historic country estate at its finest, a handsome Victorian home on thirty-nine acres of meadows and woodland, graced with noble old trees and a private fishing pond. Built in 1871 as a summer home for prominent Hannibal businessman John Garth, the mansion was the focal point for notables passing through Hannibal.

Hometown boy Samuel Clemens (Mark Twain) spent several nights here in his lifelong friend's home in 1882 and also during his last visit to Hannibal in 1902.

Amazingly, the mansion contains mostly original furnishings; they are exquisite. The library, boasting 9-foot-tall doors, is done in elegant walnut, with 1840 Empire furniture, marble fireplace with gold inlay, and a unique, Victorian, red-velvet reclining chair.

Notice the handsome ceiling medallion in the parlor and the room's seven-piece matching Eastlake furniture set.

The dining room is graced with the original table and twelve chairs. Diane pointed to the hostess chair: "It was made extra wide to accommodate the full petticoats that were the style of the day." There's also an original painting done by Mrs. Garth in the family parlor.

We walked up the magnificent flying staircase that vaults three stories high with no visible means of support. It appears even more spectacular, hanging high in the air, due to the mansion's 14-foot-high ceiling.

Guest rooms are decorated in Victorian splendor. On the second floor, the John Garth Room, occupying the old master bedroom, has a beautiful walnut Victorian bed with a 10-foot-tall headboard. The three-piece, matching bedroom set is original to the home. (Even the dresser stands nearly 10 feet high.)

I like to stay in the Samuel Clemens Room. It features an unusual Victorian button bed that has a blanket roll at its foot. There's also a Jenny Lind day bed here.

Diane said, however, that the Grape Room has become the inn's most popular lodging. It's bright and airy, with long windows, great views of the grounds, lively "grapevine" Victorian print wallpaper, and a claw-footed bathtub painted by Diane's artist/daughter, Kari. (See for yourself; she signed the tub.)

Third-floor rooms are less formal, with country and wicker themes; they also have great views of the grounds.

Breakfasts feature goodies like ham-and-cheese quiche, marmalade-filled muffins, rolls, and more. Iced tea is served on the spacious veranda during summer between 4:00 A.M. and 6:00 P.M. Hot mulled apple cider is the winter treat inside.

How to get there: From St. Louis, take I–70 west to Missouri 79 and go north into Hannibal. Turn west on Broadway, then south on U.S. 61. Turn east at Warren Barrett Drive (the first road south of the Holiday Inn) and follow signs to the inn.

Frisco House
Hartville, Missouri
65667

Innkeepers: C. C. "Charley" and Elizabeth "Betty" Roberts
Address/Telephone: Church and Rolla streets (mailing address: P.O. Box 118); (417) 741–7304 or 833–0650
Rooms: 3 share 2 baths; all with own lavatory and air conditioning. No smoking inn.
Rates: $30, single; $35, double; EPB. No credit cards.
Open: March through December.
Facilities and activities: Sitting room/parlor. Located in heart of Missouri Ozarks. Nearby: restaurants, Transcontinental Bicentennial Bicycle Route. Short drive to Lake of the Ozarks, Table Rock Lake, tourist mecca of Branson, Silver Dollar City, School of the Ozarks, old-mills area, Stockton Lake, Laura Ingalls Wilder Home & Museum, and Amish community.

"Hartville is unique because there's no commercialism here, just a self-sufficient community with town stores. Even the population hasn't changed much from the nearly six hundred people tallied seventy years ago."

The inn overlooks the town where, on January 11, 1863, Union and Confederate troops fought to a draw in the battle of Woods Forks.

Charley is a retired vice president of Burlington Northern Railroad. Railroad memorabilia is everywhere: There's an 1869 railroad route map that lists Oklahoma as Indian Territory; guests are served Betty's wonderful breakfasts on authentic railroad china and stenciled railroad glassware and use silver coffeepots and finger bowls. A side porch is fashioned after an old-time railroad depot.

The house, an 1880s log home converted into a handsome Victorian in 1895, embraces much of that period's gingerbread finery. "There are seventeen valleys in the roof," Charley said. "Repair work is so intricate that only Amish master craftsmen could match turn-of-the-century skills."

Furnishings include eighteenth-century mahogany, nineteenth-century walnut and oak, a sweeping circular staircase, and third- and fourth-generation family heirlooms.

Guest rooms are charming. The Lavender Room has a crazy quilt on its black-walnut double bed, walnut furniture, marble-topped dresser, bull's-eye woodwork, transom windows, and ceiling fan. The Yellow Room is a bright, cheery space with a big brass double bed, maple and mahogany furnishings, and yellow-green glass in its window. And the Blue Room has several family photographs on its walls.

Betty serves tea, wine, and homemade goodies upon guests' arrival. Breakfast might include black raspberries from their 450-acre Ozark farm, homemade breads, rolls, jams, jellies, freshly-squeezed juice, scrambled eggs with tomatoes and cheese, bacon, ham, and more.

How to get there: From Springfield and the west, take I–44 east to Missouri 38 east (at Marshfield) to Frisco House, 3 blocks past the school in Hartville. From the east and north, take Missouri 5 south from I–44 at Lebanon to Hartville. From the south, take Missouri 5 north from U.S. 60 at Marshfield to Hartville.

In Hartville, Missouri 5 and Missouri 38 (Rolla Street) cross at courthouse. Inn is 2 blocks west on Missouri 38 from intersection.

*

B: *Charley and Betty discovered that their ancestors were friends in settlements on Cape Cod in the 1600s. And I discovered that Betty worked with my mother in the same Chicago department store more than forty years ago!*

Captain Wohlt Inn
Hermann, Missouri
65041

Innkeepers: Lee and Harry Sammons; Edna Adams, manager
Address/Telephone: 123 East Third Street; (314) 486–3357
Rooms: 5; all with private bath and air conditioning, 1 with wheelchair access.
Rates: $55 to $65, single or double, EPB. Two-night minimum during festival weekends (Maifest and Oktoberfest). Midweek and no-breakfast discounts. Children under 12 free. Stay third night for half price.
Open: All year.
Facilities and activities: Short walk from restaurants, shops, and historic buildings of Hermann and the Missouri River. Short drive to area wineries and vineyards.

This quaint inn sits high on a hill overlooking Third Street in the middle of ethnic Hermann's historic district, which is listed on the National Register of Historic Places for its architectural and historical significance. I immediately liked it, feeling as though I were visiting a favorite aunt's house; it had a comfortable, welcome-home kind of atmosphere.

That's in large part due to the reception I received from Lee, who took me into her air-conditioned inn on a blistering hot and humid day. As we sat down in a charming dining room done in handsome slate blue, she told me that the home was built in 1886 by its namesake, a German riverboat captain who founded the Hermann ferry boat company.

She and her husband renovated the building in 1986, and they have done a terrific job. A first-floor room (the only inn room in Hermann equipped for the handicapped) boasts bright country stylings and a four-poster bed.

As I walked up the staircase, I ran my hands over a walnut handrail that's original to the home. I found second-floor rooms equally appealing: pink-and-blue-bouquet country wallpapers, country ceiling borders, handsome furnishings, including ceiling fans and a beechnut Jenny Lind bed that's been in Harry's family for years. It's also one of the prettiest I've seen in a long time.

Third-floor dormer rooms feature more pastel country prints, dormer windows, and, as in most rooms, lovely country quilts made by local artisans.

Manager Edna prepares breakfast, serving tummy-filling egg casseroles, morning sausage, ham loaf and bacon, fresh fruit and juice, and delicious sweet breads stuffed with nuts and raisins.

Lee also boasts a restored 1840 building next to the inn and her Handwoven Shop gift store that features two additional guest suites. Country furnishings, wooden decks, and a garden with tables and benches make this house a comfortable retreat.

For dinner, try Taylor's Landing, which features hearty German ethnic foods like sauerbraten, bratwurst, and schnitzel; Vintage 1847 at Stone Hill Winery offers its own schnitzel, rainbow trout, and steak fillets in a romantic setting.

How to get there: From St. Louis, take I–70 west to Missouri 19, then go south into Hermann. Turn east on Third Street to the inn. Private parking is between Second and Third streets, down an alley named Hollyhock Lane.

☀

B: Third Street, between Schiller and Market, has remained largely as it appeared in the 1800s. Lots sold in 1839 for $50. The street was cut through a high knoll, hence the inn's "hillside" site.

Seven Sisters Bed and Breakfast Cottages
Hermann, Missouri
65041

Innkeepers: Severien and P. J. Meyer
Address/Telephone: 108 Schiller Street and 126 West Second Street; (314) 486–3717 or 3528
Rooms: 5; all with private bath and air conditioning. No smoking inn.
Rates: $75, single or double, EPB and horse-drawn town tour. $65, single or double, continental breakfast. Two-night minimum on Maifest and Oktoberfest weekends. Special packages, family and seasonal rates available.
Open: All year.
Facilities and activities: In heart of historic Hermann. Walk to specialty shops, Missouri River, good restaurants nearby. Short drive to area wineries and vineyards.

Sev is one of the best sources of local Hermann history. He also is a teamster, commanding a 1910 high-wheeled antique wagon hitched to two magnificent Percheron draft horses that pull visitors along on guided tours of this history-filled, German ethnic settlement that sits on the banks of the Missouri River.

"Hermann is the first planned community west of the Mississippi River," Sev told me. "It was platted in Philadelphia in 1836, lot sizes were set at 60 x 120 feet, and local ordinances called for all house yards to be fenced to keep in livestock." That's just one bit of Sev's tidbits of local color.

His neoclassical Colonial brick cottage on Schiller Street was built in 1849, a modest but handsome home with simple moldings and yellow-pine plank floors that remain today.

"But it was the Rumford fireplace that attracted us," Sev said. "That's really an eighteenth-century design, so we knew the house was something special."

The Rose Room is a wonderful getaway haven for guests. It has handsome, German house moldings and a 1900 maple spindle bed graced with a 100-year-old quilt that's part of P. J.'s quilt collection.

"The design is called 'seven sisters,' " Sev said. "P. J. also comes from a family with seven sisters, so the cottage name seemed quite natural to us."

The other guest room is tucked upstairs under the dormers, fashioned with two French turn-of-the-century footbeds and a small sitting area.

Sev's other cottage is an 1891 brick beauty with Victorian parlors, 10-foot ceilings, and a grand piano. I especially like the bath's claw-footed tub in the main-level suite.

P. J.'s gourmet-style breakfast are another Seven Sisters treat. Count on quiche Lorraine, gourmet casseroles, fresh fruit, gooey cinnamon rolls, Swedish coffee, and more. "It's something to remember us by," Sev said.

Sev also arranges progressive dinners that take place at three additional historic homes in the course of an evening; transportation is provided by the Percherons.

How to get there: From St. Louis, take I–70 west to Missouri 19, then go south into Hermann. Turn left on First Street, then right on Schiller to the inn.

William Klinger Inn
Hermann, Missouri
65041

Innkeepers: Nancy and John Bartel; LaVerne Rickher, manager
Address/Telephone: 108 East Second Street; (314) 486–5930
Rooms: 7, with 2 suites; all with private bath. No smoking inn.
Rates: $86 to $121, weekends; $74 to $102, weekdays; single or double, EPB.
Open: All year.
Facilities and activities: Walk to restaurants, shops, stores, and craft boutiques in heart of historic German settlement. Nearby: biking, museums, historic sites, preserved architecture. Short drive to Missouri Wine Country wineries, "Big Muddy" riverscape.

"I love old Victorian homes, but so many are dark and dreary," Nancy told me. "I wanted to make this one bright and happy, while still focusing on Victorian elegance."

That's exactly why I adore the William Klinger Inn. It's an extremely cheerful place, not only because of its decor but also because of the enthusiasm and bubbliness Nancy brings to her elegant home.

The 1878 Queen Anne townhouse, built by local mill owner William Klinger for his family, is an imposing building on a quiet residential street.

The beautiful green-and-white marble tile, Nancy told me, pointing to the rich foyer floor, is original to the home and quite unusual. The tall coatrack bench also is a Klinger original, as is the colorful stained-glass window above it. The coatrack bench is one of Nancy's favorite inn pieces. She marveled that it was especially made to fit the contour of the hallway walls.

But most spectacular is an elaborate staircase leading to the upper-floor rooms, magnificently hand-carved in rich cherry, with tall columns the epitome of elegance.

The parlor is dominated by a fireplace with a finely hand-carved cherry mantel. "It took five weeks to strip the paint off this masterpiece," Nancy said, shaking her head, "and lots of elbow grease."

The only guest bedroom on the first floor is decorated in white and shades of blue, with a quilted Victorian bed, balloon draperies, and a hardwood floor.

The second-floor Klinger Suite, done in Williamsburg blue, with a blue-tile fireplace, tall windows with balloon draperies, high walnut Victorian bedboard and dressers, and period prints on the walls, is a guest favorite. But I especially like the Kallmeyer Suite, with its tall Victorian four-poster queen-sized canopy bed.

The third floor has a small sitting area, and the rooms are named for their different views. The Courthouse Room overlooks that historic building; River View is a great room, with a four-poster bed, huge antique armoire, and a view of greenery, hills, and the river.

Nancy's special breakfasts include hearty sausage casseroles, home-baked breads and muffins, sugar twists, and more. She'll be happy to recommend one of the town's many ethnic restaurants—most of them serving German fare—for dinner treats. I recommend Vintage 1847 at Stone Hill Winery or The Landing for satisfying and elegant meals.

How to get there: From St. Louis or Kansas City, take I–70 to Route 19 and go south into Hermann. Turn left on Second Street.

✳

B: *Note the original stained glass in the parlor and entry hall.*

Doanleigh Wallagh Inn
Kansas City, Missouri
64111

Innkeepers: Carolyn and Edward Litchfield
Address/Telephone: 217 East 37th Street; (816) 753–2667
Rooms: 12, including 1 suite; all with private bath, air conditioning, TV, and phone.
Rates: $60 to $110, single or double, EPB.
Open: All year.
Facilities and activities: Located between Country Club Plaza and Crown Center. Menus provided for Kansas City dinner clubs and restaurants. Fresh cookies in rooms daily. Hyde Park and tennis courts across street. Nine blocks to Nelson Art Gallery. Short drive to Kansas City Royals baseball.

Where do I start? Maybe by saying, "Hello, Dolly?"

See, entertainer Carol Channing once rented the handsome Georgian-style inn for a week while playing Kansas City. "She likened it to home and enjoyed the privacy," Edward told me. She put her musical conductor in one room and her personal assistant in another. "Now we're starting to get a celebrity clientele on a more regular basis."

That's not too surprising. Edward is used to dealing with renowned personalities. He is the former director of 20th Century-

Fox's feature-film domestic distribution, who moved with wife, Carolyn, to Kansas City after the movie-industry rat race became too time-consuming and Los Angeles became "almost unlivable."

He's brought along some mementos of his former profession. The seventeenth-century Italian bronze candlesticks that rest on the living room mantel were handled by Marlon Brando when he played Napoleon in *Desiree*. And the seventeenth-century, Italian ecclesiastical bust was an expensive prop for Charlton Heston in *The Agony and the Ecstasy*.

Let's get back to the inn, located in adjacent, architecturally interesting houses, both built in 1907. European and American antiques create a casual yet romantic atmosphere. The first floors of each house are open to guests eager to enjoy a grand piano, two pump organs, big-screen television with VCR, and a library of films and books.

The North House's Hyde Park guest room offers a sitting area with a sofa bed, wood-burning fireplace, queen-sized four-poster bed, antique Belgium chest, antique armoire from Portugal, and desk fashioned from an antique, Chickering square piano.

The Westport Room has an 1850s four-poster bed and French doors that open to a private outdoor balcony; others are similarly charming. Just ask singer Bobby McFerrin ("Don't Worry, Be Happy") and other entertainment stars who have stayed here.

A charming dining room boasts an 1840s, English oak dining table that seats sixteen people, handsome silver service, and a magnificent Waterford crystal chandelier.

Former home economics teacher Carolyn serves imaginative breakfasts, which might include puffy apple-filled pancakes, eggs Benedict, French toast lathered with fruit puree, and more, eaten to the soothing strains of classical or New Age music.

An elaborate Christmas celebration features $10,000 worth of holiday decorations that take four people three days to put in place.

Do yourself a favor; don't stay overnight in Kansas City without experiencing this inn.

How to get there: From downtown Kansas City, take Main Street south to Thirty-seventh Street, then go east 3 blocks to the inn.

Wilderness Lodge
Lesterville, Missouri
63654

Innkeeper: Stephen Apted
Address/Telephone: Box 90; (314) 637–2295, toll-free from St. Louis 296–2011
Rooms: 26 rooms, riverside suites, cottages; all with private bath and air conditioning.
Rates: $54, per person, rooms and cottages; $67, per person, suites; MAP. Children's rates available. Two-night minimum required. Special package rates.
Open: April (weekends only), daily May 1 through October.
Facilities and activities: Dining room, bar. Archery, shuffleboard, volleyball, horseshoes, frisbee golf course, walking trails, tennis courts, platform tennis. Also children's playground, swimming pool, hot tub (cold weather only), hayrides, canoeing, tube floats. Horseback riding nearby.

I drove deep into the beautiful Ozark Mountain foothills to find this woodsy retreat. Located on 1,200 rolling acres near the bank of the crystal-clear Black River, the Wilderness Lodge offers some of the best country-style fun imaginable.

A group of young canoers were excitedly telling their parents about the afternoon's adventures as I entered the Main Lodge, the oldest and largest building on the property. The heavy log-beam construction and tan pitch made me feel like a pioneer in the wilderness.

The lodge's rough-hewn country-style furniture is just what you'd expect. Especially interesting are American Indian–style rugs displayed on the walls, animal trophies, and the obligatory rifle hanging above a manteled hearth.

Later, I sat in an open dining room with a giant picture window looking out over the grounds, watching more kids frolic in the pool. A game room, just off to the side, has card and game tables for all kinds of family fun. For romantics, the lodge has a large fireplace room for snuggling on chilly evenings.

Family-style breakfasts and dinners are lodge specialties. Morning menus include eggs, pancakes, and beverages; dinner platters are heaped high with good country cooking like fried chicken, fresh bread, and sweet pastries. After dinner you might sidle up to the bar for a nightcap.

I've rarely seen guest cabins so complement the beautiful Ozark countryside. Especially attractive is the use of native rock, peeled logs, pine siding, and porches built right into the landscape. Country-antique furniture and Indian artifacts add to the woodsy ambience; many rooms feature large fireplaces and high loft ceilings.

How to get there: From St. Louis, take I–270 south to Route 21 and continue south to Glover. Then head west on Route 21/49/72. Near Arcadia, take Route 21 south, then west for about 22 miles to Peola Road. Turn left and continue down the dirt and gravel path, following the signs to the lodge.

School House
Bed and Breakfast
Rocheport, Missouri
65279

Innkeepers: John and Vicki Ott
Address/Telephone: Third and Clark streets; (314) 698–2022
Rooms: 8; 5 with private bath and air conditioning, 1 with wheelchair access. No smoking inn.
Rates: $55 to $90, single or double, EPB.
Open: All year except Christmas Day.
Facilities and activities: BYOB. Sitting rooms, outdoor garden, courtyard. Town on National Register of Historic Places, filled with nineteenth-century homes. Antiques stores and craft and pottery shops nearby. Short drive to restaurants, local winery (Les Bourgeois) overlooking Missouri River and Boone Cave. Hiking and biking on renowned Missouri River State Trail.

I walked into this 1914, three-story, brick schoolhouse just as Vicki was beginning a tour of her inn and quickly discovered that it is a magnificent example of what restoration and renovation with a visionary eye can accomplish.

Guest rooms are very spacious, almost imperial, with their 13-foot-high ceilings, cheery ceiling and wall borders, schoolhouse-sized windows, shiny oak floors, and antique furnishings. I complimented Vicki on her handsome curtains; her talented hand made all the window treatments throughout the inn.

One guest room boasts a white iron-rail bed and cane-backed chairs; another is fashioned with a brass four-poster bed that's 7 feet tall. I also found delicately carved Victorian dressers, high-back chairs, pastel wall coverings, and even a trundle bed that adds a down-home feel.

I love the second floor's executive suite, with its mahogany four-poster bed, arched doorway, and three huge windows that spill light into this happy room. It boasts the schoolhouse's original fir floors, handsomely restored by Vicki and John.

For newlyweds and incurable romantics, the Bridal Suite is a must. Imagine a heart-shaped whirlpool tub, upholstered wall coverings, and more. Or try the 100-year-old Schoolmarm's Cottage, two blocks from the main inn building, for real privacy.

Vicki does all the breakfast cooking in an expansive second-floor kitchen that opens onto the inn's main common room. "Just seems like everyone follows me up here, and we end up talking as I prepare the food," Vicki said. Prepare yourself for her "famous" egg casserole, fresh fruit and juices, and homemade bran and cinnamon muffins.

Then browse among the hallway display case's historic town and school photos and memorabilia.

Rocheport itself is a "very Southern town," Vicki said. Its history stretches back to Indian times, as early journals noted primitive, red-keel Indian paintings on limestone bluffs that edge out over the Missouri River near here. In fact, members of the Lewis and Clark expedition passed by in 1804, citing "uncouth paintings of animals."

At the height of ferryboat traffic, the town grew to more than 800 people. Today about 250 residents keep Rocheport's legacy alive; several historic structures still dot the landscape. (You can pick up a walking-tour booklet at the inn.)

How to get there: From Columbia, take I–70 west to Rocheport exit, then follow Highway BB 2 miles northwest into town. The inn is at Third and Clark streets (right on Highway BB).

261

Boone's Lick Trail Inn
St. Charles, Missouri
63301

Innkeeper: V'Anne Mydler
Address/Telephone: 1000 South Main Street; (314) 947–7000
Rooms: 6; 4 with private bath. No smoking inn.
Rates: $55 to $58, single; $58 to $61, double; EPB. Slightly higher on weekends, during Fête des Petites Côtes (Festival of the Hills), and holidays.
Open: All year except Christmas Eve and Day.
Facilities and activities: In the heart of Frenchtown, with restaurants, specialty shops, boutiques, and antiques stores. Overlooks Frontier Park, the Missouri River State Trail, and Lewis and Clark Trail. National Historic District.

I was intrigued by the numerous doors leading to rooms overlooking the gallery porch of the historic 1840 Carter–Rice building, now known as the Boone's Lick Trail Inn. It reminded me of a boarding house—but that wasn't quite it.

"Madame Duquette had her girls entertain patrons in those little rooms," V'Anne told me. "See, folklore tells us that in the 1820s, Duquette ran a brothel here. When I restored the building, those four doors still led to tiny, little cubbyhole stalls, big enough for only a cot and washstand."

The Boone's Lick Trail Inn, one of the oldest homes in town, is intertwined with all kinds of interesting history. Frenchtown is the site of many firsts, including the Lewis and Clark Rendezvous, the start of the Zebulon Pike expedition, and the beginnings of Daniel Boone's salt lick trail. It's also where the Sante Fe Trail was planned and drafted.

The 1840 inn hosted hundreds of early adventurers and settlers passing through the town on their way west. V'Anne has restored second-floor guest rooms into country-charmed quarters for modern-day visitors. Some rooms boast original plank floors, antique iron-rail beds, German lace curtains, and family antique heirlooms.

I found the inn quiet and private, a welcome respite just a stone's throw from the hubbub that engulfed me on Main Street during this summer holiday weekend.

V'Anne prides herself on her never-ending breakfasts; no one will leave here hungry. Eggs Olé is a treat; so are her French toast and special home-baked breads, homemade jams, and yummy cinnamon rolls. Then I'd suggest a walking tour that showcases the town's historic architecture (self-guided tour pamphlets can be obtained at the tourism department on Main Street).

If you work up a good appetite, I'd recommend the Mother-in-Law House on South Main for lunch, where I enjoyed their turkey-and-salad plate with a glass of white wine; Lewis and Clark's (also on South Main) arguably offers the town's finest evening dining. You'll also find restaurants specializing in local-flavored specialties like Crab Rangoon, beignets, catfish, and down-home barbecue.

How to get there: From St. Louis, take I–70 west to First Capitol Drive, exit, and continue to Main Street. Turn right; the inn is at Main and Boone's Lick Road.

✸

B: *This historic city is alive with festivals year-round, including May's Lewis and Clark Rendezvous; August's Festival of the Hills; Oktoberfest, celebrating the town's French and German heritage; and Christmas Traditions, an old-fashioned holiday extravaganza lasting from Thanksgiving to Christmas.*

The Inn
St. Gemme Beauvais
Ste. Genevieve, Missouri
63670

Innkeepers: Paul Swenson and Marcia Willson
Address/Telephone: 78 North Main Street (mailing address: Box 231);
  (314) 883–5744
Rooms: 7; all with private bath.
Rates: $40 to $50, single; $55 to $65, double; $6 per child; EPB.
Open: All year.
Facilities and activities: Dinner, Friday–Saturday, 5:30 to 9:00 P.M. Dining
  and common rooms. Walk to antiques shops, galleries, and museums
  (many specializing in pre–Civil War pieces). Historical town architecture includes some of the best examples of French Colonial homes
  in United States, including vertical-log homes. Annual Jour de Fête
  second full weekend of August.

This 1847 three-story, red-brick building is located in a town
that's been called "the finest surviving example of French Colonial
architecture in the country," with more than fifty historic buildings
dating back to the 1700s when the fur traders settled here.

Walls here are pioneer-tough—18 inches thick—and they're
only one of the inn's unique features. In the foyer, I walked under

a historic chandelier, dating from the early 1800s, that casts an amber glow over the hallway. Just to the right of the door is the inn desk, an old rolltop where you often can find Paul or Marcia ready with a touring suggestion and a welcoming smile.

The guest rooms are upstairs, decorated in a mixture of Victorian furnishings and other antiques—nothing fancy, but comfortable and cozy.

I enjoyed a French feast for breakfast, with hand-filled ham crepes an inn specialty. There are also tasty omelets, delicious homemade orange-pecan nut breads, fresh fruit cups, blueberry muffins, and more.

For dinner, the innkeepers will suggest a spot to match your tastes. I like the Cafe Genevieve, just a short walk down the street, for scrumptious steaks, fish, and chops.

Eating in the historic dining room is a treat in itself. It's cozy and quaint with white walls, a white marble fireplace, and antique tables and chairs. I also felt a bit larger than life as I walked around this room. That's because its scaled-down dimensions are typical of the town's historic French-styled homes.

There is also a common room in the cellar that at one time served as a "moonshine" tavern. It's a favorite gathering place for guests, offering books, magazines, games, and a continuously "in-the-works" jigsaw puzzle.

Just a short walk away are all the town's fabulous architectural attractions. Especially interesting is the 1770 Bolduc House, a vertical-log "fort" regarded as the most authentically restored Colonial Creole house in the country.

This is also a great town for antique hunting; my favorite place is Le Souvenir, housed in the oldest brick building west of the Mississippi River.

How to get there: From St. Louis, take I–55 south to Route 32. Turn east and continue into Ste. Genevieve. Turn right on Market Street and continue for about 3 blocks to Main Street. Turn left on Main Street and continue to the inn.

The Southern Hotel
Ste. Genevieve, Missouri
63670

Innkeepers: Michael and Barbara Hankins
Address/Telephone: 146 South Third Street; (314) 883–3493 or (800) 275–1412
Rooms: 8; all with private bath and air conditioning.
Rates: $45 to $60, single; $55 to $90, double; EPB.
Open: All year.
Facilities and activities: Billiard room, gracious common rooms, off-street parking. Located in heart of historic town, oldest settlement west of the Mississippi River. Walking tours of French Colonial architecture, other historic buildings, quaint shops, boutiques, restaurants.

"Beginning in the 1820s, The Southern Hotel was known for the finest accommodations between St. Louis and Natchez, Tennessee," Barbara said as we walked through swinging doors into the hotel's old saloon, which now acts as a guest parlor. "The Mississippi was then about 4 blocks away, and the hotel employed a young slave to sit in the belvedere atop the house and watch for steamboats arriving at St. Genevieve's dock.

"Then he'd run across the street to the stables and get a wagon to meet hotel guests."

I never suspected that this grand old dame, built in Federal

266

style with a graceful front porch around 1800, had become a deserted eyesore in the mid-1980s, "a dumping ground for everything people no longer wanted," Barbara said. It is a testament to the Hankinses' magnificent restoration work that The Southern once again exudes warmth, hospitality, and classical graciousness.

Guest rooms are charmers; much of the credit goes to Barbara, whose whimsical, artistic touches are evident everywhere. If you're one of the first guests, Barbara will let you wander among the eight rooms to choose your favorite. But let me warn you: The combination of country Victorian furnishings and fabulous folk art made the selection a difficult task for me.

The Japonisme Room is tinged with oriental influence reflecting the Victorian's fascination with the Far East and includes Chinese silk prints in the bathroom as well as a claw-footed tub painted to match the room's decor.

The River Room features a headboard of "Old Man River" carved out of Missouri cedar logs by a local artist. Buttons and Bows boasts a linen-draped canopy bed. Cabbage Rose is quite romantic, with its carved Victorian headboard, white lace, and elegant wall coverings.

But one of my favorites is Wysocki's Room, with its three-dimensional, folk-art headboard that depicts a charming village. It's perhaps one of the most unusual beds I've ever seen.

Barbara cooks ups some fabulous breakfasts in her kitchen, which she decorated with handsome rosemaling, a Scandinavian folk art. I am fascinated by the unusual gourmet breakfast that might include strawberry soup, banana bisque, mushroom quiche, freshly baked croissants, juices, and chocolate-tinged coffee. Six fine restaurants also are within walking distance; Barbara will match one to your particular tastes for evening meals.

The innkeepers have restored the "summer kitchen" behind the hotel; it's now a gracious craft boutique featuring works of local artisans and the blossom-filled Gardens surround the building and encourage visitors to stroll, sit, and enjoy.

How to get there: From St. Louis, take I–55 south to the Sté. Genevieve exit (Route 32). Continue into town and turn right at Market Street; go 1 block to Third Street; turn right to hotel.

The Schwegmann House
Washington, Missouri
63090

Innkeepers: George Bocklage, Cathy Nagel, Barbara French Lee, owners;
   Karen Jones, manager
Address/Telephone: 438 West Front Street; (314) 239–5025
Rooms: 9; 7 with private bath, all with air conditioning.
Rates: $35 to $50, single; $45 to $60, double; continental breakfast.
Open: All year.
Facilities and activities: Guest parlors, formal gardens. Across the street from
   Missouri River. In historic Washington, near historic river-front
   district and preserved 1800s architecture. Also near restaurants and
   antiques and specialty shops. In the heart of Missouri's Wine
   Country; short drive to winery tours.

The innkeepers have captured all the warmth and old-world
hospitality of this historic German-influenced Missouri River town
in this charming inn. I found it exciting to look out my window
and see the waters of the "Big Muddy" and listen to the distant
bellow of boat traffic on the river.

This stately pre–Civil War Georgian-style home was buzzing
with activity upon my arrival. A family with three tow-headed
kids was in the parlor looking over the dinner menus from area
restaurants that are provided for guests. They couldn't decide if

they wanted to "dude up" for supper or grab a hamburger and picnic next to the river.

Another young couple had bicycled to area wineries (this is the heart of Missouri Wine Country), and was showing off some of the bottles they'd purchased. They promised me samples later that evening. That's just typical of the inn's friendly atmosphere.

Most of the guest rooms are furnished with fine antiques and fun country accents. Some have river views; all have cute names. My favorites:

The Country Room, with its local handcrafts, high-back rocking chair, marble-topped lamp stand, tall armoire, and calico curtains on the window. I especially liked the hand-stitched star quilt on the bed.

The Eyelet Room, generously decorated with shockingly white lace. White eyelet curtains brighten three tall windows and sprinkle sunlight in all directions. A padded rocking chair is absolutely required for gazing out at the river. There's also a marble-topped dresser, writing desk, and a colorful hand-stitched quilt on the bed.

Karen's breakfasts are a treat. There are freshly baked croissants and a plate of imported and domestic cheeses. But save some room for homemade bread and thick fruity jams and some fresh fruit to satisfy a morning sweet tooth.

Especially interesting are the historic town's many antiques shops and fine restaurants. The Basket Case Delicatessen (a big-city deli in a tiny town) serves terrific sandwiches. At the East End Tavern, you can grab a tasty burger while listening to colorful talk about "Mizzou's" college football teams. The Landing is an informal dinner spot for families, with pizza and great burgers that are favorites. Then there's Meriweather's and Creamery Hill for fine dining.

How to get there: From St. Louis, take I–44 southwest to Route 100 and go west until you reach Washington. Turn north on Jefferson, then turn west on Front Street (along the river). The inn is at the corner of Front and Olive.

LAKE ERIE

CLEVELAND

90

271

80

75

71

10.

62

12.

1. 7.

8.

2.

36

33

36

3.

250

11

4.

70

COLUMBUS

70

9.

5.

71

6.

33

OHIO RIVER

CINCINNATI

62

125

Ohio

Numbers on map refer to towns numbered below.

The Frederick Fitting House
Bellville, Ohio
44813

Innkeepers: Ramon and Suzanne Wilson
Address/Telephone: 72 Fitting Avenue; (419) 886–2863
Rooms: 3; 1 with private full bath, 1 with private half bath.
Rates: $40 to $55, single; $50 to $65, double; EPB.
Open: All year except Thanksgiving Day and Christmas Day.
Facilities and activities: Picnic basket lunch, candlelight dinner with wine, fresh flowers, music. Golf course, tennis courts nearby. Little shops and jogging trails in all directions. Canoeing and skiing (in season) within a few minutes' drive. Two state parks a short drive away. The Renaissance Theatre, the Mansfield Art Center, and the Kingwood Gardens within a half-hour's drive. Mid-Ohio Raceway in Lexington is site of major sports car races.

Baby Kate originally discovered The Frederick Fitting House. It had been time for my then two-month-old daughter's midday feeding, so I drove down a quiet side street on this hot spring day looking for a parking spot bathed in shade. We stopped in front of a beautiful 1863 Italianate home and immediately were drawn inside.

272

It's absolutely beautiful, completely furnished in American folk art and Ohio antiques; many are family heirlooms with interesting stories behind them, so be sure to get Ramon and Suzanne to weave their magic tales.

The sight of the dining room almost took my breath away. Wonderful stencilwork is apparent everywhere; it covers even the original yellow-pine plank floor.

Breakfasts are served on a big square table that invites conversation. (In summer, breakfast is offered outside in the gazebo.) Specialties include crepes, home-baked breads, and Dutch pastries, served along with Richland County honey, fresh fruit, and juice. There's even a choice of specially blended coffee and herbal teas. Ramon and Suzanne recommend the nearby San-Dar restaurant for smorgasbord-style dining.

Walking up a magnificent, freestanding spiral staircase of walnut, butternut, and oak, I found three charming guest rooms. The Colonial Room, with a canopy bed covered in lace, is perfect for romantics. Especially noteworthy among its many fine antique furnishings is a primitive pioneer coverlet.

But my favorite is the Shaker Room, with its simple twin beds, antique writing desk, straight-back rocking chair, and wall pegs from which hang antique Shaker work utensils.

How to get there: Bellville is directly between Cleveland and Columbus. Leave I–71 at exit 165 and proceed east on State Route 97 into the village. Turn left onto Fitting Avenue. The inn is the last home on the left at the intersection of Fitting Avenue and Ogle Street.

※

B: *During the holiday season, the inn's two 10-foot Christmas trees are decorated with handcrafted ornaments, and luminarias glow along the outside walkway.*

Roscoe Village Inn
Coshocton, Ohio
43812

Innkeeper: Don McIlroy
Address/Telephone: 200 North Whitewoman Street; (614) 622–2222 or
(800) 237–7397
Rooms: 51; all with private bath, air conditioning, phone, and TV.
Wheelchair access.
Rates: $66 to $72, single or double, EP. Several seasonal weekend
packages.
Open: All year.
Facilities and activities: Full-service restaurant, tavern, sitting rooms. In
Roscoe Village, 1830 canal town; includes canal boat rides, 21 craft
shops, 5 exhibit-museum buildings, 4 restaurants, horse-drawn
trolley, Johnson-Humrickhouse Museum. Amish country nearby.
Pro-football Hall of Fame in Canton. Scenic countryside of Ohio
River Valley.

I became curious about the Roscoe Village Inn's King Charlie's Tavern. Turns out it is named after Charlie, the first white
settler in these parts. Legend has it that an heir to the throne of
England stopped in the village tavern on his way across the
country and made quite a fuss about how towns were so much
more interesting in Europe. Charlie made things a lot more

interesting for him right then and there, hiking him up by the seat of his pants and throwing him out the door.

The inn's choppy brick exterior design borrows heavily from other Greek Revival–style canal-era structures in the village. Inside, the second-floor parlor is a favorite with guests. It's easy to see why: It has exposed wood beams, a huge fireplace fronted by high-back sofas, a beautiful wrought-iron chandelier, and tall windows. Wonderful crafts are sprinkled throughout the inn (including hand-stitched quilts)—native Ohio folk art reflecting the village's canal-era heritage.

Rooms have sturdy, handcrafted wood furniture made by Amish craftsmen in nearby Holmes County. Four-poster beds, high-back chairs, and more tall windows add to the charm.

A full-service dining room, complete with china and silver, offers meals to guests in an atmosphere of early American elegance. The inn's master chef prepares the most exciting culinary delights, which have been featured in many magazines on the subject; selections might include veal, sea scallops, and roast duckling. Breakfasts offer terrific choices as well, including whole-wheat griddle cakes and hazelnut, whole-wheat waffles, served along with farm-fresh eggs, honey, and sweet butter.

Later I walked along the historic Ohio & Erie towpath north from the village to where the *Monticello III*, a reconstructed canal boat, floats passengers to Mudport Basin.

The inn also custom-tailors your schedule for your complete relaxation and enjoyment; the innkeeper will set up one-to-three-day itineraries to suit your level of fun.

How to get there: From Cleveland to the north, take I–77 south to exit 65. Follow Route 36/16 west into Coshocton. Turn west on Ohio 541, then north on Whitewoman Street to the inn. From Columbus and Indianapolis to the southwest, take I–70 and exit north on Route 60. Then turn east on Route 16 and follow into Coshocton. Next follow directions listed above.

❧

B: *Don't miss all the antiques and specialty stores along Whitewoman Street, which gets its name from the Walhonding River— walhonding is the Delaware Indian word for "white woman."*

The White Oak Inn
Danville, Ohio
43014

Innkeepers: Joyce and Jim Acton
Address/Telephone: 29683 Walhonding Road; (614) 599–6107
Rooms: 10; all with private bath and air conditioning. No smoking inn.
Rates: $50 to $80, single; $70 to $100, double; $25 for additional person or bed in room; EPB. Two-night minimum on weekends in May and October, and all holiday weekends.
Open: All year.
Facilities and activities: Dinner available. BYOB. Expansive grounds, lawn games, screen house. Good antiques in area stores. Kokosing River offers some of best smallmouth-bass fishing in Ohio; also canoe livery. Thirty minutes from Millersburg, center of Amish culture in the United States; 35 minutes from Malabar Farm State Park; 25 minutes from Roscoe Village in Coshocton, restored, canal-era town with own canal boat and towpath, specialty shops, and craft stores.

My family reached The White Oak Inn after a long drive through the central Ohio back roads, winding through pristine woods and around sweeping curves that follow the rolling hills of the Walhonding Valley. It was dusk, and the forest literally glowed thanks to the setting sun. My wife spotted a wild turkey standing off the side of the road. I fully expected deer to wander out of the brush at any time. It was peaceful, and special, and lifted our spirits.

Could there be a more perfect spot for a country inn?

Jim greeted us warmly. We sat down in the cozy common room in front of the huge brick fireplace, where Jim invited us to "put your feet up on the table and relax." He told us the house took three years to build and was finally completed in 1918.

All the magnificent woodwork is white oak; the floor, red oak. "It was fashioned from timber on this very land," Jim said. "It was cut just across the road. I still have the blade used to fell the trees."

The inn boasts all kinds of hardwoods, including oak, maple, walnut, cherry, and poplar. In fact, guest rooms are named for the type of wood featured in each of them.

The Cherry Room is very handsome, as admirers of this wood can well imagine. It has a four-poster bed, rocker, washstand, and Shaker peg rack for clothes. The quilt here, as in all rooms, is handmade. Jim said the Oak Room's bed and washstand are original to the home. I defy you to find a more beautiful shade of red maple than in the Maple Room; the color of the bed's headboard is gorgeous, and its hand-carved leaf design is simply outstanding.

Joyce serves breakfast in the dining room. It's a feast, featuring French toast made from homemade breads, scrambled eggs, muffins, sausage, bacon, coffeecake, juices, and beverages. She'll whip up dinners as well; choices may include beef Wellington with Yorkshire pudding, braised pork loin, chicken breast stuffed with ricotta cheese, and much more.

Jim and Joyce recently unearthed several Indian artifacts on their property. Perhaps you'll be there when Kenyon College sends archeology students to the site; they hope to eventually register it as an Ohio Historic Site.

How to get there: The inn is closer to Millwood than Danville. From Columbus, take U.S. 62 northeast to the junction of U.S. 36 and U.S. 62. Go east on U.S. 36 for 1 mile to Ohio 715, then 3 miles east to the inn.

❋

B: *Country inns can't get much better than this; neither can innkeepers.*

The Buxton Inn
Granville, Ohio
43023

Innkeepers: Audrey and Orville Orr, owners; Cecil Snow, manager
Address/Telephone: 313 East Broadway; (614) 587–0001
Rooms: 15, with 4 suites; all with private bath, air conditioning, phone, and TV. Wheelchair access.
Rates: $55 to $70, single; $65 to $80, double; continental breakfast. Children under school age free.
Open: All year except Christmas Day and New Year's Day.
Facilities and activities: Full-service restaurant with 9 dining rooms; full-service bar. Nearby: tennis, golf, biking, swimming, horseback riding, art galleries, antiques shops, specialty boutiques, museums, historic sites. Also near Ye Olde Mill of 1817 and Hopewell Indians' Newark earthworks.

Cecil and I sat in the charming basement dining room of The Buxton Inn, built in 1812 as a tavern by a pioneer from Granville, Massachusetts. "Stagecoach drivers would stop at the tavern during their journey across the frontier and would sleep down here on beds of straw," he said. He pointed out original rough-hewn beams and stone walls that are still sturdy after all these years. And I saw the great open hearth where the drivers cooked their meals.

The Buxton is Ohio's oldest continuously operating inn, and it's a treasure. Look closely and you'll see that the pegged walnut floors were laid with hand-forged nails. "Those windows were laid into foot-thick walls for protection from Indians," Cecil said. Black-walnut beams and timbers frame walls and ceilings; fireplaces are scattered throughout the house.

The main inn building has only four guest rooms. The Victorian and Eastlake rooms are two-room suites. One features nineteenth-century Eastlake antiques; the other boasts elegant Victorian beds, an exquisite settee, and an antique crystal chandelier. The Empire Room is my favorite because of its large sleigh beds and fine silver chandelier.

Did you know that President William Henry Harrison supposedly rode a horse up the inn stairs to the second-floor ballroom during some spirited nighttime revelry?

Down the block, on the corner, stands the 1815 Warner House, with eleven more rooms similarly decorated.

Delicious dining fare at The Buxton includes wholesome breakfasts with farm-fresh eggs, sausage, and flapjacks; lunch specialties lean toward "colonial style" fare: old-fashioned beef potpie topped with a flaky crust; and Osie Robinson's Chicken Supreme—a puff pastry filled with chicken in mushroom and pimiento sauce.

Loosen up your belt before you get to the dinner table. Inn favorites include French pepper steak with brandy, Louisiana chicken with artichoke hearts, and calf sweetbreads with Burgundy-mushroom sauce.

Cecil even makes dessert a difficult decision. Shall I choose Daisy Hunter's hot walnut-fudge cake a la mode, gingerbread with hot lemon sauce, homemade pecan pie topped with whipped cream, or "olde tyme" vanilla-velvet ice cream?

How to get there: From Columbus, take I–70 to Ohio 37. Then go north to Ohio 661 and proceed into Granville. From Cleveland, take I–71 to Route 13 through Mansfield. Go south on Route 13 until you reach Ohio 661 just outside Mansfield. Head south on Ohio 661 into Granville and the inn.

B: *Ask Cecil about the inn ghost who was once a light-opera star.*

The Golden Lamb
Lebanon, Ohio
45036

Innkeeper: Jackson B. Reynolds
Address/Telephone: 27 South Broadway; (513) 932–5065
Rooms: 18, with 1 suite; all with private bath.
Rates: $48, single; $58 to $76, double; $90, suite; EP.
Open: All year.
Facilities and activities: Full-service restaurant with wheelchair access, 9 dining areas, and tavern. Upstairs museum with Shaker furniture collection. Large gift and craft shop. Nearby: Lebanon Antique Center featuring 150 dealers. Short drive to Warren County Museum, King's Island amusement park, Jack Nicklaus Golf Center, town of Waynesville (more than 40 antiques shops).

Early 1800s stagecoach drivers and travelers (many of whom couldn't read) were simply told to drive to the sign of The Golden Lamb for a warm bed and a good meal. I saw the large wooden sign depicting a golden lamb still hanging in front of this charming and historic inn.

"It's a real friendly place," Jackson said, "the kind of place people like to come back to again and again."

I heartily agree with him. From its beginning in 1803, The Golden Lamb has offered warm hospitality to its guests. Samuel L.

Clemens paced through its hallways while in rehearsal for a performance at the Lebanon Opera House. Charles Dickens eloquently complained about the "lack of spirits" at the then-temperance hotel, circa 1842. Benjamin Harrison, U. S. Grant, and eight other presidents stayed here.

The inn is famous for both its Midwestern cooking prepared by its European-trained chef and antique-laden guest rooms named for illustrious visitors. I walked up creaking stairs and along squeaking hallway floorboards to marvel at the antique furniture gracing the second- and third-floor rooms.

Anyone can do the same; Jackson keeps the doors to all unoccupied rooms open. "We want people just coming to dinner to enjoy the antique collection of our inn, too," he said. "We encourage them to walk through the halls and look inside."

I couldn't resist bouncing up and down on the replica of the massive Lincoln bed in the Charles Dickens Room, resplendent in its Victorian finery. Another favorite was the huge four-poster Boyd bed in the DeWitt Clinton Room.

All the rooms are spacious. Besides a rocking chair, a tall secretary stuffed with books, and other antique furnishings, mine had two four-poster beds.

My family dined in the Shaker Room, with wall pegs holding all kinds of antique kitchen gadgets, pots, and pans. I thought that the roast Butler County turkey with dressing and giblet gravy was almost like Mom's—a special treat. My wife was delighted by another inn favorite, pan-fried Kentucky ham (specially cured and aged) steak glazed with bourbon. Baby Kate was fed well, too—with all the cooing and attention she received from the friendly waitresses.

The inn's display of authentic antique Shaker furniture is said to be one of the largest private collections of its kind. On the fourth floor are glass-enclosed display rooms featuring many fine pieces.

How to get there: Lebanon is midway between Cincinnati and Dayton. From I–75, take Ohio 63 6 miles east to Lebanon. From I–71, take Ohio 123 3 miles west to Lebanon. The inn is at the juncture of Ohio state routes 63 and 123.

The Inn at Cedar Falls
Logan, Ohio
43138

Innkeepers: Anne Castle and Ellen Grinsfelder
Address/Telephone: 21190 State Route 374; (614) 385–7489
Rooms: 9, with 1 suite; all with private bath and air conditioning, 1 with wheelchair access.
Rates: $45 to $60, single; $57 to $75, double; EPB.
Open: All year.
Facilities and activities: Dinner. Log-house common room, corner library, porch, log and patio dining areas. Special activity weekends. Nearby: wildlife-watching, hiking, cross-country skiing, photography. Short drive to canoeing and fishing on the Hocking River; geologic marvels like Cedar Falls, Ash Cave, Cantwell Cliffs, Conkle's Hollow, Rock House, Hocking Valley Scenic Railway, Lake Logan.

Southern Ohio's Hocking Hills offer some of the most spectacular vistas in the Appalachian foothills. And sitting squarely in the center of this magnificent landscape is The Inn at Cedar Falls.

Surrounded on three sides by Hocking State Park, the inn is a nature retreat—a wonderland of eighty acres filled with wildlife and whispering trees. Mink, red fox, and white-tailed deer abound. Woodpeckers and wild turkeys thrive in the dense forest. Spring brings a splash of colorful wildflower blossoms. Autumn hues are astounding.

I could stand on the south porch all day and look out over the hills. Or sit alongside the log house's pot-bellied stove on a cool autumn evening and enjoy a good book. Maybe just gaze out of my guest room window at more fabulous scenery.

One of the inn's log houses dates from 1840. Ellen pointed out the 18-inch-wide logs and original plank floors. "When my mother first purchased this cabin, we discovered the original mud and horsehair chinking between the logs," she said, "so we had some work to do."

The log houses have common rooms and porches filled with rockers, mountain-style folk furniture, game tables, and special room stuffed with books.

Meals often are served on the patio, where gourmet-style food vies with the scenery for guests' attention. Visit during a "guest chef" weekend and you might be treated to everything from ratatouille in eggplant shells and grilled garlic shrimp to a chocolate torte with hazelnuts for dessert.

Guest rooms, located in the new "barn," are country cozy, furnished with antiques, rag rugs on plank floors, and rocking chairs. Windows offer scenic views, and fragrant wildflower bouquets are placed in each room.

How to get there: From Columbus, take U.S. 33 south through Lancaster to the Logan-Bremen exit, which is State Route 664; turn right, go about 9½ miles to State Route 374, then turn left and continue 1 mile to the inn, located on the right side of the road (parking on the left).

☀

B: *Where else can you find a cabin in the woods featuring delicacies like apple-smoked pork loin, bean soup, bread pudding with whiskey sauce, and homemade breads, muffins and desserts?*

The Blackfork Inn
Loudonville, Ohio
44842

Innkeepers: Sue and Al Gorisek
Address/Telephone: 303 North Water Street; (419) 994–3252
Rooms: 6; all with private bath and air conditioning.
Rates: $43, single; $65 to $75, double; continental breakfast.
Open: All year.
Facilities and activities: In Ohio Amish country. Near Mohican State Park, historic Malabar Farm. Short drive to restaurants and Snow Trails ski area.

Sue will show you the handsome secretary that was brought to Ohio from Connecticut in a covered wagon by her great-great-grandfather. "He thought he'd be living in the wilderness with the Indians," Sue said, "so he was determined to bring at least one piece of fine furniture along with him."

In fact, there are several beautiful antique pieces that can be traced to Sue's family back East, including a Pembroke table in the parlor that dates back to 1760. And the lovely, Victorian, walnut bedroom suite, in the Josephine Room, was made in Painesville, Ohio, for Sue's great-grandmother. "She was born in that bed," Sue said. A photograph of her great-grandmother hangs on the wall.

284

The house itself dates back to 1865, when it was built by Phillip Black, a Civil War merchant who brought the railroad to town. That family used the house until the mid-1940s.

The inn's downstairs common rooms almost resemble a museum, so stunning are the antique furnishings. Guest rooms are more informal and are named for members of the Black family. Several have big brass beds and Victorian-style trappings, except for the whimsical Margaret Room—with its tropical feel contributed by an antique wardrobe displaying a Tahitian princess stencil.

Sue offers a hearty breakfast with some unusual choices. There are blueberry pancakes, apple fritters, cinnamon rolls, home-grown raspberries with Swiss cream, and Amish products like trail bologna and specially made cheeses. She can also arrange evening meals at the inn, prepared by one of the fine local chefs.

Or sample elegant fare at the Brass Plate, a sophisticated restaurant for discriminating tastes. Herb-tinged vegetables and delicately prepared potato pancakes, veal dishes, and seafood all offer interesting tastes and sauces you wouldn't expect to find in a town with a population of under two thousand.

How to get there: From Columbus, take I–71 north and exit on U.S. 30 east. Then take Ohio 60 south into Loudonville (it turns into Main Street). Turn north on North Water Street and continue a few blocks to the inn.

The Inn at Honey Run
Millersburg, Ohio
44654

Innkeeper: Marge Stock
Address/Telephone: 6920 County Road 203; (216) 674–0011, toll-free in
  Ohio (800) 468–6639
Rooms: 36, with 1 suite; all with private bath and air conditioning, most
  with TV.
Rates: $65 to $150, single or double, continental breakfast. Two-night
  minimum Friday and Saturday. Special winter rates.
Open: All year.
Facilities and activities: Full-service dining room (closed Sundays) with
  wheelchair access. BYOB. Meeting rooms host movies and table
  tennis on weekends, library, game room, gift shop. Hiking trails,
  sheep and goats in pastures, nature lecture and walks most weekends,
  horseshoes, croquet, volleyball. Near Holmes County antiques and
  specialty stores, cheese factories, quilt shops, 9-hole golf course.
  Short drive to Roscoe Village canal-era town and Warther Wood
  Carving Museum.

 "Just look at that," Marge said, pointing to a black Amish
carriage clip-clopping down a winding country road just below a
room deck of The Inn at Honey Run. "That's why I love spring,
fall, and winter here. You can still see sights like that through the
trees. It takes you back to the 1800s."

I had driven down a hilly, twisting road that I thought would never end to get here. "We're hard to find," Marge admitted. Her graceful inn is situated on sixty hilly, wooded acres in the middle of Ohio Amish country. Its wood and stone construction blends magnificently with the gorgeous landscape.

"Birding here is great," Marge said, as she pointed to countless feeders surrounding the inn. "Visitors have recorded about thirty different species."

I was anxious to see the rooms, and I wasn't disappointed. They're done in a potpourri of styles: early American; contemporary with slanted ceilings and skylights; and Shaker—my favorite—with many pegs on the walls to hang everything from clothes to furniture.

Marge uses Holmes County folk art to highlight each room; handmade quilts adorn walls and beds (which are extra long); and there are comfy chairs with reading lamps.

"I love books," Marge said, "so I made certain each room has a reading light and a chair that rocks or swivels, where you can put your feet up on the windowsill and read, or just stare out at the birds."

Twelve new "Honeycomb Rooms" are the "world's first commercial earth-shelter rooms," built under and into Holmes County hills. "It's the perfect place for overstressed executives," Marge said of these almost cavelike retreats that feature wood-burning fireplaces, whirlpools, and breakfast delivered to the door.

Inn food is made "from scratch," with pan-fried trout from Holmes County waters a dinner specialty. Marge's full country breakfast features juice, eggs and bacon, French toast with real maple syrup, and homemade breads.

Then you might take a hike on the grounds, perhaps followed by Luke, the inn's coon hound, or by Sandy, the beagle. And Willy (a white cat) can be borrowed for room visits!

How to get there: From Millersburg it is 3.3 miles to the inn. Go east on East Jackson Street in Millersburg (Routes 39 and 62). Pass the courthouse and gas station on the right. At the next corner, turn left onto Route 241, which makes several turns as it twists out of town. Nearly 2 miles down the road, while proceeding down a long, steep hill, you'll cross a bridge over Honey Run. Turn right immediately around another small hill onto County Road 203, which is not well marked. After 1 mile, turn right at the small inn sign. Go up the hill to the inn.

The H. W. Allen Villa
Troy, Ohio
45373

Innkeepers: Bob and June Smith
Address/Telephone: 434 South Market Street; (513) 335–1181
Rooms: 4, with 1 suite; all with private bath, air conditioning, TV, and phone.
Rates: $40, single; $60, double; EPB. Cribs and baby beds available.
Open: All year.
Facilities and activities: Double parlor, dining room, and library. Nearby: Hayner Cultural Center, Historical Courthouse, Overfield Tavern, Museum of Troy History. Short drive to golf course, Dayton Art Institute, U.S. Air Force Museum.

June's villa brochure carries a translation of "bed and breakfast" in Japanese. That surprised me, but she explained that the nearby Panasonic plant regularly sends visiting Japanese executives here while taking care of business. In fact, two Japanese businessmen were checking in during my visit. In heavily accented English, they marveled at the "big, beautiful house."

It is very big and extremely beautiful. Built in 1874 by Henry Ware Allen, part owner of the largest flour mill in the county, the three-story Victorian mansion boasts fourteen rooms, 12-foot ceilings, seven fireplaces, and white and black walnut woodwork throughout.

The Smiths opened the inn to travelers in 1986, filled with their bounty of twenty years of antiques collecting. The furnishings are remarkably distinctive; the home seems more museum than wayfarer station.

Walk into the dining room to see June's extensive set of LaBelle Flow Blue china. I also like the flamboyantly colored porcelain mantel clocks that seemingly sit in every nook and cranny.

Also note hand stenciling done in 1874 that has been restored in the library and sitting room, a handsome design that rests above 11-inch walnut baseboards.

Now for the guest rooms: They may all be bathed in Victorian antiques, but I can't help marvel at the Allen Room, with its four-poster Gamblers brass bed and extremely unusual gold Hindu-style domed lamps that would seem at home in a sheik's palace.

A breakfast of cinnamon French toast, vegetable omelets, or bacon, tomato, and eggs dishes is served on a 15-foot-long antique table in the dining room.

How to get there: From Dayton, take I–75 north to the Troy exit (exit 73, which is Ohio 55), and proceed 1 mile east, then 2 blocks north on South Market Street to the inn.

The Wooster Inn
Wooster, Ohio
44691

Innkeeper: Willy Bergmann
Address/Telephone: Wayne Avenue and Gasche Street; (216) 264–2341
Rooms: 16, with 2 suites; all with private bath, air conditioning, and phone. Pets welcome.
Rates: $50 to $56, single; $65 to $71, double; $65 to $140, suites; EPB. Special weekend packages available.
Open: All year except Christmas Day.
Facilities and activities: Wheelchair access to dining room. Sitting area, outside patio. Access to many Wooster College activities and sports facilities. Ohio Light Opera special on weekends.

Imagine an evening of professional light opera, maybe Offenbach's *La Belle Hélène*—which might be described as a Woody Allen–type version of ''Dynasty'' with ravishing waltzes—and you'll get the idea of this production's flair. Followed by a scrumptious meal featuring champagne and a juicy steak served in a Colonial-style dining room.

That's just some of the fun you'll have at the wonderful Wooster Inn. Owned and operated by the College of Wooster, and located right on its beautiful campus, the inn is surrounded by tall trees and green fields. In fact, I watched a little action on the college's golf course right from the dining room window.

The inn has an English-country feel to it. The lobby is spacious and casually gracious, with a large sitting area of high-back chairs and sofas. A stately grandfather's clock softly chimes on the hour. French doors open onto the Colonial-style dining room and terrace, which overlook the aforementioned links.

Guests may also use many of the facilities at the college. These include tennis courts and a golf course just out the back door. You can even use the library.

I stayed here recently to attend an authors' book fair. My room was very spacious, comfortable, and cheery, with windows overlooking the inn grounds, muted flowered wallpaper, oak and cherry furniture, quaint bedspreads, and a couple of wing chairs. Be sure to make reservations well in advance. College guests (and many visiting moms and dads) adore the inn.

You can choose anything from the regular breakfast menu in the morning. Inn specialties include blueberry pancakes with Ohio maple syrup. Dinner offers a wide selection of choices, including beef tenderloin in Burgundy wine and pepper sauce, Sunny-Basted Pork Chops with rosemary, fresh rainbow trout or salmon, and veal cutlets.

The dining room also offers a selection of fine wines, imported beers, and sherry.

How to get there: Five principal highways run through Wooster: U.S. 30 and 250, and State Routes 3, 585, and 83. From Cleveland, exit the 250 bypass at Burbank Road and continue south to Wayne Avenue. Turn east on Wayne to the inn.

The Worthington Inn
Worthington, Ohio
43085

Innkeeper: Shirley Black, general manager
Address/Telephone: 649 High Street; (614) 885–7700
Rooms: 26, with 5 suites; all with private bath, air conditioning, TV, and phone.
Rates: $85, single; $95, double; $110 to $140, suites; continental breakfast.
Open: All year.
Facilities and activities: Four dining rooms, pub, ballroom. Located in historic Old Worthington Village. Free maps for walking tours of area, which include several homes built as early as 1804. Antiques shops, specialty stores, and boutiques.

Masterful antiques from the Sheraton, Hepplewhite, and Victorian periods, elegant stained glass and crystal, bath mirrors imported from France, triple sheeting on beds, turn-down service, and a complimentary split of champagne transport you back to a more graceful style of traveling. I bet you never would have guessed that this magnificent inn, completed in 1831 and then known as the Central House, was originally a stagecoach stop.

Shirley told me a $4-million restoration in 1983 transformed what had become a "white elephant" into a luxurious and romantic turn-of-the-century–style getaway.

I found many of the antique pieces stunning. Every room's decor is different; some sport an early American motif complete with hand-stenciling on walls and ceilings and elegant, pine period pieces, while others are heavily Victorian, featuring fine walnut, mahogany, and cherry antique furnishings.

The Presidential Suite is a descent into pampered decadence. It offers more than 800 square feet of pomp and luxury. On one of the walls are framed papers that set the terms of an indentured servant. Shirley said those valuable documents were found within the walls during restoration.

Four more suites, located in the 1817 Snow House just down the street, offer more elegance. The center-hall staircase is black walnut, and you can notice unpeeled log joints in the cellar.

It was even a treat for me to quaff a beer in the Pub Room. The splendid marble-topped bar, with its lead- and stained-glass accoutrements, seemingly stretches on forever. Made in Austria, it originally was used as a soda fountain in Baltimore at the turn of the century. The bartender explained how the interesting Cruvinet decanter system works.

The third-floor Van Loon Ballroom has an exquisite, Czechoslovakian crystal chandelier weighing nearly 500 pounds and a romantic balcony overlooking the old village.

The inn's menu reflects a regional American influence, with veal and beef specialties abounding. And don't hesitate to try one of the rich desserts prepared daily at the inn's own bakery.

How to get there: From Cleveland, take I–71 south to Ohio 161. Exit west to Worthington, then turn left on High Street and continue to New England Avenue and the inn.

The Cider Mill
Zoar, Ohio
44697

Innkeepers: Ralph and Judy Kraus
Address/Telephone: Second Street (mailing address: P.O. Box 441); (216) 874–3133
Rooms: 2 share 1 bath; both with air conditioning.
Rates: $50, single; $55, double; EPB. Two-night minimum during fall Harvest Festival.
Open: All year.
Facilities and activities: Family room with television, deck. Zoar Historic Village tours. Antiques and specialty stores. Near restaurants, canoe livery and river trips, scenic bike paths along old Ohio-Erie Canal, fishing holes, "Trumpet in the Land" outdoor drama, National Football League Hall of Fame, Ohio Amish Country.

A rooster crowed about six times in a row. "School kids are on a tour of the village today," Judy said, "and with all the attention, he's just going crazy."

I was looking out the third-story window of Judy's restored mill building alongside tiny Goose Run Creek. The mill, which was built in 1863, served as a steam-powered mill for Zoar Village pioneers. At that time, Zoar Village was the nation's most successful religious communal settlement. Its quiet charm and serenity lured even President William McKinley here; Zoar was his summer retreat.

Well, the renovated mill lured me to this little village listed in the National Register of Historic Places. Judy's country-style antiques-and-specialty store occupies the first floor. We climbed a three-story custom-made spiral staircase to reach her beautiful guest rooms. They have original cross beams, slanted ceilings, four-poster and brass beds, and other antique furnishings.

A comfortable second-level family room has a large stone hearth; a fire would feel good here on chilly Ohio nights. The sitting room is more formal, with a collection of Victorian high-back chairs, a divan, and other antique finery that Judy and Ralph have been searching out over the years. A warming touch is added by an exposed brick wall that's more than a century old.

Judy presents guests with complimentary glasses of wine or cups of tea upon arrival, and she and Ralph will be happy to tell you everything about the historic village's seven-building museum complex that lies along tiny, narrow streets. They'll also be glad to make dinner reservations. Inn on the River serves fine gourmet-style meals, while the Zoar Tavern is a good bet for lighter fare.

Inn breakfasts, served in a bright country kitchen, are sumptuous feasts of omelets, sausage casseroles, homemade breads and rolls, and more.

Better yet, the inn's recently added outdoor deck overlooks Goose Run Creek and is a terrific place to sample Judy's breakfast goodies, weather permitting, of course.

How to get there: Take I–77 to exit 93. Then it's 3 miles to Zoar on State Route 212, following the signs. In the village, turn left on Second Street, right past the old Zoar Hotel. The Cider Mill is just down the street on the right.

∽

B: *Don't forget to say hello to Buddy the Cat, the mill's unofficial mascot. On my visit, he greeted me at the mill door.*

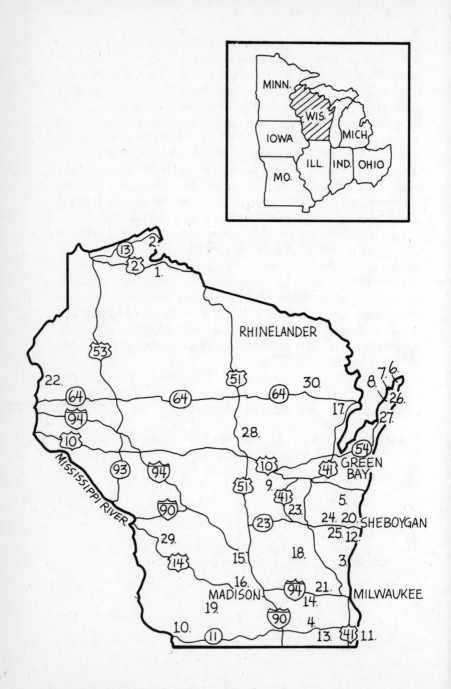

Wisconsin

Numbers on map refer to towns numbered below.

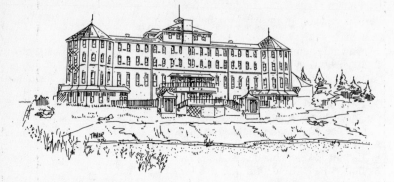

Hotel Chequamegon
Ashland, Wisconsin
54806

Innkeeper: Charles Gotschall, general manager
Address/Telephone: 101 West Front Street; (715) 682–9095
Rooms: 62, with 20 suites; all with private bath, air conditioning, TV, and
   phone.
Rates: $60 to $130, single or double, rooms; $80 to $130, single or double,
   suites; EP. Senior citizens' discount of 10 percent. Low-season rates
   from October 1 through May 1.
Open: All year.
Facilities and activities: Spa, indoor pool, 1 restaurant, lounge. Overlooks
   waters of Lake Superior and new 25-slip marina. Nearby: historic
   fishing village of Bayfield, with specialty and antiques shops; historic-
   home tours; ferry to Madeline Island, part of Apostle Islands National
   Lakeshore. Several downhill-ski hills a short drive away, including
   Blackjack, Big Powderhorn, Indianhead, and Telemark.

   The Hotel Chequamegon resembles one of those grand resort
hotels that sprang up on Great Lakes shorelines during the turn of
the century.
   Its massive white-clapboard styling harkens to more elegant
times. It is crowned on each end by rounded towers and capped
out back by an expansive veranda with two cupola gazebos
overlooking the water.

Inside, the warmth of the past enveloped me. Oak woodwork is everywhere, with posts and columns and high ceilings adding to the charm. Especially luxurious is the Northland Parlor Room, with its ornate, many-columned fireplace, brass chandelier, and high-back chairs; the room opens onto the huge veranda.

But the Hotel Chequamegon is not a historic hotel, although it rests upon a historic site. Opened in 1985, and built at a cost of $12.5 million on the site of the first hotel of the same name that burned down in 1908, it returns visitors to the days when Ashland was a booming lumber mecca.

Simple but dramatic guest rooms are examples of understated elegance. Floral prints, fluffy quilts, comfortable sofas and chairs, and great views from lakeside rooms provide special touches. Executive suites have large whirlpools, wet bar, antique-style mahogany sleigh beds, balloon drapes, lace curtains, and more.

Fifield's, the inn's elegant restaurant, features entrees like planked whitefish, fresh Lake Superior trout, blackened walleye, and an assortment of steaks and pastas. Molly Cooper's, fashioned to resemble a 1930s speakeasy, is an interesting spot for a nightcap.

How to get there: The hotel is located at the intersection of Highways 2 and 13, easily accessible from any direction.

᚜

B: *The hotel derives its name from an Indian word, the Chippewa's "shuqauwaumekong," which means a narrow strip of land running into a body of water.*

Grey Oak Guest House
Bayfield, Wisconsin
54814

Innkeepers: Mary and Jerry Phillips; Susan Larsen and Neil Howk
Address/Telephone: Seventh and Manypenny; (715) 779–5111
Rooms: 4; all with private bath.
Rates: $89 to $109, single or double, continental breakfast at Old
Rittenhouse Inn. Two-night minimum on weekends.
Open: All year, but weekends only November through April.
Facilities and activities: Located in heart of historic fishing village. Historic-
home walking tours, specialty shops, antiques stores, restaurants.
Nearby: boating, swimming, sailing through Apostle Islands National
Lakeshore; ferry to Madeline Island, with fur trader's museum, and
more.

The Grey Oak Guest House has an almost Gothic look to it.
Tall, gray oak trees tower above the handsome Victorian house,
and sunlight, piercing the dense leaf cover, shoots slender arrows
of brightness at the home. It was built in 1888 by a local
businessman.

Inside, the parlor is an example of understated Victorian
elegance. Fresh flowers color an antique marble-topped table, a
large wreath hangs over the fireplace, and soft salmon and
slate-blue pastels exude a peaceful, easy feeling that makes the inn
wear as comfortably as a favorite easy chair.

It's not surprising that guest rooms are elegantly done; the Grey Oak is co-owned by Mary and Jerry Phillips, Wisconsin inn pioneers of sorts, who also operate Bayfield's renowned Old Rittenhouse Inn and Le Château Boutin—exquisite Victorian mansions that are first-class examples of what country inns should strive to be.

Back at the Grey Oak, one first-floor room boasts an antique brass bed with lace quilt, fireplace, and an elegant Victorian lamp with fringed shade, while another features a four-poster English bed and its own fireplace.

Upstairs, a two-room suite has a huge brass bed and pretty Victorian furnishings. I walked through French doors to discover a sitting room that's more than cozy, with a handsome rocking chair and Victorian-style chandelier. The other room has a four-poster bed and working fireplace.

Just stroll down Rittenhouse Avenue to the Old Rittenhouse Inn for a continental breakfast of fresh seasonal fruit, home-baked breads, the Old Rittenhouse's own delicious preserves, juice, and beverages. Dinners here are gourmet treats, so don't hesitate to save one night for a feast.

How to get there: Wisconsin 13 brings you into Bayfield. Follow that road to the inn, located up the hill in the center of town.

Le Château Boutin
Bayfield, Wisconsin
54814

Innkeepers: Jerry and Mary Phillips
Address/Telephone: 7 Rice Avenue; (715) 779–5111
Rooms: 7, with 2 suites; all with private bath and fireplace.
Rates: $89 to $119, single or double, continental breakfast at nearby Old
   Rittenhouse Inn.
Open: All year.
Facilities and activities: Music room, sitting room, wraparound porch.
   Historic fishing village on shore of Lake Superior. Sailing, touring,
   hiking. Explore Apostle Islands National Lakeshore; visit Madeline
   Island and its fur-trading museum. Cross-country skiing (in season).
   Several village-wide festivals throughout year. Walk to restaurants.

   Jerry said that this massive sixteen-room Queen Anne mansion, completed in 1907, was home to Bayfield's first millionaire.
I could see he wasn't ashamed to show off his money.
   What a truly superb inn. I entered through heavy lead-glass
doors, stepping onto plank floors. To the left, the Music Room has
rare myrtle woodwork, Tiffany-style lamps, a lot of brass, silver
plating, and original stained glass. Several Art Nouveau pieces
(Jerry's favorites) highlight the room: a fabulous stone-and-tile
fireplace and some unusual light fixtures. Of course, there's also a
baby grand piano.

The dining room is formally gracious, with gorgeous lead glass and fine hand-carved woodwork. The huge dining room table is original to the home.

What a treat to look out the tall windows of my bedroom and see the choppy waters of Lake Superior; in fact, most guest rooms have lake views. The unique woodwork of tiger birch and maple is a handsome complement to the Tiffany-style stained-glass and lead windows.

My favorite room is an ornate master suite with a second-floor balcony. I wanted to build a roaring fire in the hearth, crawl inside the bed with its shiny brass headboard, and pull the covers up to my chin. After all, whipping breezes off the lake had added quite a chill to the spring day.

A light continental breakfast is served in the dining room at your leisure. Jerry's Old Rittenhouse Inn (just a short drive away) serves fantastic six-course gourmet dinners in an elegant Victorian setting; dishes include grilled steak sautéed in Burgundy wine, butter, and garlic; steak stuffed with oysters; and the fresh fish catch of the day. Or you can try area restaurants (like the Bayfield Inn, Greunke's, or The Pier) for some Lake Superior whitefish.

How to get there: From Duluth, take U.S. 53 south through that city to the bridge leading to Superior, Wisconsin. Pick up State Route 2 and go east. Near Ashland, turn north on State Route 13 and drive through Bayfield. Near the lakeshore, just around a bend in the road, turn left on Rice Avenue to the inn.

☀

B: *Builder Frank Boutin was a turn-of-the-century lumber baron. That's why there are so many exotic woods in this lovely inn.*

Old Rittenhouse Inn
Bayfield, Wisconsin
54814

Innkeepers: Jerry and Mary Phillips
Address/Telephone: 301 Rittenhouse Avenue (mailing address: Box 584);
  (715) 779–5765
Rooms: 11; all with private bath, 10 with fireplace, 4 with whirlpool, some
  with wheelchair access.
Rates: $69 to $169, single or double, EPB. Special off-season rates.
Open: All year.
Facilities and activities: Three romantic dining rooms. Recreational activities
  of all kinds available: fishing, sailing, Apostle Islands National
  Lakeshore; fur-trading museum and other attractions on Madeline
  Island; canoeing on Brule River; annual festivals; cross-country
  skiing (in season).

    I sat in an elegant Victorian dining room in the early morning
as an immaculately dressed Jerry, resplendent in a black velvet
vest—with a long gold watch fob and a wide bow tie—served me
an exquisite breakfast.
    After sipping freshly pressed apple cider, I started on brandied
peaches and blueberries in sour cream. Next came delicious New
Orleans–style cinnamon French toast and a tall glass of milk.
    The sound of soft classical music wafted through the room,

which was bathed in rich Victorian-print wallpaper, with brass chandeliers, and antique oak and mahogany tables and chairs. I pulled my seat closer to the roaring fire in the hearth.

"I think it's important that the feeling inside a home fits the personality of the house," Jerry said as we talked about what made a good country inn, "and it must deliver personal service that makes it a special place to stay."

The Old Rittenhouse Inn scores well on both points. It's an opulent 1890 Victorian red-brick and wood-shingle mansion, with a long wraparound veranda and gabled roof. Elegant dining rooms and sitting areas are done in formal prints, with fine Victorian furnishings and all kinds of period lamps.

Jerry's guest rooms are immaculate; many have four-poster beds, marble-topped dressers and vanities, and some have fireplaces to take the chill off cold winter days. Several boast tall windows looking out toward blustery Lake Superior.

New inn rooms are incredibly spacious; I don't think it would be an exaggeration to say that they're the largest I've ever seen in any country inn. Big brass, iron-rail, and walnut beds are inviting. Then there are pretty stained-glass windows depicting Bayfield lakeshore scenes. All the new rooms have their own fireplaces.

The inn also offers delicious multi-course gourmet meals. Here Mary is the genius. Her specialties include Steak *Bercy* stuffed with oysters, fresh trout poached in champagne, and pork ragout. Homemade breads are served steaming in heaping baskets. Save room for incredible desserts like Jerry's white-chocolate cheesecake.

How to get there: From Minneapolis–St. Paul, take I–94 east to U.S. 63. Take 63 north to State Route 2 and go east to Route 13. Take 13 north to Bayfield. The inn is on the corner of Rittenhouse and Third.

∂⃘

B: *A romantic inn along the spectacular shoreline of Lake Superior with historic islands nearby to explore—an almost perfect destination.*

Stagecoach Inn
Cedarburg, Wisconsin
53012

Innkeepers: Liz and Brook Brown
Address/Telephone: W61 N520 Washington Avenue; (414) 375–0208 or
  375–3035
Rooms: 12, with 5 suites; all with private bath and air conditioning, suites
  with double whirlpool and TV. No smoking inn.
Rates: $45, single; $55, double; $85, suites; continental breakfast.
Open: All year.
Facilities and activities: Stagecoach Pub, candy store, book shop. In heart of
  historic Cedarburg; walk to Cedar Creek Settlement, the old Woolen
  Mill, Stone Mill Winery, antiques, craft, and specialty shops, restau-
  rants, and art galleries. Also bike trails, golf, fishing, cross-country
  skiing, River Edge Nature Center, museum, Ozaukee Pioneer Village,
  Ozaukee Covered Bridge (last covered bridge in Wisconsin) nearby.

Stagecoach drivers slept on the basement's dirt floor in bunks
made of stone rubble and straw. The chimney that took the flue for
the driver's potbellied stove still stands.

The stagecoach-stop charm carries over to guest rooms that
are decorated with period antiques. "We wanted to keep the inn
authentic," Liz said. "This is a restoration-minded community."

That's an understatement. The Stagecoach Inn is in the heart of the historic downtown district, which was anchored by the Wittenburg Woolen Mills, now restored and called the Cedar Creek Settlement. (The mill provided wool uniforms for soldiers during the Civil War.)

More than 150 rare "cream city" brick and stone buildings stand throughout town, many dating back to the mid-1800s.

Everything at the inn is cozy and cheery, with many special touches. Liz created the pretty stencils on the walls and reconditioned the original pine-wood plank floors. Her antique four-poster and brass beds are covered with Laura Ashley comforters. Suites are decorated with more antiques, wicker, Laura Ashley fabrics, and boast two-person whirlpools.

The Stagecoach Pub is located on the inn's first floor. I had an imported beer from a massive antique oak cooler at a one-hundred-year-old bar. The tin ceiling adds to the frontier charm. Folk singers entertain here on evenings twice a month. Liz serves breakfast here, too, at antique tavern tables. (Or you can take your breakfast on the back deck.) She offers hot croissants, juice, cereal, fresh fruit, bran muffins, coffee, and herbal teas, and she'll recommend a good spot for dinner in the historic town. You can play games and cards here at night, in a warm coffeehouse atmosphere. Late-night sweet tooths and bookworms can find a candy shop and fine bookstore on the first floor.

Look for these inn "originals": the heavy front door dates from 1853; the intricate woodwork on the door and window frames, as well as the crown molding above the front door, is made of single pieces of wood carved to look multi-layered; and the handsome cherry staircase banister is authentic.

How to get there: From Chicago, take I–94 to I–43 and get off at exit 17 (Cedarburg). Take Pioneer Road 3 miles to Washington Avenue and turn right into Cedarburg. The inn is located on the right side of the street.

❀

B: *Newest addition—a historical annex to the main inn. Called the Weber Haus, the 1847 frame building (just across the street) is one of the oldest operating structures in Cedarburg. Honeymoon couples love the privacy, and its three suites are decorated with four-poster beds, wicker, and antiques. It also boasts a garden and picnic area.*

The Washington House Inn
Cedarburg, Wisconsin
53012

Innkeeper: Wendy Porterfield
Address/Telephone: W62 N573 Washington Avenue; (414) 375– 3550 or
   (800) 369–4088
Rooms: 29, with 1 suite; all with private bath, air conditioning, TV, and
   phone. Wheelchair access.
Rates: $59 to $139, single or double, continental breakfast. Special
   packages available.
Open: All year.
Facilities and activities: Situated in heart of historic Cedarburg; walk to
   restaurants and Cedar Creek Settlement: old Woolen Mill, Stone Mill
   Winery, antiques, craft, specialty shops. Short drive to Ozaukee
   Pioneer Village, Ozaukee Covered Bridge (last covered bridge in
   Wisconsin).

Cedarburg is a historic woolen mill town, with many rare
"cream city" brick and stone buildings dating from the mid-1800s.
In fact, the downtown area alone boasts more historic structures
than any city west of Philadelphia!
   One of these is The Washington House Inn, a country-

Victorian "cream city" brick building completed in 1886. The tall front doors and authentic frontier ambience are softened by a long lobby sprinkled with Victorian furnishings, with rich parquet floors, brass chandeliers, and a marble fireplace.

I looked at the original hotel register that recorded visitors during the months of 1895. How did anyone ever have the time to write in that fancy scroll? I also noticed an unusual display: a "wedding brick" discovered during recent restoration with the date "1886" and the names of the happy couple scratched on it.

The guest rooms are named for leading citizens of historic Cedarburg. The country-Victorian decorations are absolutely charming, with floral wallpapers, fancy armoires, cozy down quilts, fresh flowers, and more. I really like the lead-glass transom windows of some rooms.

In the newly restored rooms, there's more of a plain country feeling, but there's nothing plain about the decor. The exposed brick walls and beamed ceilings are spectacular.

Then there are some very deluxe quarters; my favorite has country-style antiques, loft beds cozied by their own fireplace, and another loft area that boasts a 200-gallon spa tub warmed by a second fireplace.

It's fun to eat breakfast in a dining room that boasts white pressed-tin ceilings, oak tables and chairs, and tall windows that wash the room in light. (Of course, you may have breakfast in bed, too.) Home-baked breads, cakes, and rolls are made from recipes found in an authentic turn-of-the-century Cedarburg cookbook. Cereal, fresh fruit, and beverages also are offered.

One of Wendy's favorite times of the day is the afternoon social hour in the dining room, with an opportunity to share with guests her love of this historic town. A manteled fireplace with Victorian sofas and chairs just off the main dining area makes things more cozy.

How to get there: From Chicago, take I–94 to I–43, just north of Milwaukee, and get off at the Cedarburg exit. This road eventually changes to Wisconsin 57; follow it into town (where it becomes Washington Street). At Center Street, turn left and park in the lot behind the hotel.

✳

B: *A historic hotel, elegant antiques—and whirlpool tubs, too.*

Allyn House Inn
Delavan, Wisconsin
53115

Innkeepers: Joe Johnson and Ron Markwell
Address/Telephone: 511 East Walworth Avenue; (414) 728–9090
Rooms: 8 share 6 baths; all with air conditioning. No smoking inn.
Rates: $75, single or double, EPB. Midweek discounts and corporate rates
available. Two-night minimum on holiday weekends.
Open: All year.
Facilities and activities: Evening social hour on weekends. Three formal
parlors, library reading room. Patio, Victorian rose and herb garden.
Nearby: restaurants, Circus Hall of Fame. Short drive to Lake Geneva
resort, Kettle Moraine State Park, Alpine Valley Music Center, skiing,
antiquing.

This 1885 Queen Anne mansion boasts one of the most
elaborate restorations of "high Victorian" style in the Midwest.
Walnut woodwork, frescoed 13-foot ceilings and ten Italian
marble fireplaces will delight inn lovers and house preservationists
alike.

Eye-catching stained, lead, and etched glass, parquet floors,
and brass chandeliers add even more elegant touches. And I felt
like royalty when ascending a magnificent three-story walnut
staircase that rises to a stunning horseshoe window.

Marvelous antique furnishings predate 1900, the bounty of Joe and Ron's multi-year collection. I especially liked the Wave Crest (New England glass, circa 1890s); it's one of the finest sets of its kind in the Heartland.

In spite of the inn's opulent stylings, Joe likes to point out Victorian era curiosities. "Who else but those Victorians would think of making a cow's hoof into an inkwell?" he said, holding up the antique for inspection.

Guest rooms are spectacular re-creations of Victorian splendor. Besides a photograph of the home's matriarch "trying to smile," according to Joe, Mrs. Allyn's Room features a piece original to the house (and my favorite Victorian gadget), a Murphy-type bed that resembles a fine walnut wardrobe, finials and all.

Mr. Allyn's Room has black print Victorian wallpaper, besides a marble fireplace and a four-poster mahogany bed. "People gave me funny looks when I chose this pattern," Joe said. "But I thought it would match the house's architectural character." It sure does.

Hallways are some of the widest I've ever seen, so rooms seem private and quiet. But even they are finely furnished. Joe pointed out that the third floor's antique Victorian sofa was ticketed for the Iowa governor's mansion before the innkeepers decided more people would see it here. "It doesn't look as though it's ever been used," I said. "It's so uncomfortable, it should last a thousand years," he retorted.

Joe and Ron make all their jams and jellies, perfect for smothering homemade muffins and breads that are served at breakfast along with fresh fruit, bacon, egg casseroles, and more.

How to get there: From Milwaukee, take Wisconsin 50 west into Delavan and continue west on Wisconsin 11 to the inn.

☀

B: *Ron used to sing in the Chicago Symphony Chorus; maybe you can convince him to croon a few bars from the musical* Les Misérables.

Siebken's
Elkhart Lake, Wisconsin
53020

Innkeepers: Doug and Pam Siebken
Address/Telephone: 284 South Lake Street; (414) 876–2600
Rooms: 53, plus 1 lake cottage; 34 with private bath. Pets OK.
Rates: $52 to $60, single; $62 to $70, double; EP. Lower rates weekdays and May and September. Two- to four-night minimum during Road America race weekends.
Open: May through September, cottage open winter.
Facilities and activities: Full-service inn, Opera House bar, antiques store, gift shop, sun porch, television and game room. Water sports, boat rentals, golf course within walking distance; horseback riding, antiquing, go-carting. Road America, internationally famous Indy-style and stock-car racing.

Siebken's really hops during Road America weekends, when internationally famous race-car drivers come to relax in the old Opera House bar after spending an unnerving day speeding down the straightaway.

Doug's family has run this turn-of-the-century summer lodge, situated just across the street from Elkhart Lake, since 1916. It's filled with country antiques, wicker furniture—and friendly critters.

I was greeted at the door by McDuff and Nigel, the inn's Irish wolfhounds. Farley, a French sheepdog, rounds out the four-legged menagerie. Their gruff barking is just a friendly welcome. After I became part of the inn "family," I was often called upon to gently stroke these lugs behind their ears while they tapped their paws in delight.

A large enclosed sun porch on the first floor, one of my favorite spots, reminds me of beach houses on Cape Cod. The television/game room is another favorite, especially when I visit in the fall during the major-league baseball playoffs.

Pam's antique-filled dining rooms serve large portions of Wisconsin-style homemade foods. My roast duck on a bed of wild rice virtually filled a platter-sized dish. The rest of the meal, including fresh vegetables, broccoli soup, a large salad, and home-baked bread and rolls, was overwhelming. Of course, I made room for the dessert platter: a choice of homemade chocolate cherry cake, raspberry tortes, or ice cream.

Rooms in the main building and annex are eclectically styled, comfortable, and airy. My room was quiet and cozy, with a bouncy spring bed covered with a brightly colored quilt. Summer guests can use ceiling fans to cool their rooms; hallway radiators provide heat for chilly Wisconsin nights; fluffy comforters and wool blankets further ward off chills.

There's a small bar in the main house, but the real fun is at the Opera House bar across the courtyard, where locals often come to down a few. See if you can get Doug to roll out the piano and sing some of his wacky tunes.

How to get there: Siebken's is about 60 miles north of Milwaukee. Take I–43 to Wisconsin Highway 57 (Plymouth exit). Continue north past Plymouth; then turn left on County Trunk J and right on 67 to Elkhart Lake.

The Griffin Inn
Ellison Bay, Wisconsin
54210

Innkeepers: Jim and Laurie Roberts
Address/Telephone: 11976 Mink River Road; (414) 854–4306
Rooms: 10 share 2½ baths; all with air conditioning. No smoking inn.
Rates: $63, single; $67, double; $69, cottages; EPB. Winter weekend
  packages available.
Open: All year.
Facilities and activities: Sitting room, sports court, and gazebo on grounds.
  Fishing, boating, and swimming within walking distance. Golf,
  horseback riding, tennis, art galleries, potters, antiques shops, restau-
  rants, and the Peninsula Players theater group within short drive.

Here's a little bit of New England on the rugged Door County
peninsula. New owners Jim and Laurie have done lots of restoration work on their charming white clapboard inn, built in 1921,
which rests among nine quiet acres that include an apple orchard
and lovely gazebo.

I like the cozy country feeling of the main floor, with its
library and large stone fireplace surrounded by high-back Queen
Anne–style chairs that make it a popular spot for night talkers.

The dining room is all rich wood tones with lots of antiques,
and a decorative wood-burning stove in the corner that brings
back memories of North Woods winter adventures.

Ten quaint rooms line the hallway of the second floor. Each boasts country prints and is decorated in antique and country style reproductions. All have antique double beds adorned with handmade quilts. You'll also find Victorian dressers, tall armoires, and comfy rockers in your room.

Laurie prepares a huge country breakfast, prepared fresh in her kitchen daily. Treats may include fresh seasonal fruit, German apple pancakes or a soufflé, freshly baked breads and muffins, homemade coffee cake, and coffee, teas, and cocoa.

For cottage guests, Laurie offers a breakfast basket with the day's fresly baked selections, juice, and coffee.

Bring your bicycles to explore the backroad beauty of "The Door's" rugged countryside, or the spectacular shoreline of Green Bay and Lake Michigan. Or drive to the many art galleries and specialty shops that line the streets of tiny lakeshore villages that dot the peninsula. Maybe you'll even want to take a ferry across "Death's Door," a sometimes turbulent channel of water, to Washington Island—itself a great getaway.

How to get there: Take Route 42 to Ellison Bay and turn east on Mink River Road. The inn is about 2 blocks up the road.

Eagle Harbor Inn
Ephraim, Wisconsin
54211

Innkeepers: Ronald and Barbara Schultz
Address/Telephone: Route 42 (mailing address: P.O. Box 72B); (414) 854–2121
Rooms: 9, plus 12 cottages; all with private bath.
Rates: $64 to $96, single or double, EPB. Two-night minimum on advance reservations; 3-night minimum in July, August, first 2 weekends in October, holiday weekends.
Open: All year (inn only).
Facilities and activities: Front parlor, fireplace room. Outdoor basketball court. Nearby: hiking, cross-country skiing at Peninsula State Park south of the inn. Famous Wilson's Ice Cream Shop up the road. Art galleries, craft stores, and specialty shops in harbor towns. Several area restaurants serving Door County fish boils. Charter fishing, water sports, seasonal Door County apple and cherry festivals.

Eagle Harbor Inn is a charming white clapboard building near the bay shore of fabulous Door County in perhaps the most picturesque town this peninsula has to offer.

Ronald and Barbara are former Chicagoans: She owned a boutique in that city's fashionable Lincoln Park area; he is a graphic designer. Now they've retreated to the beauty of "The

Door" to get away from that hurried life-style. "We deserved something different after twenty years of work," Barbara told me.

Nine cozy guest rooms are in the main house; during summer, there are also housekeeping and do-it-yourself sleeping cottages, which do not have breakfast privileges.

I found the guest rooms warm and intimate, yet unusually roomy. "We've added more special touches to guest rooms," Barbara said. They are handsome and antique-filled, with chests of inlaid wood, dressing tables, tall headboards, and other treasures.

Pegged floors made of pine run along the first floor. The front parlor, with its comfy sofa, is a good place to relax and unwind from a day's boutique-and-art gallery hopping. In back, the quaint fireplace room is littered with collectibles: antique pewter mugs on the mantel, branding irons, and baskets of colorful yarn. A 1960s-style Grundig console stereo looks exactly like the one my Mom had.

Breakfast is taken on an enclosed porch overlooking the handsome grounds. It includes freshly squeezed orange juice, fresh baked coffeecakes, eggs and ham, French toast, pancakes, blintzes, and more.

For dinner, I head over to the White Gull Inn at nearby Fish Creek for a local specialty—the famous Door County Fish Boil, where whitefish is boiled in a huge flaming caldron. Al Johnson's Swedish Restaurant in Sister Bay, a short ride away, serves tasty food, including incredibly good, paper-thin Swedish pancakes with lingonberry topping. Another attraction here are goats grazing on top of the grass-thatched roof of the building.

How to get there: Take Wisconsin 42 north from Sturgeon Bay and continue to Ephraim. The Eagle Harbor Inn driveway is on the right side of the road.

The Ephraim Inn
Ephraim, Wisconsin
54211

Innkeepers: Nancy and Tim Christofferson
Address/Telephone: Route 42, (mailing address: P.O. Box 247); (414) 854–4515
Rooms: 17; all with private bath, air conditioning, and TV.
Rates: $75 to $125, single or double, EPB. Two-night minimum throughout year. Three-night minimum during Memorial and Labor Day weekends, Fall Festival, and Regatta weekend.
Open: April through first weekend in October; weekends during winter.
Facilities and activities: Across the street from bay and beach. Next to Wilson's Ice Cream Parlor; short walk to specialty shops and studios, sports facilities and activities (boating, sailboarding). Short drive to restaurants, golf, hiking trails, ski trails, Peninsula Players Theater, and Birch Creek Music Center.

I believe Ephraim has the most beautiful harbor in all Door County. And the Ephraim Inn, located in the heart of this charming village's historic district, faces that harbor, affording guests one of the finest vistas around.

The inn itself, despite its conspicuous setting right next to the always packed Wilson's Ice Cream Parlor, is a haven for relaxed hospitality. Built about six years ago, it exudes the warmth of a

318

fine country home, and its wood beams, exposed brick, and country antique reproductions add to the charm.

More than half of the guest rooms enjoy a magnificent view of the harbor and the tiered green bluffs that rise above it. Each is identified by a hand-carved and hand-painted wooden plaque affixed to the door.

Tulip Heart is one of my favorites, with its four-poster pine bed, fluffy bed quilt, and country cupboard for clothes. I especially liked the Shaker-style wall pegs that circle the room. An antique jelly cupboard keeps modern conveniences like the television out of sight.

Forget-Me-Not has more of the same, including an iron-and-brass-rail day bed and hand-stenciling; and Tulip Star, on the second floor, boasts a four-poster English bed and an alcove window that affords more great harbor views.

For breakfast, count on fresh fruit and juices, Colombian coffee, homemade granola, freshly-baked muffins, egg dishes, omelets, and more, all served in cozy dining areas. Perhaps you'd enjoy a table across from a crackling fireplace on a brisk fall morning.

The inn common room also faces the harbor and exudes a very masculine feeling. It's all oak paneling and exposed brick, with another fireplace and soft sofas for cozy night talk.

How to get there: From Sturgeon Bay, take Wisconsin 42 into Ephraim. The home is just after Wilson's Ice Cream Parlor.

❋

B: *Wilson's Ice Cream Parlor, a Door County landmark since 1906, is where I first caught a glimpse of my wife-to-be. We were both staying at different country inns at the time.*

The Whistling Swan
Fish Creek, Wisconsin
54212

Innkeepers: Jan and Andy Coulson
Address/Telephone: Main Street (mailing address: P.O. Box 193); (414) 868-3442
Rooms: 7, including 2 suites; all with private bath.
Rates: $85 to $100, single or double; $106, suites; EPB at White Gull Inn, November 1 through April 30 only; at other times, continental breakfast served on veranda. Children $10 per day (free if in crib).
Open: Daily May through October, Christmas week, and weekends throughout the rest of the year.
Facilities and activities: Sitting and music rooms, elegant Whistling Swan Shop (women's and girls' fashions). Located in the heart of historic Fish Creek. Walk to restaurants, scores of specialty shops, antiques stores, art galleries. State parks and golfing nearby.

What do you say about a house that originally sat in Marinette, Wisconsin, 18 miles across the waters of Green Bay, was dismantled, loaded on sleds, moved across the ice during winter, and reassembled at its present location—as a gambling casino?

"I'd say it had one of the most interesting histories of any house in Door County," Andy said.

320

Just a few years ago, The Whistling Swan was a grand, but tired-looking reminder of the turn-of-the-century resort era that boomed on the Door County peninsula. Things improved dramatically, however, after Jan and Andy purchased the historic, white-clapboard building.

Now The Whistling Swan, built in 1887, is not only Door County's oldest inn, but one of the most comfortable, too.

Andy and Jan have lovingly restored inn antiques and have added new ones to the building's collection. The handsome foyer, a welcome respite on both cold winter and hot summer days, once again boasts a baby grand piano at which the original owner's wife, Henriette Welcker, entertained Victorian-era guests.

Jan designed and decorated all the guest rooms. I especially like Number One, with its antique four-poster pine bed and windows overlooking bustling Main Street.

I noticed the old-fashioned transom windows above all guest room doors—another charming reminder of days gone by. Inside Room Four, a tall Victorian headboard commanded my attention. But what really caught my eye was a hand-painted claw-footed bathtub.

A long enclosed porch with huge windows facing the shops, sights, and sounds of Fish Creek is a great spot to eat breakfast and watch people. Your summer meal might include freshly-squeezed juice, homemade rolls, muffins, and croissants, freshly made granola, fruit in season, cereal, and beverages.

You'll also eat in style. Handsome lace napkins and place settings, linen tablecloths, English garden china, and fresh flowers on the table are pampering pluses.

Winter breakfasts, served at Andy and Jan's White Gull Inn just down the street, might mean pancakes, eggs, bacon, and more.

How to get there: From Sturgeon Bay, go north on Wisconsin 42 into Fish Creek. Turn left at Main Street, to the inn.

❧

B: *Just walk to the White Gull Inn for evening meals. Romantic candlelight dinners feature beef Wellington and baked Door County whitefish. Or try an authentic fish boil, served Wednesday and Friday through Sunday evenings in summer and Wednesday and Saturday nights in winter.*

White Gull Inn
Fish Creek, Wisconsin
54212

Innkeepers: Andy and Jan Coulson
Address/Telephone: 4225 Main Street (mailing address: P.O. Box 159-C);
(414) 868–3517
Rooms: 14, plus cottages and buildings for multiple couples; 9 rooms and
all cottages and buildings with private bath, all with air conditioning.
Rates: $58, single or double with shared bath; $70 to $105, single or
double with private bath; EP. Midweek winter packages. Two-night
minimum on weekends, 3-night minimum on holidays.
Open: All year.
Facilities and activities: Wheelchair access to dining room; famous Door
County fish boil featured on Wednesday, Friday, Saturday, and
Sunday nights. Situated in the heart of historic Fish Creek: Walk to
art galleries, specialty, and antiques shops. State parks and golfing
nearby.

Russ Ostrand, the inn's "Master Boiler," is a bear of a man.
He sits perched on a small chair in the dining room, pumping his
concertina and singing "oom-pah" songs to guests as they devour
his latest fish boil—whitefish, potatoes, and a secret recipe boiled
outside in a huge caldron with flames darting toward the sky.
Served with hot loaves of bread, homemade coleslaw, and mugs of

ice cold beer, it's a Door County institution. A tasty extra is home-baked cherry pie for dessert.

I like the casual atmosphere of the White Gull Inn; it makes me feel right at home. The landmark 1896 white clapboard inn also looks "New England picture perfect."

Andy said that, according to local legend, the inn originally sat on the other side of Green Bay, 18 miles away, in Marinette, Wisconsin. During a frigid Door County winter around the turn of the century, it was dragged on a crudely fashioned log sled by draft horses across the frozen waters to its present location. Sort of a Victorian mobile home.

The guest rooms are small and cozy, comfortably furnished with country-Victorian antiques that create an intimate, romantic retreat. I love the iron-rail beds that Andy has painted a cheery white. There are also high ceilings and plank floors covered with braided scatter rugs.

The inn lobby has a large fireplace often ablaze to take the chill off a typically nippy Door County morning. Besides Russ's famous fish boils, the dining room also serves dinner feasts like beef Wellington, baked whitefish (a local favorite), and Chicken Piccata.

How to get there: From Milwaukee, take Wisconsin 43 north. Near Manitowoc, take Wisconsin 42 north past Sturgeon Bay into Door County. In Fish Creek, turn left at the stop sign at the bottom of a hill along the twisting road and proceed about 3 blocks to the inn.

*

B: *Don't miss the fish boil, especially you first-timers. It's not just a dinner; it's a real happening.*

Oakwood Lodge
Green Lake, Wisconsin
54941

Innkeeper: Marcy Klepinger
Address/Telephone: 365 Lake Street; (414) 294–6580
Rooms: 11; 7 with private bath, some with balcony.
Rates: $40 to $60, single; $50 to $70, double; EPB. Children, cribs, $5 extra per night. October through April winter rates available. Two-night minimum on weekends; 3-night minimum on holiday weekends.
Open: All year.
Facilities and activities: Family room, dining room, room balconies, patio, private lake pier and raft. Water sports and activities. Will arrange midweek golf packages. Three golf courses nearby; horseback riding; specialty shops in town; cross-country skiing.

The huge white cottage with the arched second-floor balcony jumped out at me as I approached the bend in the country road. It was surrounded by tall trees, perched lakeside in a perfect getaway setting.

I discovered that this is one of only a few buildings remaining of the original massive Oakwood Hotel complex built in the 1860s. Now it's a charming inn with "the best view of the Green Lake," according to Marcy.

324

We sat outside on her back-porch dining terrace, just a stone's throw from the lake. Marcy suggested that I try one of her breakfast specialties: homemade buttermilk pancakes. She needn't have said more. There were also hearty helpings of her homemade breads and rolls, and cakes and sweet rolls for morning sweet tooths. What a fabulous way to enjoy the day's first meal—lakeside al fresco.

Marcy has fashioned eleven charming rooms in this historic building; my favorites are four upstairs facing the lake. I like to just sit and watch all the colorful sails bob along the waters. Some of the rooms have high walnut headboards and brass beds. And she's constantly adding to the inn's antique collection.

Marcy doesn't serve dinner, but the romantic Viennese dining room of The Heidel House resort is a one-minute drive down the road. Marcy also recommends Norton's, a nearby seafood restaurant right on the lake—a local favorite. I also like Carver's on the Lake (open only in summer), specializing in French cuisine, and Alfred's.

How to get there: Travel Wisconsin 23 west to Business 23 and then turn left on South Street. Take South to Lake Street and turn right. Oakwood Lodge is at the intersection (bend of the road) of Lake Street and Illinois Avenue.

❋

B: *Marcy claims her inn boasts the best view of Green Lake. Just take breakfast on her lakeside porch, and you'll agree with her.*

Wisconsin House
Stage Coach Inn
Hazel Green, Wisconsin
53811

Innkeepers: Betha and John Mueller
Address/Telephone: 2105 East Main Street; (608) 854–2233
Rooms: 9; 5 with private bath and air conditioning.
Rates: $35 to $60, single; $40 to $65, double, second night $5 less; EPB.
Open: All year.
Facilities and activities: Sitting room, antiques shop, gazebo, stagecoach.
Nearby: biking, canoeing, skiing, Fever River Trails, historic archi-
tecture, antiques and crafts shops in Galena, Illinois, riverboat rides,
and dog racing in Dubuque, Iowa.

This 1846 stagecoach inn served travelers on the Milwaukee-
to-Galena, Illinois, stage. An old tin horn from one of those
historic stagecoaches sits in the upstairs hallway. And there's a
copy of the original stagecoach handbill on the wall in the parlor.

John, a tinsmith, makes the stencils for patterns adorning the
walls and plank floors and entertains visitors with his Swiss
heritage–style yodeling. Betha collects antique cookie cutters and
maple-syrup molds and sometimes sings some of her Norwegian
heritage folk tunes.

The inn is handsomely decorated with all kinds of antiques and collectibles, the passion of more than thirty years' antiquing by the innkeepers. My favorite is a 16-foot-long breakfast dining table found at the nearby New Diggings Methodist Church. "We were lucky enough to find these balloon-back chairs, the type made in Galena in the 1840s," John added.

Upstairs, the guest rooms are furnished with country antiques, including some with canopy beds, high-back chairs, bright curtains, and more. All are named for noteworthy inn visitors, including one for U. S. Grant, once a frequenter of the Wisconsin House.

New rooms are graced with hand stenciling; two are decorated to celebrate the innkeepers' Swiss and Norwegian heritages.

"We like to keep on schedule, so breakfast is served at 8:00 A.M. sharp," Betha said. It consists of family-style fare, with meat, eggs, French toast, home-baked muffins, toast, cheese, and potatoes. Or maybe Betha's prize-winning recipe for applesauce pancakes or scrambled eggs with chili sauce. Specially prepared gourmet dinners are offered by reservation Friday and Saturday, with cocktails offered before the meal; some of the choices include Yankee pot roast, *torsk* (broiled codfish), beef barbecued ribs, and more—all made from authentic country inn recipes. (Here's a secret: Betha and John surprise guests with Swiss folk songs and yodeling after their hearty meals.)

Some new additions include a large gazebo out back, which is the centerpiece for polka and *bratwurst* parties; a stagecoach (built to three-quarter size) that John uses on special occasions to give rides to guests; and Ole and Olga's Place, a one-bedroom, 1850s miner's cottage, country-furnished in Norwegian antiques, located nearby. Ask about rental rates.

How to get there: Take U.S. 20 west from Galena to Highway 80 north into Wisconsin and continue to the town of Hazel Green. In town, the name of the road changes to North Percival. Turn right on Fairplay and go to East Main Street. The inn is on the corner.

❀

B: *This handsome inn has been featured in several magazines, including* Midwest Living *and* Country Living, *and Betha's recipes have been selected for inclusion in a number of cookbooks.*

The Manor House
Kenosha, Wisconsin
53140

Innkeepers: Ronnie and Mary Rzeplinski
Address/Telephone: 6536 Third Avenue; (414) 658–0014
Rooms: 4; all with private bath, air conditioning, and TV.
Rates: $80 to $110, single or double, continental breakfast.
Open: All year.
Facilities and activities: Formal parlor, sitting room. Formal gardens, sunken lily pool, water fountain, and gazebo. Walk across street to lakeside park. Walking tours of Kenosha Lakeshore historic places. Short drive to restaurants, Lake Michigan charter fishing, boating, beaches, bike trails, golf, downhill and cross-country skiing. Lakeside Players theater, Chiwaukee Prairie conservation area, Palumbo Civil War exhibit.

If you consider a stately, historic Georgian mansion overlooking Lake Michigan to be the perfect getaway, get into your car immediately and proceed to The Manor House.

This magnificent home, the largest in Kenosha, was built in the mid-1920s for a vice president of Nash Motor Company, forerunner to the American Motors Corporation. Ronnie and Mary have tastefully restored it to elegance with English antiques and furnishings from the 1800s; you'll lounge on Chippendale,

Queen Anne, and even a smattering of furnishings from the Rothschilds' Mentmore Manor in Buckinghamshire, England.

Rich oak paneling, glistening crystal chandeliers, arched hallways, and marble fireplaces add to the splendor. I was overwhelmed by the grand oak staircase that greets visitors as they step into the home's entryway. And the formal dining room, sparkling with antique crystal, is an especially handsome room in which to eat breakfast and get acquainted with other guests.

The Purple Room is the manor's largest; a unique touch is the small nurse's bed at the foot of a massive antique four-poster bed that dominates the room. A tall Victorian dressing mirror adds another touch of elegance, as do the room's small chandelier and manteled working fireplace. It also has separate men's and women's dressing rooms and a lake view.

I especially like the Rose Room's canopied Sheraton bed, which dates from 1780. With brass chandelier, a connecting dressing room, and a view of the manor's formal rose garden, it provides an especially romantic ambience for couples celebrating a "special" day.

Several common rooms, and the grounds themselves, hold their own excitement. A grand sitting room features wonderful Chippendale sofas and a baby grand piano. The second-floor foyer is an antique lover's paradise. And the manicured lawns, gardens, and fountains invite romantic hand-in-hand walks in a colorful and fragrant haven.

Breakfasts of home-baked goods, fruits, tea, and juices are served in the elegant dining room.

How to get there: From Chicago or Milwaukee, take I–94 to Wisconsin 50 and turn east. Follow to Third Avenue and turn left, continuing to the inn.

❀

B: *Stroll across the street to an unspoiled 11-acre lakeside park and enjoy breathtaking sunrises.*

The American Club
Kohler, Wisconsin
53044

Innkeeper: Susan Porter Green
Address/Telephone: Highland Drive; (414) 457–8000 or (800) 344–2838;
   FAX (414) 457–0299
Rooms: 160; all with private Kohler whirlpool bath, air conditioning, TV,
   and phone. Wheelchair access.
Rates: May 1–October 31: $99 to $255, single; $122 to $292, double; EP.
   November 1–April 30: $86 to $230, single; $109 to $267, double; EP.
   Each child over 10, $12 extra; children 10 and younger free.
   Two-night minimum on weekends from July 1 through Labor Day,
   and December 30–31.
Open: All year.
Facilities and activities: Nine restaurants and full-service dining rooms.
   Renowned for extravagant buffets, special-event and holiday feasts;
   large Sunday brunch. Ballroom. Sports Core, a world-class health
   club. River Wildlife, 500 acres of private woods for hiking, horseback
   riding, hunting, fishing, trapshooting, canoeing. Cross-country skiing
   and ice skating. Also Kohler Design Center, shops at Woodlake,
   Kohler Arts Center, Waelderhaus. Nearby: antiquing, lake charter
   fishing, Kettle Moraine State Forest, Road America (auto racing).

   Just 4 miles from the shoreline of Lake Michigan, amid tall
pines, patches of white birch, scrubbed farmhouses, and black soil,

is one of Wisconsin's best-kept secrets. It's The American Club, a uniquely gracious guest house.

I found an uncommonly European ambience at this elegant inn. With its Tudor-style appointments of gleaming brass, custom-crafted oak furniture, crystal chandeliers, and quality antique furnishings, The American Club looks like a finely manicured baronial estate. It's also the only Five-Diamond resort hotel in the Midwest.

Built in 1918 as a temporary home for immigrant workers of the Kohler Company (a renowned plumbing manufacturer, still located across the street), the "boarding house" served as a meeting place where English and citizenship classes were taught—a genuine "American Club."

My room in the main building boasted handsome oak paneling and furniture. Handmade European comforters with four fluffy pillows adorned each bed, adding a cozy touch. It's more of the same opulence in the Carriage House, with skylights, remote-control cable television, and more.

Some rooms boast four-poster canopied brass beds and huge marble-lined whirlpool baths. Special suites contain a sauna-like environmental enclosure with a pushbutton choice of weather—from bright sun and gentle breezes to misty rain showers. And consider these guest rooms amenities: fluffy bathrobes, scales, twice-daily maid service, daily newspapers—the list goes on!

The inn's showcase restaurant is The Immigrant, where I dined on a gourmet meal of smoked Irish salmon. The wine list was impressive, too. For dessert, I walked to the Greenhouse, in the courtyard. This antique English solarium is a perfect spot for chocolate torte and other Viennese delights.

The hotel's Pete Dye–designed Blackwolf Run golf course, until recently comprising three distinct 9-hole courses, is one of the most dramatic links around. Players select whichever two courses appeal to them to play a normal round or just play a single nine. Upon its opening in 1988, it was named the "Best New Public Course in the Nation" by *Golf Digest*. Now that the hotel has added a fourth 9 holes, I cannot get there often enough.

How to get there: From Chicago, take I–94 north and continue north on I–43, just outside of Milwaukee. Exit on Wisconsin 23 west (exit 53B). Take 23 to County Trunk Y and continue south into Kohler. The inn is on the right. From the west, take I–94 south to Wisconsin 21 and go east to U.S. 41. Go south on 41 to Wisconsin 23; then head east into Kohler.

French Country Inn
Lake Geneva, Wisconsin
53147

Innkeeper: Dane Hime
Address/Telephone: Highway 50 West, Route 4, Box 690; (414) 245–5220
Rooms: 24, including 1 suite; all with private bath, air conditioning, TV, and phone.
Rates: Monday through Thursday, $95 to $105, single or double; Friday and Saturday, $125 to $145, single or double; EPB. Two-night minimum on weekends. Special midweek and weekend packages.
Open: All year.
Facilities and activities: Full-service restaurant and bar, afternoon tea, outdoor swimming pool. Nearby: golf, horseback riding, and winter ski areas. Short drive to Lake Geneva specialty shops, boat tours, water activities.

What looks like a modest lakeside retreat from the outside reveals itself to be a magnificent showplace. I marveled at the lobby's intricate parquet floors, hand-carved solid-oak staircase, and rich chandeliers—all shining and sparkling from rays of the sun sprinkling in through a large skylight.

The inn's main house, including that magnificent staircase, was completely hand-built by master craftsmen in Denmark in the 1880s. Later it was dismantled in piecemeal fashion, shipped by boat and rail to Chicago, and reassembled as the Danish Pavilion for the 1893 Columbian Exposition. After that famed event, the building was purchased and moved to its present site.

Anxious to see the guest rooms, I wasn't disappointed. Located in annexes just steps from the main building, the rooms are gracefully done in country-French styles, with brass beds, high-back chairs, balloon drapes, and more. Some have cathedral ceilings and skylights; all have their own gas fireplaces and private balconies overlooking Como Lake. In fact, the balconies are only 25 feet from the shoreline.

Late afternoon tea, featuring samples from the inn kitchen, is served in the parlor, itself a warm retreat dominated by a fireplace and more country-French furnishings. A full breakfast of cheese and sausage omelets, fresh fruit, juice, and homemade croissants is offered in a quaint nook off the main lobby.

The inn restaurant, boasting a graceful panorama of the shoreline, delights in traditional European specialties. You might choose *Le blanc du dindon* (turkey breast filled with mushrooms, sausage, and chestnuts, with sauce Madeira), *Cassoulet* (trilogy of duck, sausage, and pork with lima beans in chef's classic sauce), *L'homard en croute* (lobster tail in a puff pastry with shrimp sauce), or one of more than a dozen specialty entrees.

And do leave some room for dessert. I can personally recommend the bourbon pecan pie in champagne-sabayon sauce and the flourless double-chocolate cake with raspberry cream. Or perhaps you're in the mood for some Mississippi mud pie. What else can I say but, "Bon appetit."

How to get there: From Chicago, take I–94 to Wisconsin 50 west and proceed about 3 miles out of Lake Geneva. Then turn north at the inn sign off Highway 50 and proceed down the winding road to the inn.

B: *The inn's colorful past includes a stint as a speakeasy and gambling casino during Prohibition.*

Fargo Mansion Inn
Lake Mills, Wisconsin
53551

Innkeepers: Tom Boycks and Barry Luce
Address/Telephone: 406 Mulberry Street; (414) 648–3654
Rooms: 9; with 2 suites; all with private bath and air conditioning, phone and TV on request.
Rates: $65 to $150, single or double, EPB.
Open: All year.
Facilities and activities: Parlor, sitting room. Perennial flower garden. Bicycles-built-for-two available to guests. Nearby: Rock Lake beaches, boating, swimming. Short drive to restaurants, hiking trails, Indian burial grounds, Aztalan State Park, Drumlin Bike Trail, golf, tennis, trapshooting.

I arrived on a warm springtime day to find the grounds of the inn masked by a cover of bright-blue flowers. "Mr. Fargo planted the scilla more than one hundred years ago," Tom said. "They only last about two weeks, but they continue to come up every year."

Tom and Barry have done a masterful job restoring this 1881 mansion built by Enoch J. Fargo, a local entrepreneur and descendant of the famed Wells Fargo family. The foyer alone is a stunning Victorian masterpiece of Queen Anne architecture, with a 30-foot-high ceiling and handsome winding staircase of quarter-sawn oak.

Guest rooms, named for Fargo relatives and friends, are elegant and comfortable. The Elijah Harvey Suite celebrates that period when Victorians became fascinated with Turkish stylings. Earthy colors, Turkish rugs, an ornate Victorian double bed with marble-topped washstand, and a reading nook are inviting enough. But the bathroom includes a whirlpool surrounded by hand-cut Italian marble done in earth-tone colors that carry out the Turkish theme to the hilt. It's addictive, so don't be surprised if you begin to utter remarks like, "Take me to the Casbah."

Tom and Barry call the E. J. Fargo Suite their "grandest." It has an 8½-foot Victorian queen-sized bed, a working marble fireplace warming a cozy sitting area, ceiling-to-floor bay windows providing a panorama of the grounds, and a private porch done up in wicker furniture during summer weather, perfect for sunset watching and relaxing.

Where's the bathroom? Go to the bookcase and "remove" a title called *The Secret Passage*. The bookcase swings open to reveal a secret passageway and a bathroom done entirely in Italian marble, with a whirlpool built for two and an oversized glass-enclosed shower. The effect is memorable.

Breakfast—which includes egg casseroles, morning meats, croissants, juice, and coffee—is often taken in the music room; the massive table can seat twenty. For dinner, there are several restaurants nearby; the innkeepers will recommend one to suit your tastes.

How to get there: From Milwaukee, take I–94 west to Lake Mills exit (Wisconsin 89). Go through town to Madison Street, turn left, then turn left on Mulberry Street and proceed to the inn.

☀

B: *Barry said the sidewalks surrounding the inn were the first in the state of Wisconsin. Fargo, himself, went to Germany to learn how to mix the cement for them.*

Victorian Treasure
Bed and Breakfast
Lodi, Wisconsin
53555

Innkeepers: Linda Bishop and Joe Costanza
Address/Telephone: 115 Prairie Street; (608) 592–5199
Rooms: 4; 1 with private bath, all with air conditioning. No smoking inn.
Rates: $48 to $105, single; $55 to $105, double; $160, suite (2 adjoining bedrooms with private bath); $285, whole house; continental breakfast.
Open: All year.
Facilities and activities: Sitting rooms, porch. Guest speakers on first Saturday of every month include experts in history, art, wildlife, crafts. Water activities on nearby Wisconsin River and Lake Wisconsin. Hiking, rock climbing, bird-watching on Baraboo Range. Also nearby: restaurants, downhill and cross-country skiing; Devil's Lake State Park, with 500-foot bluffs; American Players (Shakespearean) Theater in outdoor amphitheater; Taliesin, home of Frank Lloyd Wright; golf; bald eagle–watching.

"We've always owned old houses and restored them ourselves," said Joe, who hails from upstate New York. He and Linda have done an outstanding job here.

It's hard to imagine that this rambling Victorian, with its expansive wraparound veranda, was built for only $3,000 in 1897 by lumber baron and Wisconsin State Senator William G. Bissell. The innkeepers have the original bill of sale and Bissell's canceled check. They also dug for more house history, hiring a genealogist who traced a great-granddaughter to Rockford, Illinois, and obtained some early-1800s photos of the house from her. These now hang on the inn walls.

Many original chandeliers, brass door fittings, and woodwork harken back to fine Victorian-era craftsmanship. The tulip-drop brass chandelier in the sitting room, which casts a warm glow over Victorian high-back chairs and sofa, is one of the home's original gas fixtures.

As we walked up a grand staircase, coming to a wide hallway that leads to guest rooms, Joe told me they searched little towns within a 150-mile radius for period antiques. You can see the results for yourself.

The Queen Anne's Lace Room has a queen-sized, four-poster brass bed in front of three floor-to-ceiling windows draped with antique lace panels for privacy. It also has an expansive bath featuring a two-person whirlpool.

In the Wild Rose Room, a full-sized bed with antique head-board and footboard is set amid a blaze of bold Victorian printed wall coverings. Yet the effect is light and airy, with three huge windows that allow sunlight to filter into the room. It also has a small private porch.

And the Wild Ginger Room has handsome furnishings and a porch perfect for star-gazing and comes with a special inn privilege—the use of an outdoor hot tub, located on the back porch, that Joe made from a circa-1865, 500-gallon wine barrel.

All beds have dual-control electric blankets, down comforters, and four pillows—real European style. Breakfasts of homemade breads and muffins await guests each morning. Afternoon tea is a tradition here. And the inn library holds a large collection of books and parlor games.

How to get there: From Chicago and Milwaukee, take I–90/94 to Wisconsin 60 and go west into Lodi. In town take Route 60 (now called Lodi Street) 1 block west, then turn right on Prairie Street. It's the first house on the left.

The Collins House
Madison, Wisconsin
53703

Innkeepers: Barb and Mike Pratzel
Address/Telephone: 704 East Gorham Street; (608) 255–4230
Rooms: 4 suites; all with private bath and air conditioning, 2 with sitting room.
Rates: $65 to $85, single or double, continental breakfast on weekdays, EPB on weekends and holidays.
Open: All year.
Facilities and activities: Sitting room, library, living room. Inn on shoreline, with neighboring beach. Madison is state capital: art museums, galleries, theater, ethnic restaurants, specialty shops. University of Wisconsin main campus here, with major arts, sports, and entertainment activities.

Barb had just finished her latest baking binge as I stepped in the door. "It's a compulsion," she joked. Lucky for me and other guests who reap the considerable benefits of her "compulsion." I devoured delicious chocolate marzipan bars that were still warm from the oven.

This landmark turn-of-the-century inn features the distinctive architecture of the Prairie School made famous by Frank Lloyd Wright. And it hugs Lake Mendota, boasting striking views of its glistening waters.

I loved the open interiors and natural woods, all characteristic of Wright's designs of simple lines and open spaces. Mike was stoking a fire in the living room graced with striking mahogany woodwork while we tried to decide which classic movie to watch from their video library of more than eighty films.

The guest rooms are very spacious and decorated with period furniture. Some have bay windows that overlook the shoreline of the white-capped lake; others boast lead glass that peers out at the historic "Old Market Place" neighborhood.

I stayed in the largest suite, the Claude and Stark, named after the house's architects. The arched entryway is a nice touch, framing an elegant solid cherry, lead-glass cabinet.

"Guests remark that the house constantly smells like freshly baked bread," Barb said. "I'm always experimenting with new goodies, too, so our guests get to be my master samplers." For that, we're very lucky! (I wonder if Barb caught her baking bent from Mike; his family owned a large bakery in the St. Louis area.)

Barb's home-baked breads and scrumptious pastries, juice, fruit, cheese, and coffee are the weekday breakfast fare; on weekends, and some weekdays, and holidays, she serves a full breakfast that might include house specialties like Swedish oatmeal pancakes with cinnamon apples, chicken tarragon roulades, and potato pancakes made from a secret family recipe. (She now also boasts a full-time custom catering business based on the same homemade foods that gained renown for the inn.)

For dinner, I drove to the nearby Fess Hotel restaurant, located in a historic Victorian building, for roast duckling with brown sauce and Montmorency cherries. Madison's best restaurant, however, might be L'Etoile, specializing in fabulous fresh seafood creations and fish terrines; if you enjoy a European menu utilizing fresh local ingredients, this could be your gustatory nirvana.

How to get there: From the Interstate, follow Wisconsin 30 to Highway 151 (East Washington Avenue) and continue to North Blount Street; then turn left. The inn is at the intersection of Blount and East Gorham streets.

❧

B: *Barb's homemade truffle chocolates are becoming a Madison-area favorite.*

Mansion Hill Inn
Madison, Wisconsin
53703

Innkeeper: Polly Elder
Address/Telephone: 424 North Pinckney Street; (608) 255–3999
Rooms: 11, including 3 suites; all with private bath, air conditioning, cable
    TV, stereo, VCR, and mini-bar.
Rates: $80 to $230, single; $100 to $250, double; continental breakfast.
    Two-night minimum on holidays and football weekends.
Open: All year.
Facilities and activities: Victorian parlor, dining room (with catered dinners
    available), belvedere, private wine cellar, garden. Access to health
    spa, private dining club. Mansion Hill Historic District invites touring,
    especially Period Garden Park. Madison is state capital; many fine
    ethnic restaurants, specialty shops, art galleries, recitals, theaters,
    nightclubs. Also University of Wisconsin main campus nearby.
    Swimming, fishing, boating in surrounding lakes.

An extraordinary inn! I knew it would be special as soon as a
tuxedo-clad manservant opened a tall door, graced with elegantly
stenciled glass, to officially greet me.

This 1858 building is an architectural showplace. Its fine
construction materials include white sandstone from the cliffs of
the Mississippi, Carrara marble from Italy, and ornamental cast

iron from Sweden. The original owner imported old-world artisans to do all the construction work. It shows.

Nearly two million dollars have been spent to restore the mansion to its former magnificence. I love the handsome arched windows and French doors that let the sunlight spill in. Hand-carved white marble fireplaces blaze with warmth, and a spectacular spiral staircase winds four floors up to the belvedere, which provides a panoramic view of the city.

All the rooms are exquisitely furnished in beautiful antiques—some of the finest I have ever seen. I stayed in the McDonnell Room, which evokes a bold Empire atmosphere. I felt like royalty in these surroundings: arched windows, French doors, a large crystal chandelier, and an incredible 10-foot-tall tester (canopy) bed that one might find in the sleeping quarters of the Prince of Wales.

It also had an oval whirlpool tub, where I soaked in the swirling hot waters with a set of tub-side stereo headphones clamped on my ears.

Another extraordinary room has floor-to-ceiling bookcases with a hidden door opening into an incredible bathroom with arched windows, classical Greek Revival columns, and a huge marble tub.

And a deliriously romantic retreat is the Turkish Nook, swathed in Victorian silks, strewn with pillows and ottomans, and boasting a tented sultan's bed—all evoking the sensual delights and intrigues of the mysterious Middle East.

You can dine on gourmet meals, which are specially arranged on request. Or explore Madison's gustatory delights on your own, perhaps at L'Etoile, L'Escargot, or The White Horse Inn.

How to get there: From Milwaukee, take I–94 west to Madison. Exit west on Wisconsin 30 to Wisconsin 113. Go south to Johnson; then west to Baldwin. Turn south on Baldwin to East Washington, and then turn west toward the capitol building. At Pinckney Street, turn north. The inn is on the corner of Pinckney and Gilman.

❋

B: *"Too much is not enough"* is the inn maxim.

Lauerman Guest House Inn
Marinette, Wisconsin
54143

Innkeepers: Sherry and Steve Homa, Tony and Doris Spaude
Address/Telephone: 1975 Riverside Avenue; (715) 732–4407
Rooms: 7; all with private bath, air conditioning, TV, and phone.
Rates: $57, single; $68, double; EPB.
Open: All year.
Facilities and activities: Restaurant serving Sunday brunch, lunch during
    the week; wheelchair access. Menominee River marina 2 blocks
    away. Two golf courses within 2 miles. Restaurants, Theater on the
    Bay, University of Wisconsin at Marinette a short drive away.

This stately mansion is a real traffic stopper.

With towering Corinthian pillars, a commanding white-rail
balcony overlooking the Menominee River, and an ornate portico
that once welcomed horse-drawn coaches containing formally
attired gentlemen and their handsomely dressed ladies, the Lauer-
man Guest House Inn was hailed as one of the most outstanding
examples of Colonial Revival architecture in this part of the
Midwest.

Built in 1910 by its namesake—a local businessman who was

grossing more than one million dollars a year from his department store—the inn exhibits all the special touches of turn-of-the-century elegance.

I was immediately drawn to beautiful Art Deco lamp figurines that grace staircase posts on the main floor. (These exquisite pieces, fashioned after Grecian goddesses, were named *Naiade* and *Diane* by the artist.)

Oak and black walnut shine throughout the rich interior, and the commanding brass chandelier, leaded-prism windows, and timbered ceilings are original to the home.

Guest rooms are charming. One of my favorites is the Bow Room, with its hand silk-screened wallpaper done in an English garden floral pattern. Through the huge window I could gaze at the stately black-walnut trees that dot the grounds. I even liked the bath, with its original soaking tub, pedestal sink, and cameo window.

Other rooms are equally comfortable. Cecilia's boasts a ceramic-tiled fireplace with an ornate cast-iron screen and the home's original wall safe; Freda's Room has handsome mahogany woodwork as well as a whirlpool; and the Master Suite offers more mahogany and bird's-eye woodwork and French doors that open to an expansive private porch overlooking the Menominee River.

For breakfast, choose from the inn's regular menu, which includes Eggs Benedict Duchef, French Toast Romanoff, the Lumber Baron's Breakfast (smoked ham steak, eggs, fried potatoes, bakery basket, preserves, and coffee), or eggs with a 4-ounce tenderloin steak.

How to get there: From Green Bay, take U.S. 41 north into Menominee. Turn left on Riverside Avenue, and continue 1½ blocks to the inn.

The Audubon Inn
Mayville, Wisconsin
53050

Innkeeper: Linda L. Anderson, manager
Address/Telephone: 45 North Main Street; (414) 387–5858
Rooms: 18, all with private bath, air conditioning, TV, and phone. Pets OK.
Rates: $89 to $99, single or double, EPB.
Open: All year.
Facilities and activities: Lunch, dinner. Sitting rooms, dining room, bar with
  lounge. Nearby: Horicon Marsh, spring and fall geese migration;
  Kettle Moraine State Forest hiking, biking, and backpacking; golfing;
  cross-country skiing; lake activities.

It's difficult to articulate the scope of this elegant renovation. An 1896 hotel that had fallen into disrepair now sparkles as a community showplace thanks to Wisconsin country inn king Rip O'Dwanny.

Rip and his partners invested more than $500,000 in handsome woodworking alone, then imported hand-dyed carpets from Great Britain, commissioned fourteen fabulous stained-glass windows that adorn the dining room and bar, and also commissioned a master craftsman from Wisconsin to create marvelous handmade etched-glass panels that decorate the inn. Did I say decorate? These are not mere decorations, but fine works of art.

Guest rooms are superbly crafted, boasting four-poster canopy beds handmade in New Hampshire and adorned by handcrafted quilts, Victorian-inspired wall coverings "imported" from California, double whirlpool Kohler tubs, Shaker-inspired writing desks, brass lamps, wooden window blinds, and more.

"I feel that this is the ultimate country inn," Rip said. "Not only does the inn offer luxurious comfort and privacy, but a great restaurant that employs four master chefs and a pastry chef."

In fact, my gourmet dinner rivaled anything I've ever tasted in a fancy New York restaurant. The menu changes monthly, but when offered, I highly recommend the Swordfish Moutarde (a charbroiled steak served atop a Grey Poupon cream sauce, and wonderfully presented).

Also impressive: Grilled Barbarie Breast of Duck, served with raspberry sauce, and New York Strip Steak aux Poivre, adorned with cracked peppercorn sauce.

And you'll be sorry if you don't sample an incredible strawberry dessert tart.

The bar is quite special. Consider that Rip had the second and third floors above the bar removed to the ceiling; then he fashioned skylights on the third-floor roof and opened the second floor completely so that natural light could fall on a massive, hand-etched glass depiction of geese in flight over the marsh (the hallmark of this wetland bordertown) that is the lounge's incredible centerpiece and ceiling. It's already been called the most beautiful bar in Wisconsin.

Simply put, it would be difficult to discover a full-service Midwest country inn that could match the Audubon's class, style, and menu selections.

How to get there: From Milwaukee, take U.S. 45 north to Wisconsin 67; then go west into Mayville's downtown district and the inn.

❋

B: In the heart of Canada goose country, the inn is named in honor of famed naturalist John J. Audubon. A stained-glass window in the dining room depicts the renowned wildlife artist.

Chesterfield Inn
Mineral Point, Wisconsin
53565

Innkeeper: Shawn Huffman, general manager
Address/Telephone: 20 Commerce Street; (608) 987–3682
Rooms: 8 share 4 baths; all with air conditioning.
Rates: $50 to $70, single or double, continental breakfast.
Open: All year.
Facilities and activities: Full-service dining room. Pendarvis, Cornish miners' homes built during Mineral Point heyday as lead-mining boom town, 5 blocks away. Artists and craftspeople of Shake Rag Alley, Jail Alley, nearby. House on the Rock in Dodgeville, 15 miles. Frank Lloyd Wright buildings in Spring Green, about 20 miles. American Players Theater (classical/Shakespeare) in Spring Green.

I wanted to know about ghosts, but I was told there were none in this building. Some locals, however, said that several places in the area have had some strange happenings.

Now I was getting somewhere. Mineral Point, an old lead-mining boom town largely inhabited by Cornish miners in the early 1800s, with many of the original stone buildings still intact, ought to have some doppelgangers floating about.

Perhaps Shawn will tell you where to spot the spirits.

Ghostbusting aside, make sure a Mineral Point getaway

includes a stay at the Chesterfield Inn. Opened in 1834 as a stagecoach stop, this handsome inn built in the Cornish stone style served newly arrived miners from Cornwall, England, who came to carve "mineral" out of the ground.

Now charming guest rooms host other kinds of miners—modern-day travelers bent on discovering a shiny nugget of a vacation gem.

Guest rooms at the main inn building are small but very attractive. Room 1 is downright cozy, with a big antique brass bed, Empire country dresser, and shake rag rug. Room 2 boasts a bird's-eye maple bed, homemade quilt, and original plank wood floors. Others are equally quaint. All the rooms have ceiling fans, quite important in a small building with low ceilings.

The inn restaurant is attractive, with original exposed wooden timbers, huge antique quilts hanging on walls, old tavern tables—and terrific food. Operated by the Ovens of Brittany from Madison, Wisconsin, the menu fare includes Cornish Pasties (meat pies); Cajun Shrimp Diane (sautéed shrimp, mushrooms, scallions, and hot spices); Scallops Fettuccine; and desserts like the Queen of Sheba (a hearty chocolate cake doused with liqueurs).

Or take your dinner out on the garden terrace. A natural rock wall, colorful flowers, herb garden, and gazebo make it a popular gathering place.

How to get there: From Madison, take U.S. 18/151 west; follow 151 to Mineral Point. Follow signs to downtown, then turn right on Commerce to inn.

∽

B: *In the 1830s the inn was known as the "kiddlywink," or pub, and food included "figgyhobbin," pasties and pudding taken down to the mines, along with a pint of ale.*

Silver Springs
Inn and Resort
Mitchell, Wisconsin
53073

Innkeepers: Larry Gentine, owner; Sarah Staples, manager
Address/Telephone: N4621 Silver Springs Lane, Plymouth 53073; (414)
    893–0969
Rooms: 4 cedar chalets, sleeping maximum of 6 people or 3 couples each;
    all with 2 private baths, kitchenette, air conditioning, and TV.
Rates: $99 one couple/one night, $189/two nights, $279/three nights; two
    couples, $198/one night, $359/two nights, $519/three nights. EP.
    Additional persons to a maximum of six, $10 per person/per night.
    Includes free gear and trout fishing in private trout ponds, streams.
Facilities and activities: Dining room. Private trout hatchery, trout ponds
    and streams, hiking, and snowmobile trail edging property. Adjacent
    to 45,000-acre state forest. Downhill skiing nearby, along with
    Greenbush, one of state's top cross-country spots.

Don't let the word "resort" fool you. This is a most enchanting, secluded, and private paradise, which should be high on
everyone's getaway itinerary.

It's 184 acres of tall red and white pines, trout streams, and
artesian-fed ponds, nestled in a bowl-shaped valley surrounded by

the Ice Age hills and swells of breathtaking Kettle Moraine State Forest. The surroundings create powerful impressions. "Its scenery is as pretty as anything we just saw out in Colorado," said Marge Laughlin, another inn guest, from Milwaukee.

I met Marge in the dead of winter, while my family was angling for rainbows in one of thirty-eight trout ponds on the property. Open water during a Midwest winter—that's another part of Silver Springs's magic. Artesian springs pump three million gallons of pure water per day through the ponds, keeping them at a constant 47 degrees. That's why I could fish here on my first visit even as outside temperatures dipped to 15 degrees below zero.

Before long, my pa hooked a whopping three-pounder that my then 22-month-old daughter, Kate, held proudly for a few snapshots, talking incessantly for the rest of the evening about "Grandpa's big fishy that go wiggle, wiggle, wiggle."

Obviously, treasured family memories are part of the fun at Silver Springs. "There is a magic here that people don't soon forget," Larry said. "A feeling of peace and solitude my wife calls 'part of tomorrow and a thousand years ago.' It's only a few hours' drive from Chicago, yet it's a whole world apart."

The inn's fanciful history includes the site of an 1830 Blackhawk Indian War battle; a stint as an 1848 Fourierite utopian community admired by visitor Horace Greeley; a trout-rearing club, formed in 1936, which soon grew to be the largest in the North Central states; and a private fishing club. Get Larry or Sarah to show you photos of the old Milwaukee Braves' Warren Spahn and Joe Adcock trying their luck.

The four attractive, roomy, and comfortable chalets have decks with floor-to-ceiling windows overlooking the woods and trout ponds, a wood-burning fireplace in the great room, extra-long beds adorned with handmade quilts, and two baths. And dinnertime is a special treat, with the inn restaurant featuring the most delicious rainbow trout I've ever tasted.

How to get there: From Chicago, take I–94 into Wisconsin. In Milwaukee, continue north on I–43 to I–57 (Plymouth exit). Go north to Wisconsin 23, turn west, then south on County S to the inn.

Inn at Pine Terrace
Oconomowoc, Wisconsin
53066

Innkeeper: Linda Moore, manager
Address/Telephone: 371 Lisbon Road; (414) 567–7463
Rooms: 13; all with private bath, air conditioning, phone, and TV.
   Wheelchair access. Well-behaved pets OK.
Rates: $69.50 to $139.50, single or double, EPB.
Open: All year.
Facilities and activities: Sitting room, swimming pool on grounds, breakfast
   room, conference room. Short walk to Lac La Belle for swimming,
   fishing, boating, and 3 beaches. Restaurants and Olympia Ski Area,
   with downhill and cross-country skiing, a short drive away.

Cary O'Dwanny and wife, Christine, two of the inn's principal
owners, greeted me outside their inn, an impressive three-story
Victorian mansion built in 1884 by the Schuttler family, well-
known wagon makers from Chicago. In fact, two Schuttler sons
married girls whose families used those wagons to haul barrels of
beer for their breweries; one was an Anheuser, another a Busch.

As soon as I stepped inside the massive double-doors of the
tiled foyer, accented with stained and etched glass, I knew the inn
would be quite special.

The restoration, which took more than two years to complete, is an accomplished one. Cary spent over $750,000 in millwork alone to bring back the elaborate butternut and walnut moldings that are everywhere. Furniture, done in antique Eastlake style, was custom made especially for the inn. A curving walnut handrail that crowns the three-story staircase is valued at $55,000. Most bathrooms have marble-lined two-person whirlpools; guest-room doors boast brass hinges and hand-carved wooden doorknobs; custom wall coverings and brooding Victorian paint colors evoke the period as almost no other inn has before.

Once the town was an exclusive vacation spot for wealthy Southern families escaping the summer heat. "The mansion was the 'in' place to be," Cary said. "Five U.S. presidents were guests here, beginning with Taft." Other notables included the likes of Mark Twain and Montgomery Ward.

Elegant guest rooms are named for historic residents of Oconomowoc. Most are huge by inn standards, with the first-floor beauty perhaps the showcase. It features a massive bedroom area with a crowning touch: marble steps leading to a marble platform, upon which sits a white enamel, brass–claw-footed bathtub illuminated by a bank of three ceiling-to-floor windows—shuttered for privacy, of course.

Rooms on the third floor are smaller, since these are the old servant's quarters; however, they are no less attractive. My room, named for Captain Gustav Pabst, was a charming hideaway with slanting dormer ceilings that create a small sitting-room alcove; its brass lighting fixtures, rich woodwork, deep-green wall coverings, double whirlpool, and tiny window offering a view of Lac La Belle made it one of my favorites.

Breakfast, served in the dining room on the lower level, means Linda's French toast, quiches, egg bakes, and homemade muffins. Later you can lounge at the inn's swimming pool, or take a dip in the refreshing water while already making plans for your return visit here.

How to get there: From Milwaukee, take I–94 west to U.S. 67. Exit north and continue through town to Lisbon Road. Turn right; the inn is just down the street.

St. Croix River Inn
Osceola, Wisconsin
54020

Innkeeper: Vickie Farnham
Address/Telephone: 305 River Street; (715) 294–4248
Rooms: 7; all with private bath and air conditioning, 2 with TV.
Rates: $85 to $150, single or double, EPB. Midweek discounts. Gift certificates.
Open: All year.
Facilities and activities: Outdoor porch, sitting room overlooking St. Croix River. Several area antiques shops, canoeing, fishing. Downhill and cross-country skiing nearby at Wild Mountain or Trollhaugen. Short drive to restaurants and Taylors Falls, Minnesota—lovely, little river town with historic-homes tours and cruises on old-fashioned paddlewheelers.

This eighty-year-old stone house is poised high on a bluff overlooking the scenic St. Croix River. It allows unsurpassed, breathtaking views while providing one of the most elegant lodgings in the entire Midwest.

I'm especially fond of a suite with a huge whirlpool set in front of windows, allowing you to float visually down the water while pampering yourself in a bubble bath.

"The house was built from limestone quarried near here,"

Vickie said. "It belonged to the owner of the town's pharmacy and remained in his family until just eight years ago."

Now let's get right to the rooms (suites, really), which are named for riverboats built in Osceola. Perhaps (and this is a *big* perhaps) Jennie Hays is my all-time favorite inn room. It is simply exquisite, with appointments that remind me of exclusive European hotels. I continue to boast about a magnificent four-poster canopy bed that feels as good as it looks and a decorative tile fireplace that soothes the psyche as well as chilly limbs on crackling-cool autumn or frigid winter nights.

Then there is the view! I'm almost at a loss for words. A huge Palladian window, stretching from floor to ceiling, overlooks the river from the inn's bluff-top perch. It provides a romantic and rewarding setting that would be hard to surpass anywhere in the Midwest. The room has a whirlpool, and there's also a private balcony with more great river views.

The G. B. Knapp Room is more of the same: a huge suite, with a four-poster bed canopy adorned with a floral quilt, tall armoire, its own working gas fireplace, and a whirlpool tub. Then walk through a door to the enclosed porch (more like a private sitting room), with windows overlooking the river. There are also exquisite stenciling, bull's-eye moldings, and private balconies.

Pampering continues at breakfast, which Vickie serves in your room or in bed. It might include fresh fruit and juices, omelets, waffles, French toast, or puff pastries stuffed with ham and cheese, and home-baked French bread and pound cake.

Vickie also delivers to your room a pot of steaming coffee and the morning paper a half hour before your morning meal. She can recommend a great place for dinner. But you simply may never want to leave your quarters.

How to get there: From downtown Osceola, turn west on Third Avenue and follow it past a hospital and historic Episcopal church (dating from 1854, with four turreted steeples). The inn is located on the river side of River Street.

*

B: *One of the Midwest's most romantic retreats—smothered in grace and elegance.*

353

Tiffany Inn
Oshkosh, Wisconsin
54901

Innkeepers: Tom and Mary Rossow, managers
Address/Telephone: 206 Algoma Boulevard; (414) 231–0909
Rooms: 11, with 2 full suites, 2 half suites; all with private bath, air conditioning, TV, and phone. Pets OK.
Rates: $69.50 to $89.50, single or double, EPB. Rates increase during Experimental Aircraft Association fly-in convention held each summer.
Open: All year.
Facilities and activities: Large living and dining rooms, library. Short drive to Lake Winnebago and the Fox River, restored Opera House, Paine Art Center. Also near Experimental Aircraft Association museum, where midsummer air show draws nearly a million visitors; Oshkosh B'Gosh clothing outlet stores, Manufacturer's Market Place Outlet Mall.

Mary and Tom were expecting their first child during our last stay, so my wife and I entertained them with tales of our child-rearing experiences. (With our two young daughters, we could talk forever, and we nearly did.)

We eventually got around to the inn itself, an exquisite Victorian home graced with manicured grounds, tall trees, and a wonderfully colorful flower garden in the summertime.

354

Rooms in the main house exude classical Victorian charm, while those in the seven-room carriage house exhibit more country-Victorian touches. All are named for family members of the famous American art-glass creator, Louis Comfort Tiffany.

We stayed in the magnificent Louis Comfort Tiffany suite, one of the largest inn rooms I have ever seen. Our canopied queen-sized bed was especially comfortable, and the Victorian dressers and wicker chairs blended perfectly.

A huge bathroom sporting original tiles is bigger than most offices. And an expansive dressing room with its own window was a perfect spot to set up a portable crib for Dayne, our special traveling companion when she was four months old.

Another terrific choice is the Charles Louis Tiffany suite, which stretches the width of the house, boasts elegant furnishings, and affords views of the signed Tiffany window gracing the Episcopal Church across the street. It's subtly illuminated at night, producing a warm, ethereal feeling.

The inn also boasts a beautiful manteled fireplace surrounded by high-back chairs (a great place for serious book reading on a cold winter night), beamed ceilings, and terrific sun room.

My wife and I feasted on Mary's cinnamon rolls, which were hot out of the oven. Her other breakfast creations include home-made muffins, egg bakes, quiches, and more.

There are lots of choices for dinner. I suggest The Granary, a 106-year-old flour mill turned restaurant that served us excellent shrimp and has a few choice selections of wine.

How to get there: Approach Oshkosh either from the south (Chicago) or north (Green Bay) on Highway 41. Exit on Ninth Avenue and turn east. Count five stoplights, including the one at Highway 41, and you'll come to South Main Street. Turn left; go across the Fox River bridge to the fourth stoplight. That's Algoma Boulevard. Turn west 2 blocks to the inn at Algoma and Division.

52 Stafford
Plymouth, Wisconsin
53073

Innkeeper: Cary O'Dwanny
Address/Telephone: 52 Stafford Street (mailing address: P.O. Box 565); (414) 893–0552
Rooms: 20; all with private bath, air conditioning, TV, and phone. Wheelchair access. Well-behaved pets OK.
Rates: $64.50 to $94.50, single; $69.50 to $99.50, double; EPB. Two- or three-night minimums on Road America race weekends.
Open: All year.
Facilities and activities: Full-service restaurants, sitting room, Irish folk singer/entertainment in bar. Nearby: Road America in Elkhart Lake, state parks with hiking, biking, nature trails, cross-country skiing (in season), Old Wade historic site, swimming and fishing at local lakes, charter fishing on Lake Michigan.

Cary, better known as Rip, has created a little bit o' Ireland in the middle of cheese country: 52 Stafford, an "authentic" Irish country house complete with imported European appointments, classy guest rooms, and Guinness Stout on tap.

"I wanted the feeling of casual elegance," Rip told me as we shared a pint of bitters, "where you could feel at home in blue jeans or a tuxedo.

356

"I also decided to use only the finest materials when decorating the inn," he said. First-floor hardwoods are all solid cherry, with crown moldings and solid brass chandeliers (weighing eighty pounds apiece) adding classical touches.

He picked the yarn colors for the handmade floral carpet imported from England that graces the inn. Much of the lead glass comes from West Germany. Chinese silk adorns lobby wing chairs.

The bar is imposing. It's solid cherry, stretching almost to the ceiling. Green and white tiles cover the footrest. Then there's beautiful hand-sandblasted etched glass, with deep relief designs of harps and wreaths done by a local craftsman. The glass gave off a lilting greenish glow. Just pull up a bar stool, order a Guinness on tap, and you'll be close to heaven.

All rooms are individually decorated. Mine had a handsome English four-poster bed and "fox hunt" wall prints, tall shuttered windows, crown ceiling moldings, and an elegant brass chandelier.

Another special inn feature is a first-floor antique lead-glass window—*above* a fireplace. It has more than four hundred jewels and beads in it, with a flue that must swing to the left, around the window.

Rip's breakfast, served in the inn's handsome dining room, offers huge omelets, French toast, homemade muffins, and much more.

But his dinner chefs have fashioned quite a gustatory reputation for 52 Stafford and one of its sister inns, The Audubon Inn, located in Mayville, Wisconsin. Consider Guinness Brisket (a beef brisket simmered in Irish stout and served with boiled carrots, Kilkenny potatoes, leeks, and cabbage). Or try the Stafford Steak (a certified eight-ounce Black Angus beef tenderloin served with a shiitake mushroom sauce). And how can you resist Bailey's Irish Cheesecake for dessert?

How to get there: From Milwaukee, take I–43 north, switching to Wisconsin 57 just past Grafton. At Wisconsin 23, turn west and drive into Plymouth. At Stafford Street, turn south. The inn is on the right side of the street.

$$*$$

B: *52 Stafford's St. Patrick's Day celebration lasts from March 1 to March 17 and culminates with a huge parade.*

The Rochester Inn
Sheboygan Falls, Wisconsin
53085

Innkeepers: Dan and Ruth Stenz
Address/Telephone: 504 Water Street; (414) 467-3123
Rooms: 5, with 4 suites; all with private bath, air conditioning, TV, and phone. Well-behaved pets OK.
Rates: $79.50 to $99.50, single or double, Sunday through Thursday; $89.50 to $109.50, single or double, Friday and Saturday; EPB. Two-night minimum on special festival weekends.
Open: All year.
Facilities and activities: Short drive to restaurants, Kettle Moraine State Forest for biking and hiking, Lake Michigan fishing and boating, Road America (automobile racing), Blackwolf Run for golfing, Kohler Design Center.

Yet another of Wisconsin country-inn king Rip O'Dwanny's elegant creations, this 1839 National Historic Landmark has been transformed from a pioneer general store into a den of opulence.

Lest my adjectives overwhelm my pen, suffice it to say that the Rochester Inn's cozy rooms are quite breathtaking. Imagine guest rooms, each with its own parlor, fashioned with quality antique reproductions that include wingback chairs, Chippendale-style sofas, and finely polished armoires.

Though each has its own distinctive look, they are similar in their Victorian-inspired stylings. For example, the Charles D. Cole Room (named after the Sheboygan Falls settler who built this structure) is swathed in handsome wall coverings produced in California and boasts a pencil-post bed adorned with a handmade quilt, its own wet bar, and a double whirlpool bath.

I also liked the triangular window just above the bed. "That's original to the house," Ruth said. "It was discovered when the old clapboard was ripped off."

A tiny dining room downstairs makes breakfast reservations a necessity. But this treat includes a choice of quiche, French toast or pancakes, scrambled eggs with ham or sausage, cinnamon and butter croissants, and fresh fruit. Joan can arrange a prebreakfast sip of juice or coffee in your room.

Also take a peek at the photo hanging above the dining-room table. It shows the building in its early days. Note that there seems to be no sidewalks—not even a road.

For dinner, wander to Rip's flagship inn, 52 Stafford, for wonderful gourmet-style meals. Or just enjoy the Irish folk music performed by artists brought directly from the Auld Sod; might as well take a pull on a Guinness, since your stay at the Rochester entitles you to two complimentary drinks from the 52 Stafford bar.

(By the way, early settlers named this town Rochester, only to discover that a village in New York claimed the same name—so they changed it to Sheboygan Falls.)

How to get there: From Milwaukee, take I–94 to U.S. 43 north and continue to the Sheboygan Falls exit (Exit 51); turn west and proceed about .8 mile to County A, turn north until reaching Wisconsin 28, and take Wisconsin 28 west into the town and to the inn.

~

B: *Rip calls this "the classiest little inn in America." He might be right.*

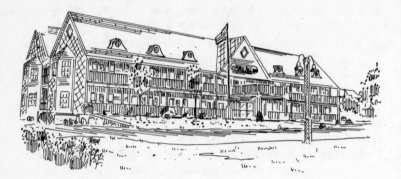

Church Hill Inn
Sister Bay, Wisconsin
54234

Innkeepers: Paul and Joyce Crittenden
Address/Telephone: 425 Gateway Drive; (414) 854–4885
Rooms: 35; all with private bath. Wheelchair access.
Rates: $89 to $124, single or double, EPB. Three-night minimum on summer weekends.
Open: All year.
Facilities and activities: Sauna, whirlpool, exercise room, heated outdoor pool. Located in heart of Door County peninsula, one of the Midwest's premier vacation spots. Golf courses, water sports, shopping, antiques, orchards, shoreline nearby. Country Walk specialty stores steps away. Town's beach, dock, and downtown 2 blocks down road.

This inn sits high on a hill, glistening in the Door County sunlight like a regal jewel in the crown of the royal family.

It is designed and decorated in English country style, striving to blend the best of an elegant, small hotel with the intimacy of a European bed-and-breakfast inn. I think it succeeds quite well.

Masterful guest rooms are beautifully done in antiques and reproductions. In fact, many of the antiques were purchased in England and brought back especially for the inn.

Each of the inn's stately wings features its own separate sitting areas, complete with fireplace, high-back chairs, and books and magazines; there are also a wet bar and a porch. These areas feel much like the library of an English country estate and are nice places to unwind and relax.

That is, if you ever leave your room. They are handsome; many feature four-poster canopy beds done in rich mahogany, queen-sized mattresses, Empire-style dressers, and private balconies.

For total luxury, enjoy a room with double whirlpool bath, refrigerator, and huge bay windows with quaint bench seats that might offer a view of the flower-filled terrace.

Or maybe you'd like a room that has delicate French doors opening directly onto the inn's swimming pool and its elegant sunbathing deck?

You'll breakfast on tasty treats like cherry crisp, poppyseed bread, sausage-and egg-soufflés, and more.

And don't forget that complimentary snacks or hors d'oeuvres are served in the lobby sitting room every day from 4:00 to 6:00 P.M. It's a great way to unwind and swap Door County stories at the same time.

How to get there: From Sturgeon Bay, go north on Wisconsin 42 and continue into Sister Bay. The inn is on a hill near the intersection of Wisconsin 42 and 57.

Bay Shore Inn
Sturgeon Bay, Wisconsin
54235

Innkeepers: John Hanson and Paul Mathias
Address/Telephone: 4205 North Bay Shore Drive; (414) 743–4551
Rooms: 36; all with private bath, air conditioning, and cable TV.
Rates: $120 to $140, for single bedroom unit; $170 to $225, for 2-bedroom unit; EP. MAP available for $18 per day adults, $12 children 7–13, under 7 free.
Open: All year.
Facilities and activities: Full-service dining room, game room, indoor pool, hot tub, outdoor pool, children's playground area, barbecue picnic area, private beach. Rowboats, sailboats, canoes, and pontoons. Nearby: biking, hiking, fishing, specialty shops, antiques stores, restaurants. Short drive to state park, golfing, maritime museum.

The last time my family stayed at the Bay Shore Inn, we rented lakeside rooms with views of the beach and bay. My daughters, Kate and Dayne, were in heaven—their own private beach to splash about, build sandcastles, play tag, you name it. We had a blast.

You'll still experience a fun-filled adventure at the Bay Shore, but things sure have changed. Gone are the main building guest rooms, lakeside motel-style rooms and A-frame cabins; in their place are two large condominium buildings housing thirty-six deluxe-style rooms—some boasting whirlpools, full kitchens, huge living rooms, large bedrooms, and decks with panoramic views of the bay.

The setting remains spectacular. Paul said the land is part of a mid-1800s homestead begun by an immigrant sailing captain, Jacob Hanson, who settled here on Door County's rugged western shore—amid tall trees, bays, and bluffs—because it reminded him of home.

His wife, Matilda, began serving food to summer vacationers, using cherished Swedish and Norwegian recipes. (Paul still uses them to create the inn's renowned butter-fried chicken.) A historic apple orchard out back, along with a vegetable farm, supplies the inn with garden delights.

The rustic main lodge, which houses the inn restaurant, was built in 1921. I love the massive stone fireplace that stretches to the ceiling; it's a favorite spot for toasting icy toes before dinner.

Hearty Midwestern-style food selections include Swedish pancakes smothered with tangy lingonberries and hot-cooked oatmeal that will stick to your ribs during cross-country season. There are also lots of homemade breads, jellies, and special sweets like cinnamon-swirl loaf and Elizabeth's Swedish Ginger Cookies (Elizabeth is Matilda's daughter).

You shouldn't miss Paul's Door County Fish Boil, held Friday evenings during the summer season and Saturday year-round. This feast of whitefish, potatoes, and vegetables is boiled in a huge, fiery caldron outside the dining room on the beach. It's great fun to watch the flames lick the sky.

How to get there: In Sturgeon Bay, take the Route 42/57 bypass to Gordon Road. Turn west and continue to Bay Shore Drive (Third Avenue). Then turn north until you reach the inn, located on the shoreline.

*

B: Paul is so proud of the inn's historic recipes that he published his own recipe book; try them out in your own kitchen.

The Inn at Cedar Crossing
Sturgeon Bay, Wisconsin
54235

Innkeeper: Terry Wulf
Address/Telephone: 336 Louisiana Street; (414) 743–4200
Rooms: 9; all with private bath and air conditioning, TV on request.
Rates: $65 to $109, single or double, continental breakfast. Two-night
minimum on weekends.
Open: All year.
Facilities and activities: Full-service restaurant, 2 dining rooms. About 3
blocks from waterfront. Walk to quaint shops, restaurants, Miller Art
Museum, historic district, downtown area. Half-hour's drive to
beaches, antiques shops, tip of Door County peninsula. Cross-
country ski rentals available at inn through local outfitter.

This handsome inn, housed in a 100-year-old-plus merchant's
building modeled after European markets, was the scene of one of
my most embarrassing moments as an inn-hopper.

As Terry talked with me about her beautiful restoration work
(the building is located in Sturgeon Bay's historic district), she
suddenly looked at my wife, who was holding Dayne, then four
months old, and exclaimed something like, "Debbie, it looks like
Dayne had an accident on your shorts."

After we all stopped laughing and got Dayne (and Debbie) cleaned up, we explored gorgeous guest rooms that make this inn one of my Door County favorites.

"My mom made all the chair coverings, ruffles, curtains, pillows, and lamp shades," Terry told us. That's some talented mom. Rooms have a homey, comfortable feel to them, while exhibiting gracious, country antique furnishings.

Number Three has an exposed brick wall, original to the century-old building, that adds a special touch. There are lots of warm country fabrics, a beautiful red-maple armoire, a brass four-poster bed graced with a lace canopy—and a single electric candlestick resting on the window sill.

Even though Number Two is the smallest inn room, you'd hear no complaints from me; it offers a four-poster pine bed, stenciling, and "bent twig" folk art chairs.

My favorites, however, are Number Seven and Number Nine. In Number Seven (the Anniversary Room), you'll find a four-poster mahogany canopy bed (whose mattress is so high you must ascend a few wooden steps to reach it), crewel wallpaper, antique walnut writing desk, exposed brick wall, and two-person whirlpool. Of course, Terry's mom made the handsome curtains and Roman shades for this room, too.

And Number Nine has a European feel, or more accurately, a touch of Scandinavia. "The bed is an intricately painted, cottage-style piece of folk art from the 1800s," Terry said. "The armoire is from Norway, the wallpaper imported from Denmark." And the room is done in Danish blue.

The new inn restaurant boasts stenciling, antique chairs, exposed brick walls—and great food. Consider home-baked coffeecakes, apple crisp, and Scandinavian fruit soup for breakfast; scrumptious dinners include apple-stuffed pork loin, whitefish baked in brown butter with capers and pine nuts, grilled New York strip steak, and sinfully decadent desserts.

How to get there: Go north on Wisconsin 42/57, around Sturgeon Bay, over the new bridge. Turn left on Michigan Street about 1 mile to the first stop sign. Then turn right on Fourth Avenue, go 1 block, then left on Louisiana. The inn is just before the stop sign, on the right.

The Scofield House
Sturgeon Bay, Wisconsin
54235

Innkeepers: Bill and Fran Cecil

Address/Telephone: 908 Michigan Street (mailing address: P.O. Box 761); (414) 743–7727

Rooms: 5; all with private bath and air conditioning, some with TV, VCR, double whirlpool, fireplace. No smoking inn.

Rates: $60 to $110, single or double, EPB. Two-night minimum for weekends, 3-night minimum for holiday weekends. No credit cards.

Open: All year.

Facilities and activities: Walking distance to historic district and downtown Sturgeon Bay, specialty shops, restaurants. Walk to Green Bay shore, park with tennis courts. Near Miller Art Center, Maritime Museum. Potawatomi State Park a short drive; offers miles of hiking and cross-country ski trails, biking roads, observation tower. Golf courses nearby.

Okay. I admit it. The Scofield House is so elegantly restored to Victorian opulence that I'm at a loss for words. So I'll just give you the facts.

Built in 1902, the three-story, fifteen-room, Queen Anne–style home was referred to as the "grandest" house in Sturgeon Bay, Bill told me. It was designed for Herbert Scofield, a former

366

mayor of the city from 1899 to 1901 and a member of a prominent local lumber-and-hardware family. The magnificent turn-of-the-century craftsmanship (hand-carved and inlaid woodwork, beveled and stained glass, tall posts and columns) attests to his good fortune.

Some highlights are oak woodwork and gingerbread, all original, with a unique sheen to it. "Workers applied an orange shellac to it that gives off that glow," Bill said. It's exquisite.

The parlor's formal Victorian couch and chair are a rich mahogany and date from 1870; they're some of the finest pieces I've ever seen. ("When I look at them I see my Yamaha 850," said Bill, who sold his bike several years ago in order to buy the furniture.)

The dining room features recessed oak paneling, bead chandelier, rose-and-gold stained-glass window, and hardwood floors with original inlay and parquetry (composed of five different woods: cherry, birch, maple, walnut, and oak), which are found throughout the house. Distinctive bow-and-ribbon carvings above windows and doors also are found throughout the home.

Family heirlooms are showcased throughout guest rooms. The Rose Room, with inlaid maple floors and 7-foot headboard, displays an original oil painting done by Fran's great aunt Ida. The Blue Room has Bill's baby quilt made by his grandmother in 1932, complete with a likeness of Peter Rabbit, who holds a letter addressed to "Billy Cecil." Great Aunt Chrissy's signed, 1912 "wave pattern" quilt hangs on another wall.

There's so much more, including Bill's delicious gourmet breakfasts, which might include hot apple crisp, carrot rolls and raisin muffins, and eggs Benedict with his famous no-name red sauce. Fran's contributions include nightly sweet treats fresh from the oven.

How to get there: Take Wisconsin 42/57 north and follow this road along the Sturgeon Bay bypass. Turn left at Michigan Street and continue to Ninth Street and the inn.

✳

B: *One of the newest inn additions: The Gazebo Room, with corner fireplace, stained-glass window, inlaid maple floor, Laura Ashley watersilk print linens, and more stunning Victorian luxury.*

White Lace Inn
Sturgeon Bay, Wisconsin
54235

Innkeepers: Bonnie and Dennis Statz
Address/Telephone: 16 North Fifth Avenue; (414) 743–1105
Rooms: 15 in 3 historic houses; all with private bath and air conditioning, some with fireplace, whirlpool, TV, and wheelchair access.
Rates: $58 to $128, single; $65 to $135, double; continental breakfast. Special winter or spring fireside packages available.
Open: All year.
Facilities and activities: Five blocks to bay shore. Close to specialty and antiques shops, restaurants, Door County Museum, Miller Art Center. Swimming, tennis, and horseback riding nearby. Short drive to Whitefish Dunes and Potawatomi state parks, Peninsula Players Summer Theater, Birch Creek Music Festival. Cross-country skiing and ice skating in winter. Gateway to the peninsula.

Bonnie and Dennis call their inn "a romantic fireside getaway." I can't think of a better place to spend a cozy, pampered weekend for two.

And things have only gotten better since my last visit. Now the White Lace Inn resembles a private, Victorian-era park, with three handsome historic buildings connected by a red-brick pathway that winds through landscaped grounds filled with stately rees, wildflower gardens, and a rose garden featuring varieties dating from the 1700s. You will also enjoy the "Vixen Hill" gazebo, a great place to pause among the inn's many gardens; it is a beauty from Pennsylvania.

The Main House was built for a local lawyer in 1903; what's surprising is the extensive oak woodwork put in for such a man of modest means. Stepping into the entryway, I was surrounded by magnificent, hand-carved oak paneling.

Bonnie has a degree in interior design and has created guest rooms with a warm feel, mixing Laura Ashley wallpaper and fabrics with imposing, yet comfortable, antique furnishings like rich oriental rugs and high-back walnut and canopied beds. Fluffy down pillows are provided, handmade comforters and quilts brighten large beds, and lacy curtains adorn tall windows.

The 1880s Garden House has rooms with their own fireplaces. They're done in myriad styles—from country elegant to the grand boldness of oversized Empire furniture.

This time my wife and I stayed in the Washburn House, the third and newest "old" addition to the White Lace. All rooms here are luxurious; ours had a brass canopied bed with down comforter, fireplace, and two-person whirlpool. It was graced with soft pastel floral chintz fabric and white-on-white Carol Gresco fabrics that tell a story; in fact, some of her work is part of the Smithsonian Design Institute's collection. The bath's Ralph Lauren towels are heavenly.

Back in the main house, Bonnie's homemade muffins are the breakfast treat, along with juice, coffee, and delicious Scandinavian fruit soup (a tasty concoction served cold), or old-fashioned rice pudding. It's a great time to swap Door County stories. For dinner, the innkeepers will recommend a restaurant that suits your tastes. I'm always pleased with the Bay Shore Inn, whose family-style meals are just a short drive away. Or try Oliver Station, a restored railroad station converted into a casual restaurant and microbrewery. Great beer and beer cheese soup.

How to get there: From Milwaukee, take U.S. 41 north to Wisconsin 42, toward Sturgeon Bay. Just outside the city, take Business 42/57 and follow it into town, cross the bridge, and you'll come to Michigan Street. Follow Michigan to Fifth Avenue and turn left. White Lace Inn is on the right side of the street.

Or you can take the 42/51 bypass across the new bridge to Michigan Street. Turn left on Michigan, go to Fifth Avenue, and take a right on Fifth.

Rosenberry Inn
Wausau, Wisconsin
54401

Innkeepers: Jerold, Patricia, and Doug Artz
Address/Telephone: 511 Franklin Street; (715) 842–5733
Rooms: 8; all with private bath, air conditioning, TV, and phone.
Rates: $40, single; $50, double; continental breakfast.
Open: All year.
Facilities and activities: Gathering room, porch. Walk to downtown Wausau and the Mall, Washington Square shopping complex, antiques shops, boutiques, restaurants, Leigh Yawkey Woodson Art Museum. Short drive to Dells of Eau Claire nature trails, rock climbing, rappelling, fishing, and canoeing. Five miles from Rib Mountain skiing; cross-country ski trails nearby.

I have just arrived at the Rosenberry Inn early on a weekend morning. Inside on the guest-book stand rests a cowbell to alert the innkeepers of new arrivals.

It's library quiet in the house. I just know I'll wake the entire place if I ring that bell, and I don't want a guilty conscience—especially on Sunday.

Oh, what the heck. *Cllaaannnngggggg!*

A smiling Jerry came down the stairs. "Well, well—we've been waiting for you." Let's say that I was relieved.

Jerry, Pat, and Doug worked endlessly to rescue this wonderful house from ruin and restore it to its early-1900s splendor. There's rich woodwork everywhere. Lead and stained glass cast prisms of light on the stairwell. Antique photographs and prints add to the bygone-era feeling.

"We've named all the guest rooms after relatives we cherish," Pat said. All the rooms are graced with Victorian antiques and some country primitives; four have fireplaces, and teddy bears are everywhere.

In the rose-colored Agnes room, I like the iron-rail beds and the working fireplace—good to take away the winter chill after a day of skiing at Rib Mountain nearby. Leona has antique Victorian bedspreads, homemade comforters, and a fireplace that transforms the room into a cozy retreat.

My favorite is John, with its pressed-tin ceiling, fireplace, and collection of *bierhaus* steins.

Pat created the charming apple-design stencils on the walls of the third-floor card room. It's also filled with cheery country crafts.

I like eating breakfast (juice, Pat's home-baked banana bread, muffins, and coffee) up in the old attic, now cheerily decorated with wall stencils of farm animals, along with antique tables and chairs. The innkeepers can recommend a restaurant to suit your tastes.

How to get there: From Milwaukee, take I–94 west to U.S. 51 and head north until you reach Wausau. At Highway 52, go east to Franklin Street and turn left to the inn.

⤴

B: *The Artzes also have two additional homes, located in the Historic District just 1½ blocks away. Rooms at the 1887 Mercer House and the Bardeen House (built in the early 1900s) are furnished with antiques and feature hardwood floors and stained glass. They're a cozy retreat for big-city visitors.*

Westby House
Westby, Wisconsin
54667

Innkeeper: Patricia Benjamin Smith
Address/Telephone: 200 West State Street; (608) 634–4112
Rooms: 6, with 1 suite; 3 with private bath, all with air conditioning, TV, and phone.
Rates: $50 to $85, single or double, continental breakfast.
Open: All year.
Facilities and activities: Full-service restaurant. Short walk to specialty stores and antiques shops. In Wisconsin Amish country, with quaint back-road exploring. Winter cross-country skiing, major ski-jump park and training site. Town celebrates many Norwegian holidays.

This charming Queen Anne–style inn, located in a fun Norwegian community, is a Westby landmark. The eighteen-room mansion, built in the 1890s, has all the special Victorian touches: a tall tower, stained-glass windows, gingerbread finery, and elegant interior woodwork.

I saw a 1915 photograph of the house in the hallway. Doesn't look as though it's changed much since then. Lucky for me—and you, too.

The elegant chandeliers with cranberry-colored shades cast a rose-tinted glow. The antique Amish quilts hanging on walls make an attractive backdrop.

372

To reach the second-floor guest rooms, I walked up a long staircase. Note the old butler's pantry. It's fun to imagine servants scurrying about up here, preparing breakfast for the turn-of-the-century household.

The guest rooms are small-town charming. The spacious Anniversary Suite has a large brass bed, lacy curtains on windows, and a Victorian love seat and chair; it's a guest favorite.

There are two white iron-rail beds in the Greenbriar Room. And the Squire Room has cheery country accents like eyelet lace curtains, and a hand-painted queen-sized bed that looks awfully inviting.

Sure to quickly become the most requested room is the inn's newest addition—the Fireplace Room. This two-room suite boasts regal antiques (including a fainting couch), lots of lacy finery, a fireplace, and a cozy nook inside the home's tall tower—high Victorian and very romantic.

Downstairs, the busy Victorian dining room draws people from all over town for its delicious, hearty food. I sat in front of a manteled fireplace at an antique table complete with bentwood chairs, and devoured my lunch: a hot crabmeat sandwich with tomato slices and jack cheese. Dinner also looked pretty inviting, with choices like fresh trout or sautéed shrimp with mushrooms and onions. (Of course, everything at the inn is made from scratch, right down to the salad dressing.)

I suggest that you try the *torsk,* an inn specialty. It's eight ounces of Norwegian cod baked in lemon butter and served with egg noodles. Then opt for a luscious dessert—the Victoriannie—a homemade brownie topped with ice cream, whipped cream, and a cherry.

How to get there: The inn is located halfway between Chicago and the Twin Cities. From LaCrosse, take U.S. 14/61 southeast into Westby. Turn west a half block at the corner of 14/61 and West State Street and continue to the inn.

❋

B: *Westby's Olympic-style ski jump draws top athletes to its winter competitions every year. It's a great time to enjoy the Westby House hospitality.*

Wolf River Lodge
White Lake, Wisconsin
54491

Innkeepers: Joe and Joan Jesse, owners
Address/Telephone: White Lake; (715) 882–2182
Rooms: 9, plus 1 carriage house; 2 rooms and carriage house with private bath.
Rates: $50, single; $60 to $80, double; EPB. Carriage house $120 per night. Most reservations are made through week-long or weekend package rates: winter ski season (Christmas season to mid-March), $130 per person/3 days, 2 nights; spring, summer, fall, $125/3 days, 2 nights; packages include 3 meals Saturday, 2 meals Sunday.
Open: All year.
Facilities and activities: Full-service dining room, bar, wine cellar, parlor and game rooms, gift shop, outdoor hot tub. Located on Wolf River, with world-class white-water rapids during high-water periods. River is always runnable, April through October. Excellent trout fishing May and June. Ideal terrain for cross-country skiing, horseback riding.

Where can you find world-class white-water rapids, kayaking, and fly-cast trout-fishing in a spot where eagle and osprey soar overhead and roadsides are smothered by early summer wildflowers? The Wolf River Lodge, of course.

This rustic lodge is a center for river rafting on the Wolf River.

In the majestic Nicolet National Forest country, frothing white-water rapids tumble over boulders and ledges, dropping 12 feet per mile for 25 miles. The crystal-clear water is often icy cold.

The log building is surrounded by tall trees and teeming wilderness. A large, rustic dining room, with exposed logs, long oak dining and tavern tables, offers solid fare.

A cozy sitting room with a crazy-quilt arrangement of chairs and sofas is a favorite guest gathering spot—the large stone fireplace is the reason. Some relax here after a long day of cross-country skiing; others just watch the glow of the fire.

I browsed through piles of books sitting on a large coffee table. Naturally, lots of them give tips on white-water rafting, canoeing, and kayaking. The wackiest offering was a surfing handbook.

The guest rooms are small but cozy, with pine furniture and country finery. I like the brightly colored quilts and braided rugs that add color to the rustic charm.

The food is simple but delicious. Breakfast means a morning treat: the lodge's renowned crepes. Most evening meals feature delectable trout, delicious roast duck, thick, juicy steaks or baked stuffed pork chops with pine-nut dressing.

The lodge's newest wrinkle: a carriage house loft (with its own private bath) that sleeps two to six people; this handsome log home should be a real family-pleaser.

How to get there: From Milwaukee, take I–43 north to Green Bay; then take U.S. 41/141 north to Wisconsin 64. Head west to White Lake. Turn north on Wisconsin 55 and then watch for the Wolf River Lodge signs that direct you there.

❧

B: *George Washington didn't sleep here, but one senator who became our thirty-fifth president did.*

Indexes

Alphabetical Index to Inns

377

Inns with Full-Service Restaurants

Bed and Breakfast Inns
(serve breakfast only)

Island Inns

Riverside Inns

Inns on Lakes

Inns with Swimming Pools

Inns near Downhill or Cross-Country Skiing

Inns Especially Good for Kids

Pets Welcome

Historic Hotels

Historic-Town Inns

Rustic-Area Inns

Romantic Inns

No Smoking Inns

Inns with Wheelchair Access
(*to at least one room*)

About the Author

Bob Puhala is an award-winning journalist who writes a weekly travel column for the *Chicago Sun-Times*. His articles have also appeared in other newspapers and national magazines, including the *Chicago Tribune*, *USA Today*, *Travel & Leisure*, *Travel-Holiday*, *Columbia Journalism Review*, and *Consumers Digest*.

Puhala has written seven books and is a member of both The Authors Guild and the Society of American Travel Writers. He lives in Chicago with his wife, daughters, and family.